MILITARY SYSTEM OF THE MARATHAS

Owing to the antiquity and rarity of this book, certain pages are regrettably absent, and readability is compromised due to the blurring of the original text. If you possess any insights regarding the availability of these missing sections, kindly inform us. Your assistance is crucial in ensuring the completion of this significant work for the benefit of future generations.

MILITARY SYSTEM OF THE MARATHAS

BY

SURENDRANATH SEN

GYAN

Published by

Gyan Publishing House
5, Ansari Road
Daryaganj, New Delhi-110002
Phone: 011-47034999, 9811692060
E-mail: books@gyanbooks.com

Distribution Network
gyanbooks.com
India, USA, Canada, UK, Australia

ISBN: 978-93-6433-385-6 (PB)
First Published, 1928

2nd Impression 2024

Printed at: Gyan Press, Delhi.

MILITARY SYSTEM OF THE MARATHAS
Author: SURENDRANATH SEN

MILITARY SYSTEM OF THE MARATHAS

WITH A BRIEF ACCOUNT OF THEIR MARITIME ACTIVITIES

BY

SURENDRANATH SEN,

B. LITT. (Oxon.) M.A., PH.D. (Cal.),

LECTURER IN HISTORY, CALCUTTA UNIVERSITY

THE BOOK COMPANY LTD.

4/4A, COLLEGE SQUARE, CALCUTTA

1928

To

Sir EWART GREAVES, Kt., M.A., D.L.

IN TOKEN OF

GRATITUDE AND ESTEEM

PREFACE

A civilian writing about military matters labours under obvious difficulties, and it is necessary to offer an explanation for undertaking a task for which neither my training nor my profession qualifies me. Nearly ten years ago I began a study of the civil institutions of the Marathas with a view to explore the causes of the rapid expansion of their empire and its speedy collapse. The Maratha empire was primarily a military organisation and its civil institutions were closely connected with its military system. Every state forms an organic unit, and even a cursory examination of its character demands an enquiry into the nature of its component parts. This is the only excuse I can offer for trespassing into domains other than my own, but I am fully conscious of my limitations and I have carefully avoided all technical matters as far as possible and confined myself to those broad questions to which even a layman can do some justice. The need for such a survey was pointed out by the late Mr. Sydney Owen more than fifty years ago.

If the civilian student of military history suffers from some disadvantage due to his lack of technical knowledge, he is further handicapped when he selects the military history of the Marathas as the subject of his enquiry. In England a large number of useful works on the art and science of war was written and published in the 16th and 17th centuries, but the Maratha commanders and strategists have left us nothing of that kind. Their military theories must, therefore, remain a subject of conjecture. Luckily facts and figures, on which such conjectures can safely be based, are not wanting, though they are still buried in unpublished records scattered in different parts of India and Europe. All the information we need cannot be found in Marathi records, but these can be profitably supplemented by contemporary English, Portuguese, French and Dutch records; and for the last phase of the Maratha military organisation we have the valuable accounts left by European military experts like Tone and Smith, who wrote from personal knowledge. On the naval history of the Marathas their own records do not throw much light, and we have to rely almost entirely on foreign sources. It has been my endeavour to piece together these widely scattered scraps of information in the following pages; with what success, it is for my readers to judge. I have examined, as far as possible, all the manuscript records available in London, Paris, Lisbon, Evora and Goa, and I have not neglected the rare old publications likely to throw light on my subject. But these old records and manuscripts are without any index and in some cases they are not in a good state of preservation. It is, therefore, quite possible that some papers bearing on the subject may have escaped my scrutiny.

The political history of the Marathas is now fairly well known, thanks to the monumental work of Grant Duff. It has been, therefore, possible to avoid a detailed narrative of their campaigns, but, as the average reader is yet unfamiliar with their naval activities, I have deemed it necessary to deal with that subject in greater detail; though a fuller account of the exploits of Kanhoji Angria and his sons has to be postponed for a future occasion from consideration of space.

It is necessary to add a few words here about my references to Factory Records and Bombay Public Consultations. The date indicated either in the text or in the foot-notes will supply a surer means of locating the extracts than the page or folio number, as each copyist seems to have numbered his own pages according to his own convenience. To avoid confusion, I have sometimes given the number of the particular part of the volume as well, but it should be noted that in the original volumes the different parts have not been separately numbered. It is also necessary to point out that in the following pages the word Maratha has not been (except when otherwise indicated) used in the caste sense.

My thanks are due to Mr. Otwell, Superintendent of Records, India Office, for kindly permitting me to read the Bombay Public Consultations from 1700 to 1756. I take this opportunity for offering my grateful thanks for similar courtesy to Dr. Jaime de Cortesao of Biblioteca Nacional of Lisbon, Senhor Pedro de Azevedo of Archivo Ultramarino of Lisbon, Dr. Lopes da Sylva of Bibliotheca Publica of Evora and Monsieur Paul Roussier of the Colonial Office of Paris. Col. C. E. Luard has placed me under great obligations by lending me several rare publications on Maratha history and I am also indebted to Sir William Foster and Professor Alfred Martineau for their expert guidance in my search of English and French records. Professor Nripendra Chandra Banerji and Dr. Hem Chandra Ray Chaudhuri have very kindly gone through my manuscripts and my friend and colleague Mr. Sailendra Nath Mitra has read the proofs with his usual kindness and patience. The late Mr. S. M. Edwardes very kindly revised some of the earlier chapters and I am indebted to him for some valuable suggestions. They are not, however, in any way responsible for any short-coming that may still disfigure this work.

The bibliography indicates the fact, and not the extent, of my indebtedness.

It has not been possible to print Portuguese words correctly for want of proper types, but it is hoped that this unavoidable defect will cause my readers no serious inconvenience.

SURENDRA NATH SEN

Senate House
CALCUTTA
The 8th October, 1928.

CONTENTS.

MILITARY SYSTEM OF THE MARATHAS

INTRODUCTION

The Marathas were the last indigenous empire builders of India[1]. They leapt into prominence suddenly and swiftly; in the third decade of the seventeenth century the Maratha name was unknown to the world outside; three decades later it became a terror to the rulers of the land. In the second decade of the next century the Emperor of Delhi had to recognise their *de facto* supremacy in the Deccan by granting them *chauth* and *sardeshmukhi* of six provinces of the South. But their activities were not long confined to the immediate neighbourhood of their home. Balaji Vishwanath entered Delhi in the train of Syed Husain Ali, his son appeared in its environs at the head of his victorious army, his grandsons became arbiters of the fate of the Mughal empire and carried the Maratha banner to the banks of the Indus, while their cavalry scoured the country from Lahore to Murshidabad, from Delhi to Seringapatam. The rapid expansion of their empire was once arrested by the defeat of Panipat, but the Marathas quickly recovered from the shock, and Mahadaji Sindhia founded a new empire in Hindustan. In 1794 they inflicted a crushing defeat on the Nizam at Kurdla and compelled him to cede half his territories. Hardly eight years elapsed before the Peshwa became a feudatory of the British Government in India, the grand armies of Daulat Rao Sindhia and Raghuji Bhonsla were defeated and destroyed by Lake and Wellesley, and the Maratha empire collapsed like a house of cards. If their rise was sudden and swift, the fall of the

1. The later Sikh and Gurkha states never transcended the provincial limits of the Indus valley and the Himalayan region respectively.

Marathas was no less sudden and unexpected. The Empire was apparently at the zenith of its power, it had reached its greatest extent, its man power was almost unlimited, yet it was destroyed by a foreign power with a small army after a brief campaign of fifteen weeks.

What led to this quick and complete collapse? The plea of accidents cannot be seriously considered. In History accident plays no prominent part, and seldom turns the tide of national fortunes. It is true that Mahadaji Sindhia died while still in the prime of life, and about the same date died a lesser person Hari Pant Phadke. It is true that the early death of the first Madhav Rao, the murder of Narayan Rao, the unfortunate suicide of the second Madhav Rao were national calamities of no mean order and certainly accelerated the pace of the Maratha fall. It is also true that after Nana Fadnavis there was no one competent to unite the divergent forces that constituted the complex organisation called the Maratha empire. But why did the Maratha race suddenly grow barren of great men? If the Marathas could survive Shivaji's death, why could not they survive Nana Fadnavis? If able leaders came forth to save the nation in 1690, why were they lacking in 1802? The death of Cavour did not arrest the progress of Italian unity; why should the death of Nana Fadnavis or Mahadaji Sindhia cause the downfall of the Maratha empire? Accidents offer no satisfactory explanation.

Social reformers have attributed the misfortunes of the Marathas to their caste dissensions. Yet the Maratha empire came into being under the shadow of the caste system, it expanded and flourished while that system was in full vigour. Shivaji, a Maratha, recruited his highest officers from the Brahman caste; the two greatest generals employed by the Brahman Peshwa in Northern India were both Marathas; Yamaji Shivdev, a Brahman, once intrigued against the Brahman Peshwa; the pretender Sadoba found an ardent supporter in the Chitpavan governor of Ratnagiri, while Jaswant Rao Holkar, a Maratha (more accurately a Dhangar), fought against Daulat Rao Sindhia, another Maratha. Govind Pant Bundele, a Karhada Brahman, complained that there was none in the Brahman Peshwa's court to recommend his devoted services as he was only a Brahman servant of His Highness. Caste system has been responsible for many evils in India, but for the real cause of the downfall of the Marathas we must look elsewhere.

It has been suggested that the Marathas fell because they neglected their civil Government; and they lived on plunder and did not encourage trade and industry, agriculture and commerce. Defective as their civil institutions were they were no worse than similar institutions in contemporary Europe[2]. Their Government certainly degenerated in the closing years of the eighteenth century, but that was a result rather than the cause of the decline and fall that had already commenced.

Nor was their fall due to their policy of aggression. An imperial power in a country like India must be aggressive, until its supremacy is fairly established over the whole country. In pursuance of such a policy they had often recourse to diplomacy of a kind condemned by their critics. Whatever may happen in future, in the past abstract principles of morality played little or no part in diplomacy, oriental or occidental. Neither Clive nor Cavour, nor Bismarck, nor Napoleon III would hesitate to hoodwink a rival or dupe an enemy. In the eighteenth century the standard of diplomatic morality in Europe was certainly not very high as Albert Sorel tells us. In India things were no better and no worse. If the Marathas coveted the lands of their neighbours, their neighbours on their part were not free from land hunger. Every envoy that the Bombay Government sent to Poona was instructed to take advantage of the disunion and dissension that existed among the Marathas. Vansittart seriously contemplated a general invasion of the Maratha empire from all sides when he learnt of the disaster of Panipat, although there was peace between the two powers at the time. It is true that had the issue of that battle been different, Vansittart's protege at Murshidabad would almost

2. This subject has been exhaustively treated in the present writer's *Administrative System of the Marathas.*

immediately have felt the weight of the Maratha military power.

But a policy of aggression proves futile if it is not provided with a proper implement. An imperial power with an aggressive programme must have an efficient instrument of war. So long as its army remained efficient the empire flourished and prospered; when the army grew weak and inefficient the Marathas naturally lost the pre-eminence and prestige they once enjoyed and had to make room for their better equipped rival. An enquiry into the causes of the decline and decay of the Maratha army may therefore reveal the real causes that led to the decline and decay of the Maratha empire.

The Army is an instrument of the State. Every change in the constitution and organisation of the State is therefore bound to be reflected in the organisation of the army. The rules and regulations by which an army is governed always bear an impress of the ideals by which the State is inspired. The history of the Maratha army does not offer any exception to this axiom.

The Maratha State in its infancy was governed by an enlightened autocracy in the shape of a national monarchy. The army which gave expression to the ideals and aspirations of this state was naturally a national institution with strict rules and regulations. It formed a homogeneous body commanded by a regular cadre of officers who had to obey one supreme commander. The monarchical autocracy was however soon replaced by a feudal despotism, and the national army had consequently to make room for a feudal force. Discipline in such a body is necessarily lax and homogeneity is impossible. During the Peshwa period therefore we no longer find a single army under one central organisation led and commanded by one supreme leader but a conglomeration of different armies led by different feudal chiefs who were not always inspired by common ideals or united by common interests. The total military strength of the State was under such circumstances not available at any given moment and one military officer of the State could be, and in fact was, often pitted against another. This necessarily reduced the general military resources of the State and rendered unity of command impossible.

Unfortunately this was not all. With the change of its constitution the Maratha State gradually forsook its original ideal and the national elements in the army were in consequence largely replaced by foreign mercenaries. But this defect of the Maratha army, important as it is, does not explain its discomfiture; for the English army, against which it fought, was also composed of the same elements; and disunited as the Maratha chiefs were, some of them could and did bring to the field a much bigger force than the English could hope to muster. Their defeat must therefore be attributed to inferiority in discipline, equipment and command.

The Marathas owed their early success against their Muslim rivals to superior discipline. But as their empire expanded and the hoarded wealth of Hindustan flowed into the saddle bags of the Maratha horsemen, they began to emulate the grandees of the Mughal empire in their military customs and ways of living. Discipline was in consequence sadly impaired and the Maratha army of the later Peshwa days suffered from the very defects that had led to the fall of their Muslim rivals.

The arms and equipments of the Maratha army were of a heterogeneous character. While they adopted new arms they did not reject the old ones. Consequently the weapons used by the Maratha soldiers represented all stages of civilisation, and some of them were certainly handed down from the early stone age. In the battle of Udgir bows and arrows were employed with matchlocks and muskets and among the missiles *hat dhonda* or stones are mentioned.

In their choice of weapons no evolution is perceptible but there was accretion. The same remark is applicable to their tactics. When they began to adopt the new tactics with which they had become familiar in their warfare against the Europeans, they did not reject their traditional system of fighting. The two methods were found in practice to be irreconcilable, but they persisted in their useless efforts at hybridization in a way calculated to be disastrous. The Maratha chiefs with their old cavalry force clung to the traditional ways without in any way improving it, while the new battalions consisted of foreign mercenaries commanded by foreign officers of doubtful character, diverse nationality and very little knowledge of their profession. Such an army had of course no chance against their English opponents.

The inefficiency of the command in the Maratha army can be directly traced to its feudal organisation and their inability to improve their military and civil institutions was also due to the same cause.

In short the decline and fall of the Maratha military power was due firstly to the revival of feudalism after the death of Sambhaji, which caused disunion and dissension from which Shivaji had tried to save his people; secondly to the rejection of Shivaji's ideal of racial amity on a religious basis in favour of the principle of personal aggrandisement which led to the denationalisation of the Maratha army, and thirdly and lastly to the failure of the Maratha leaders to keep pace with the scientific progress in other parts of the world, to learn and assimilate what others had to teach and improve upon what they had learnt. In Europe there was steady progress from feudalism to national monarchy and from national monarchy to democracy; in Maharashtra the process was reversed by the Peshwas, and the result was the decline, decay and fall of the Maratha empire.

CHAPTER I

SHIVAJI AND HIS FOLLOWERS

Splendid soldiers alone cannot make a splendid army and a nation of fighters does not necessarily rank as a military power. Military efficiency demands discipline in the men and imagination tempered with common sense in their leaders. A military power needs above all an ideal to defend, an ideal to fight for. The Marathas had earned the reputation of good soldiers as early as the first half of the seventh century A.D., but it was not before the second half of the seventeenth that they emerged from comparative insignificance and obtained a place among the great powers of India. Till then they were disunited, disorganised and a prey to petty internal animosities.

Of the military organisation of the Marathas in the early times we know next to nothing. They must have followed the Chalukya banner and later fought under the valiant Rashtrakuta kings; that they were good fighters is beyond doubt, for Huenth Sang was highly impressed with their warlike qualities. He sang the praises of the Maratha warriors, but how they were armed and accoutred, how they were paid in peace time and mobilised in times of war, whether they had any regular cadre of officers and any military tactics of their own, the Chinese pilgrim either did not know or did not think fit to record[1]. After the Chalukyas and the Rashtrakutas came the Yadava and the Silahara dynasties, both of undoubted Maratha origin[2]. The latter ruled over small principalities in

1. The Chinese pilgrim says of the people of Maharashtra—"The inhabitants were proud-spirited and warlike, grateful for favours and revengeful for wrongs; self-sacrificing towards supplicants in distress and sanguinary to death with any who treated them insultingly. Their martial heroes who led the rear of the army in battle went into conflict intoxicated, and their war elephants were also made drunk before an engagement". Thomas Watters, *On Yuan Chwang*, Vol. II, p. 239.

2. The Silaharas were feudatories to the Rashtrakutas and the Yadavas and did not ever possess the same power and enjoy the same influence as the two latter. The Rashtrakutas also according to some authorities belonged to the great Ratta tribe from whom the modern Marathas are said to have been descended.

the Konkan and Karad but the kingdom of the former was of considerable extent. In the few inscriptions that have come down to us the Yadava kings boast of their huge elephants and mention also their Dandanayakas. But these were common features of all Indian armies of those days, and the fact that the kingdom collapsed at the first attack delivered by an external foe does not argue well for its military capacity. Nor do we find any trace in the chronicles of the Pathan conquest of the Deccan of those harassing tactics that the Marathas of the seventeenth century used with such remarkable success against the imperial army of Delhi. Ramchandra Deva, the last independent Yadava king, became a feudatory of the Pathan ruler of Delhi after his numerous forces had been beaten by a small Muhammadan army. His son-in-law made an unsuccessful attempt to throw off the Muhammadan yoke, and after his defeat we lose sight of the Marathas for centuries. They do not reappear on the scene till the fall of the Bahmani kingdom. But in the meantime they had not been slothful. They had lost their political independence but their country had not been completely conquered. The physical features of their land formed a natural bulwark, while their villages, though few and scattered, were each provided with a defending wall. The Deshmukhs[3] or petty feudal lords could defy an invading army for months in their impregnable strongholds perched on the summit of inaccessible hills. They had no exaggerated regard for national honour for the idea of nationality was yet unborn, and as practical people they were not reluctant to acknowledge the suzerainty of the Muhammadan Prince, provided that the latter guaranteed to them peaceful possession of their hereditary lands and hereditary rights. The Muhammadan conqueror on his side recognised the limits of his own supremacy and did not seek to extend them. Thus the Maratha chiefs continued to exercise their petty sovereignty over their hill girt principalities, long

3. The term Deshmukh has been derived from Sanskrit Desha, country or province and Mukhya chief. The Deshmukh enjoyed almost sovereign authority over his small principality or district. For the rights and perquisites of a Deshmukh in the Peshwa days see Sen, *Administrative System of the Marathas*, pp. 243-251.

after the Yadava and the Silahara princes had made way for a stronger military power from the North.

Yet peace was not the keynote of this primitive society. The climate and the physical features of the land, which engendered courage and endurance in the Maratha, made him also self-centred and crafty. The isolation of his daily life led also to a certain parochialism in political affairs. The ambition of the average Maratha villager was confined to his own village and the ambition of the average Maratha chief seldom extended beyond the narrow confines of his paternal principality. But to every Maratha high or low one thing was of paramount importance. He lived and died for his *watan*[4]. What his *bapoti*[5] was to the Rajput, the *watan* was to the Maratha. There was no sacrifice he could not make for it; even apostacy from his religion was not too high a price to pay for its retention. As each *watan* had more than one claimant, it caused continual strife between rival chiefs and rival families. And as the Maratha of those days did not readily forget a loss or forgive an injury, these quarrels inevitably led to blood feuds, which could only be ended by the complete extermination of one of the rival families[6]. These animosities kept the Maratha so busily engaged that he had hardly time or inclination to notice the movements and progress of the external world. The habit narrowed his vision but made a good soldier of him; and thus when the time came, he was ready to take advantage of the new situation and improve his fortunes.

After the dissolution of the Bahmani kingdom the Maratha chiefs began to extend their view and sought civil and military situations in the new courts. They were welcomed by all the new houses who had partitioned the old

4. Watan is an Arabic word and originally meant country, but in Marathi it has acquired a special significance, and stands for any hereditary right or property.

5. Bapoti is patrimony and has the same significance as Watan.

6. Many instances of such blood feuds will be found in the papers published by Mr. V. K. Rajwade in Vol. XV of his *Marathyanchya Itihasachin Sadhanen* and only two instances have been quoted in Sen, *Administrative System of the Marathas*, pp. 30-34.

kingdom. The policy of these houses was uncertain and shifting and their alliances were not of long duration; and they had no hesitation in joining their Hindu neighbour of Vijayanagar against a brother Muhammadan Prince. After the battle of Talikota they employed their energy and resources in the conquest of the weakest members of the confederacy, Berar and Bidar. Yet when this was accomplished, the survivors found themselves unable to compose their differences, and while in this position, were suddenly confronted by a new menace from the North. These continual wars offered excellent opportunities to Maratha soldiers and Maratha diplomats, who were as eager to earn new as to retain their old *watans*.

The beginning of the 17th century saw many Marathas in high positions in the military and the civil services of the Ahmadnagar, Bijapur and Golkonda Governments. In 1615 Malik Ambar employed a Brahman diplomat, Kasi Pandit, to negotiate peace between Ahmadnagar and the Portuguese state in India[7]. Four copies of the treaty resulting from this negotiation were made—two in Portuguese and two in the "Hindu language," or, more accurately, "Hindu alphabet." (Dous de letra endu e dous em portuguez). This clearly testifies to the growing influence of the Hindus in the court of their Muslim rulers. A fresh treaty was concluded two years later and as before two copies of the treaty, apparently for the use of the Indian signatory, were prepared in the Hindu language instead of Persian[8]. In this interesting document the date of the Hindu calendar (o premeiro do mes asar dos gentios) is given side by side with those of the Persian and Portuguese reckoning.

It was, however, in the army that the Marathas particularly distinguished themselves. The art of war was still

7. Biker *Tratados da India*, Vol. I, p. 192. But there is earlier evidence of the employment of Hindus of Maharashtra in the diplomatic service of Muslim rulers. In 1547 Nizamshah sent two envoys to Goa. One of these was a Muhammadan Xeraffiecao (Sharif Khan?) by name and the other was, as his name Catymagy or Timagy Aldeu shows, a Hindu. Biker, Vol. I, pp. 120-122.

8. Biker, Vol. I, p. 193.

in its infancy, primitive weapons like sword and spear, bow and arrows, lance and dagger, which demanded little or no technical knowledge were still in general use, so that every able bodied man was a potential soldier. He could enlist as a *Bargir*[9] or, if he had means enough to buy a horse and the slender outfit that a soldier needed in those days, he could join as a *Silhedar*[10] with much better prospects of advancement. A well-to-do *Silhedar* was really a *condottiere* leader with his own followers whose services he could utilise as he chose. Naturally he tried to secure the best market for his commodity. This was the time-honoured system in India and it is at least as old as the *Shukranitisara*[11]. Neither time nor foreign conquest had affected it in the least. Success added to the *Silhedar's* reputation and following and of course improved his worldly prospects, for his reward generally came in the shape of a *jahgir* or military fief. It was in this way that some Maratha families rose to prominence. The most important of them in rank as well as in power were the Mores of Jawli with the twin titles of Raja and Chandra Rao. Next came the Savants of Wari, the Ghorpades of Mudhol, the Nimbalkars of Phaltan, the Jadhavs of Sindkhed, the Shirkes, only lately dislodged from their paternal principality, the Surves with whom the Shirkes had found an asylum, the Mahadiks, the Mohites and the Ghatges. Of less note were chiefs like the Jedhes, the Manes and the Dafles.

These families formed the military aristocracy of the land, but it should not be forgotten that in Maharashtra the profession of arms was not limited to the noble few. The social barrier was neither strong nor insuperable. The Shelars and the Jadhavs[12], descendants of royal houses, had declined in

9. Persian *Bargir* literally means a burden taker but in the Mughal as well as in the Maratha army the term signified a soldier who rode a horse furnished by his employer.

10. *Silhedar*, more properly *Silahdar*, literally means equipment holder, *i.e.*, a soldier who finds his own horse and arms.

11. *Shukranitisara* is the digest of a work on polity attributed to the legendary sage Shukracharya. The school of Shukracharya is mentioned by Kautilya in his *Arthashastra*, but I am of opinion that the digest in its present form cannot be older than the 15th century A. D.

the scale, the Pawars, another princely family, had reconciled themselves to their humble lot and no longer hesitated to marry Kunbi girls of lowly origin[13]. They still affected the title of "Raje" after their first name, but that was the only trace of royalty now left to them. This society was naturally democratic, and the common dangers, common risks, and common adventures of a soldier's life levelled what difference might have survived. A promising young man who had only recently rejected the plebeian plough for the more aristocratic sword, could aspire to the hand of a daughter of the proud Nimbalkars, and could demand a matrimonial alliance with the princely family of the Jadhavs. Social intercourse was more intimate and less formal than what is possible in a modern barrack, and an able leader of magnetic personality commanded not only the admiration but also the affection of his following. The common soldiers except the few who formed the King's bodyguard, had nothing to do with the state but looked for pay, promotion and preference to the *Jahgirdar* under whom they immediately served. A loyal *Jahgirdar* contributed to the strength of the Government; but in those days it was no discredit to set up as a "*pund palegar*" or lawless chief, as once did a Nimbalkar and a Jedhe[14]. Yet the state continued its policy of multiplying the military fiefs and conferring fresh *jahgirs* on each enterprising *Silhedar*. Even a wise prince like Muhammad Adilshah laid down that while a disloyal Zemindar should be deprived of his fief, the loyal lord should on no account be discouraged or disturbed[15]. The inevitable result of this policy was that the civil

12. The Shelars claim to be the descendants of the Silaharas and Lukhji Jadhav was a direct descendant of Ramchandra Deva the last independent Yadava ruler of Devgiri. Similarly, the Mores are supposed to be connected with the ancient imperial Mauryas.

13. In the family history submitted to the Inam Commission the Pawars confess that after they had settled in the South they behaved like Shudras and married Shudra girls. *Kaifiyats yadis, etc.*, ed. Mawjee and Parasnis, p. 71.

14. Mudhoji Rao Nimbalkar set up as a rebel chief. See *Itihas Sangraha, Prachin Marathe Sardar*, p. 28. Kanhoji Jedhe also defied the authority of the Bijapur Government; Sen, *Administrative System of the Marathas*, p. 33.

15. *Itihas Sangraha, Aitihasik Sphuta Lekha*, p. 25.

Government of the country was subordinated to military needs and the major portion of Maharashtra was held by a number of military leaders serving under three different masters. When Shivaji rose to power, the principality of Ahmadnagar had already been annexed by the Emperor of Delhi and the kingdoms of Bijapur and Golkonda were awaiting a similar fate.

The question may very well be asked why did the Maratha *Jahgirdars* not make common cause against their Muslim masters and assert their independence. The answer is that everybody acted for himself and would not co-operate with his brother chiefs (in another kingdom) except for personal reasons. The Mughal power was deemed invincible ; the weakness of the two surviving offshoots of the Bahmani kingdom was not yet apparent ; they were still planning and effecting fresh conquests in the Karnatak. And people who have anything to lose do not generally favour a change. While the Marathas claimed a common origin, spoke a common language, professed a common faith, in normal circumstances religious persecution alone could assemble them under a common banner. The Muslim rulers of the South normally pursued a policy of religious toleration, and on occasions when a chief of note was compelled to forsake his father's faith, the pangs of conscience were forgotten in the arms of a royal princess[16]. The Mughal annexation of Ahmadnagar, however, introduced a new element in southern politics, the more orthodox, the more uncompromising and the more bigoted belief of Shahjahan and Aurangzib ; and the repeated invasions from which the subjects of Bijapur and Golkonda suffered and the scant consideration with which solemn treaties were treated by ambitious Viceroys like Aurangzib created an atmosphere of distrust and disquiet. Simultaneously a new spirit had been infused into Hinduism in the Deccan by what is popularly known as the Pandharpur movement. This, in short, was the situation when Shivaji appeared in the political arena.

16. It is said that Bajaji Rao Nimbalkar married a princess of Bijapur after his conversion to Muhammadanism. *Itihas Sangraha, Prachin Marathe Sardar*, p. 30.

With the advent of Shivaji a new era opened in the military history of the Marathas. He had a clear conception of military efficiency, definite plans of military reform and had views and prejudices based upon past experience. He believed in personal selection but had no faith in hereditary genius. He approved of unity of command, but would not tolerate military interference in the civil administration of the country. He desired a strong monarchy as the only antidote to the prevailing discord, dissension and anarchy, and could not therefore reconcile himself to feudalism and all that it stood for. He had some advantage over his antagonists. His hands were not tied by precedents; but, at the same time, as the founder of a new kingdom and a new house, he could not ignore the tradition of the land, nor could he afford wholly to alienate the vested interests.

His first steps were naturally cautious and circumspect. He started operations with a small force attached to his father's *jahgir*, which probably needed few officers. But as soon as this force was augmented by the addition of Sambhaji Mohite's cavalry[17], a *Sarnobat* or commander-in-chief was appointed. During the *Sarnobatship* of Mankoji Dahatonde the strength of the army was 3,000 and by 1659, if we can believe Krishnaji Anant Sabhasad, Shivaji was in a position to bring ten thousand cavalry and ten thousand Mawle infantry into the field. In this army the *Silhedars* did not preponderate although at first Shivaji had to depend mainly on these free lances. Of the three thousand horsemen under Mankoji Dahatonde, fully two thousand were *Silhedars*; but by 1659 the strength of the *paga* or regular cavalry had risen to seven thousand, while the *Silhedars* numbered only three thousand[18]. In other words the numerical proportion of the *Silhedar* had fallen from 66% to 33% of the whole cavalry force available for service. This feature of the Maratha army did not escape the notice of the Muslim historians. Khafi Khan writes :—" It is said that

17. Sabhasad, p. 8. Sen, *Sivachhatrapati*, p. 4.
18. Sabhasad, p. 11. Sen, *Sivachhatrapati*, p. 8.

Sivaji got together some ten or twelve thousand of Kachh and Arab horses, so that when he sent out an army most of the horsemen were *bargirs*, i.e., they rode horses belonging to him "[19]. Bhimsen, who served under Dalpat Rai, a Bundela chief, informs us that Shivaji employed *Silhedars*, " but the Mahrattas, who had most pay, were *bargirs* "[20]. Krishnaji Anant Sabhasad is more positive in his statement:—" The strength of the *paga* (regular cavalry) was rendered superior (to that of the *Silhedar*). The *Silhedars* were placed under the jurisdiction of the *paga* "[21]. It is needless to point out that the numerical superiority of the regular cavalry over the irregular *Silhedar* horse contributed to better discipline in Shivaji's army. But he did not stop here. A born military leader, he early recognised the supreme need of unity of command in the battle field and this he attained by establishing a regular cadre of officers both for the infantry and for the cavalry.

Of the cavalry officers, the lowest in rank was the *Havaldar*. He commanded a unit of 25 horsemen, and to each of these units was attached a water carrier and a farrier. Over five such units was placed a *Jumledar*, while a *Hazari* had under him ten *jumlas*. The *Panchhazari* commanded five *hazari* units, and the chief command of the cavalry rested with the *Sarnobat*, who was subordinate to none but the King, the supreme military and civil head of the state.

A number of civil officers were attached to the army. A *Jumledar* was assisted by a *Majumdar* or accountant with 100 to 125 *Hons* a year. A *Hazari's* civil establishment consisted of a *Majumdar*, a *Karbhari* and a *Jamenis*; and a similar staff, probably with more pay, was attached to the *Panchhazari*'s office. Besides these there were the regular news writers of the camp, who held their office independently of the military commanders and reported to the King or his *Vaknavis*[22].

19. Elliot and Dowson, *History of India*, Vol. VII, p. 287.
20. J. Scott, *History of the Dekkan*, Vol. II, p. 55.
21. Sabhasad, p. 28. Sen, *Sivachhatrapati*, p. 30.
22. The Vaknavis or Mantri, as he came to be styled, after Shivaji's coronation was in charge of the intelligence department. See Sen, *Administrative System of the Marathas*, p. 52.

In the infantry the smallest unit consisted of ten men, commanded by a *Naik*. Five such units were placed under a *Jumledar*, and two or three *jumlas* formed a *Hazari's* division. When this cadre was introduced, there were apparently only seven divisions of Mawle infantry, and these were placed under the *Sarnobat* Yesaji Kank who held the chief command. The *Sarnobat* of infantry was inferior in rank and status to the *Sarnobat* of cavalry, for, while the latter was admitted to the *Ashta Pradhan Council* the former had no place in that body. For their civil assistants the *Jumledar* and the *Hazari* of the infantry had each a *Sabnis*, who kept the account and the muster roll. The *Sabnis* of the *Jumledar* drew a salary of 40 *Hons*[23] while the officer of that name on the *Hazari's* staff was given 100 to 125 *Hons*.

As was natural the military officers were much better paid than their civil assistants. The *Jumledar* of the cavalry had five hundred *Hons* a year besides the proud privilege of riding in a palanquin. The *Hazari*, his official superior, drew a salary of 1,000 *Hons* while the *Panchhazari* received double that amount. Krishnaji Anant Sabhasad, to whom we are indebted for these figures, does not tell us the precise salary of the *Sarnobat* or the commander-in-chief; but from a memorandum drawn in the first year of the coronation era[24], it appears that the clothes of honour awarded to the *Senapati* were in every respect similar to those of the crown prince and the Peshwa or prime minister. The document throws no light on the emoluments of the office.

The infantry officers were not so well paid as their colleagues in the cavalry. The *Jumledar* received only one hundred *Hons* or about thirty Rupees per month, and a *Hazari's* pay was five hundred *Hons* or about 2,000 Rupees per annum. It should, however, be remembered that the purchasing power of money was much higher in those days, while the general scale of pay was nowhere very high. The Portuguese Captain of

23. The value of a *Hon* varied from four to five rupees.

24. A new era was started from the year of Shivaji's coronation. This was known as *Rajyabhisheka* or coronation era. For the memorandum see Sane, *Patre Yadi Bagaire*, pp. 357-361.

Chaul was paid 400,000 Reis or 1,000 Rupees per year[25], while the salary of Captain Keigwin, who commanded the English forces on the island of Bombay during the rebellion against the East India Company and Sir John Child, must appear according to modern ideas absurdly exiguous[26].

The Bijapur officers obtained hereditary *jahgirs* in lieu of pay. In the Mughal army the *mansab* was not hereditary but the *Mansabdar*[27] held a *jahgir*. Even civil officers were granted *mansabs* and their pay or more accurately their *jahgir* depended on their military rank. The private was as a rule very poorly and irregularly paid. Even in the life time of Aurangzib the commanders frequently found themselves, specially on occasions of sudden and unforeseen transfer, unable to pay the arrears due to their soldiers as we learn from the interesting memoir of Eradut Khan[28]. This irregularity caused indiscipline in the army and the *jahgir* system was incompatible with the ideas of a strong monarchy. Shivaji did not favour the *jahgir* system nor did he approve of hereditary appointments. Most of his principal ministers were expected to take a military command when necessary. The *Peshwa* Moro Trimbak Pingle and the *Sachiv* Annaji Datto were often

25. *Notes on the History and Antiquities of Chaul and Bassein*—By J. Garson da Cunha, p. 69. The pay of the Portuguese soldiers continued to be poor when Hamilton visited the west coast of India in the second decade of the 18th century. He wrote :—"Their soldiers' pay is very small and ill paid. They have but six Xerapheens per month and two suits of calico, stript or chequered in a year. Their two suits may amount to forty Xerapheens; and a Xerapheen is worth about sixteen pence half peny ster. Out of their six Xerapheens in money that they are to receive, their Captain who is Barrack-Master and Victualler to his Company detains five, and the other one is paid in small money to discharge the Accounts of the Shoemaker, Tailor, Barber, Washerman and Tobacconist." *A New Account of the East Indies*, Vol. I, pp. 249—250.

26. Keigwin's salary was six shillings a day with an allowance for diet. See Ray and Oliver Strachey, *Keigwin's Rebellion*, p. 67. The salary in Indian money amounted to 72 Rupees per month according to the exchange then current.

27. The *Mansabdar* literally means the holder of a *Mansab* or command; the lowest *Mansab* was that of ten horsemen.

28. See John Scott, *Memoirs of Eradut Khan*, p. 1. He says, "I had entertained numerous followers, a tenth of a tenth of whom, the suddenness of my recall rendered incapable of paying; but as my life was yet to remain, I made my escape from among them in the best manner I could with my family."

employed on active service. On such occasions they held independent commands but the *Sarnobat* was on no account permitted to interfere in the civil administration of the land. Shivaji laid down that soldiers and officers should be punctually paid, partly in kind and partly in cash. In an age when barter was in vogue payment in kind could not, if fairly made, cause any hardship[29]. Shivaji's men and officers were paid either in cash from the central treasury or by *varat* or assignments on the provincial revenue. In the latter case payment was made by the district officers but the assignee was not on any account to interfere with the collection. In case he held any land of the Government, the rent payable by him was deducted from his salary and the balance was paid in cash or by *varat*. Shivaji had tried his utmost to undo the evils of feudalism by depriving the old Deshmukhs and Deshpandes of some of their obnoxious rights and prerogatives. He had, like Henry II, pulled down the fortified castles of the petty local tyrants[30] and he was determined not to create new fiefs and renew the evils of military tyranny and feudal anarchy. No office in his army was hereditary, and all officers, high or low, were liable to dismissal, transfer or censure as the case deserved.

Shivaji had no less than five *Sarnobats* of cavalry. Of the first, Tukoji, we know practically nothing, nor why he was removed in favour of Mankoji Dahatonde. After Mankoji's death, Netaji Palkar, a commander of exceptional ability, was raised to the chief command. He was dismissed for his failure to succour Panhala and replaced by a dashing cavalry leader, Kadtoji Gujar. Death caused a vacancy for the fourth time, and Hasaji Mohite[31], who had served with

29. Payment in kind was fairly common in those days. The East India Company's officers used to pay the wages of their Indian labourers partly in kind and partly in cash. See Anderson, *The English in Western India, Second edition*, pp. 221—222.

30. *Sabhasad bakhar*, p. 33. Sen, *Siva Chhatrapati*, p. 38.

31. Prof. Jadunath Sarkar is of opinion that Pratap Rao was succeeded by Anand Rao. He writes, (*Shivaji and His Times*, first edition, p. 260) "I here follow the account of Narayan Shenvi, written at Raigarh, only a month later, on information supplied by Shiva's ministers." I have carefully gone through Naran Sinay's letter. (Factory Records, Surat,

distinction under the late *Sarnobat*, was promoted. It should be noted that in no case did a relative or heir of the last incumbent obtain the office. When Tanaji Malsure, the brave leader of the Mawles, fell in the assault on Sinhgad, his office passed to Suryaji, not because he was brother of the fallen hero, but because he had retrieved the fortunes of the day by rallying the demoralised assailants after their general's death. According to the old feudal traditions the command ought to have passed to young Rayaba, who, according to the writer of an old ballad, was taken into Shivaji's favour[32].

But while he rejected the time honoured *jahgir* system for the remuneration and reward of his adherents, Shivaji did not neglect to confer on them other marks of appreciation as occasions demanded. Both Kadtoji Gujar and Hasaji Mohite obtained high sounding titles. The right of carrying *aftabgir*[33], an ornamental circular sun shade, and of riding in a *palki* or a *nalki* was granted to deserving officers. Presents of gold and silver ornaments and money were made to officers and men for acts of conspicuous bravery. Wounded men received allowances according to the nature of their injuries, and widows of soldiers killed in action were suitably pensioned. A similar pension was granted to the minor children of fallen soldiers, and these were taken into service as soon as they came of age[34].

The abolition of the *jahgir* system was not the only reform at which Shivaji aimed. He wanted to introduce strict

Vol. 88, fols., 78—83). He does not say that he got his information about Shivaji's army from any of his officers or ministers. He prefaces his report on military affairs as follows :—" By other Conveighances Your Honour will have received newse of the proceedings of Sevagees army nevertheless I cannot be excused without giving some account." As for the sources of his information he is absolutely silent. This is all the more remarkable as he specifically mentions that the account of the naval action between the Sidi and the Maratha fleet he had heard from Shivaji, (" this news Sevajee told me himself "). Moreover the appointment of the Sarnobat was not made at Rairi, as Naran Sinay himself tells us. And as all the Maratha accounts contradict his statement on this point, I do not feel inclined to reject them. Naran Sinay, it is evident, had been wrongly informed.

32. Acworth and Shaligram, *Aitihasik Povade*, p. 60.

33. Sen, *Siva Chhatrapati*, pp. 35—36.

34. *Sabhasad bakhar*, p. 25. Sen, *Siva Chhatrapati*, p. 25.

discipline in his army. His success in this direction was far from complete for he had to fight against tradition and environment. None the less he deserves credit for his attempt. His army was employed in *mulukgiri* or foreign expedition for eight months in the year. They returned to cantonment when the monsoon broke and the four months of the rainy season they had to spend in barracks in enforced idleness. Shivaji laid down that provision and medecine for men and fodder for their horses should be carefully stored in the cantonments. During the active season, if we may call it so, the Maratha army subsisted on the spoils of war but here again it was clearly laid down that the spoils belonged to the state and not to the army. Women, Brahmans and cows were not to be molested on any account. It was a capital offence to bring a female slave or a dancing girl into the camp. It was probably military discipline and not moral reform that he strove to achieve[35]. Krishnaji Anant Sabhasad tells us that Shivaji inflicted exemplary punishment on some of his soldiers for breach of discipline during the Karnatak expedition. But it was impossible to effect such a moral revolution all at once. From the preamble of a Portuguese treaty it appears that Shivaji's men had carried away men, women, children and cattle from Portuguese territories[36]. In 1672 some soldiers had been guilty of disorderly conduct at Chafal[37]. In 1676 Shivaji had to address a letter of admonition to the regiment encamped at Chiplun[38]; from the text of the letter it appears that they had taken away from the civil population by force what could be and should have been obtained by peaceful purchase. But when we remember how the Mughal soldiery destroyed the standing crops on their marches, drew out the straw from the thatch to feed their horses, and compelled the unoffending villagers to carry their baggage, we feel inclined to judge Maratha delinquencies more

35. *Chitnis bakhar*, ed. K. N. Sane, p. 180.

36. Biker, *Tratados da India*, Vol. IV, pp. 131—32. Sen, *Historical Records at Goa*, p. 10.

37. Bhate, *Sajjangad Wa Samartha Ramdas*, p. 122.

38. V. K. Rajwade, *Marathyanchya Itihasachin Sadhanen*, Vol. VIII, pp. 23—25.

leniently[39]. War does not bring out the best side of human nature. But in some of his disciplinary reforms Shivaji was notably successful, and his camp was entirely free from the undesirable presence of women of doubtful character as we are informed by two European travellers. John Fryer, the East India Company's physician, tells us that "whores and dancing wenches" were not allowed in Shivaji's camp[40]. Bishop Navarette went to Surat and spent a few days there in 1671. "I was told at Surat," he writes, "that Sabagi Mogal was extraordinarily careful that no woman should be in his army; and, if he happened to find one, he immediately turned her out, first cutting her hair and ears. This to prevent the effect of sensuality on the alertness and activity of his troops, for the same reason as the Tartars"[41]. The good Bishop did not know that Shivaji was not a Mughal but his evidence shows what reputation the Maratha leader enjoyed as a strict disciplinarian[42]. There is good reason to believe that women were very seldom molested by Shivaji's soldiers; for a brave Mughal governor once deemed it safest to leave

39. Manucci, *Storia do Mogor*, ed. Irvine, Vol. II, p. 452. "When the soldiery passes through they plunder everything they can lay hands on,—cattle, food supplies, grass, straw, they destroy houses to get firewood, and on the villagers' heads they load their luggage, and by dint of blows force them to carry it." Military discipline was very slack even at Bombay as we can infer from the following passage in a letter dated 5th October, 1669, "as to the strictness of discipline we shall goe as farre as wee dare." Factory Records, Surat, Vol. 88, fol. 147. In a consultation held at Swally on the 17th October, 1670, occurs the following statement : "Mr. Streinsham Master having formerly advised us of some irregular actions committed by the seamen that were sent up for the defence of the Company's house at Suratt they being very prompt to offer violence to the estate of the natives; Wee then to remedy and stopp their proceedings in such an unlawful manner and keep up our wonted creditt and reputation thoughtt good to enorder Mr. Master to promise the seamen a gratuity for their encouragement in case they behave themselves decently and soberly, which Mr. Master accordingly did." Factory Records, Surat, Vol. III, fol. 96. Things were much worse in Bijapur where the "Naikwadis" did not permit a Governor to enter the fort until he had granted all their unreasonable demands. See letter from Carwar dated the 20th September, 1671. Factory Records, Surat, Vol. 106, fol. 14.

40. Fryer, *A New Account of East India and Persia*, (Original edition), p. 174.

41. Navarette quoted in Orme's *Historical Fragments of the Moghul Empire*, p. 91.

42. Cosme da Guarda, *Vida e accoens do famoso e felicissimo Sevagy da India Oriental*, p. 69.

in a woman's garb when the Marathas appeared at the gates of his city[43]. This was accomplished in an age when a Mughal general had in his camp 400 dancing girls from Kabul and Lahore to enliven his leisure[44].

On their march the Maratha army of Shivaji's day was not encumbered with much baggage or equipment. Their arms were of the simplest and most primitive kind. Field-artillery they had none; and the elaborate and comfortable camp equipage of their Mughal adversaries they did not require. The men wore turban, a simple jacket and tight fitting trousers; their officers were better protected with a helmet and an armour of chain or more frequently with thick padded coats of quilted cotton. In their saddle bag they carried with ease the scanty provision on which they and their mounts could subsist for days. In his second expedition to Surat Shivaji had no tent with him and the Dutch spy found him sitting on the ground[45]. In his longer and more elaborately organised Karnatak expedition he had only two small tents, one for himself and the other for his minister, as we learn from Martin, the French Governor of Pondichery[46], and it is no wonder that, thus lightly equipped, the Maratha army was able to cover 45 to 50 miles in a single march[47]. In fact this constituted their greatest advantage over their heavily armed and heavily armoured Muhammadan adversaries. Man for man the Maratha horseman was no match for the Mughal or the Bijapuri, but where they were not absolutely sure of victory they would not risk a pitched battle. Superior discipline,

43. Factory Records, Surat, Vol. 105, fol. 93.

44. Scott, *History of the Dekkan*, Vol. II, p. 28. But Mahabut Khan was not the only delinquent in this respect. William Minchin wrote about the Sidi Admiral who had no money to pay his men: "The Siddy minds nothing but his dancing women whom he hath continually dancing before him." Factory Records, Surat, Vol. 90, Part I, fol. 29, (the date of the letter is 25th July, 1678).

45. Dutch Records, India Office transcripts, English translation, Vol. 27, D.C.C.XIX, Jan. 18th, 1664.

46. *Indian Historical Records Commission, Proceedings of Meetings*, Vol. VI, p. 25.

47. Sir William Foster, *The English Factories in India*, 1661—1664, p. 236.

greater hardihood, and greater speed more than compensated for the slighter build and the lighter weight of the Maratha soldiers.

Let us now see how the contrast impressed two European contemporaries, an English Doctor of Medicine and an Italian Doctor of Law. John Fryer gives the following estimate of the merits and demerits of the rival armies, " Seva Gi's Men thereby being fitter for any Martial Exploit, having been accustomed to Fare Hard, Journey Fast, and take little Pleasure. But the other will miss of a Booty rather than a Dinner; must mount in State and have their arms carried before them, and their women not far behind them, with the Master of mirth and jollity; will rather expect than pursue a Foe; but then they stand it out better; For Seva Gi's men care not much for a pitched Field, though they are good at Surprizing and Ransacking; yet agree in this, that they are both of stirring Spirits "[48]. Francis Gemelli Careri visited India in 1695 and the Shivaji he speaks of was Ram Raja or Ram Rao as he calls him. " This *Shivaji*," he writes, "whom his Subjects call *Raja*, which signifies petty King, is so Powerful, that he maintains war at once and the same time with the Great Mogul, and the Portuguese. He brings into the Field 50,000 Horse, and as many or more Foot, much better Soldiers than the *Moguls*, for they Live a Day upon a piece of dry Bread, and the Moguls will March at their Ease carrying their Women, abundance of Provisions, and Tents so that their Army looks like a moving City "[49].

The achievements of Shivaji's army need not detain us long. They are well known. The Maratha chroniclers assert with evident pride that he fought with success against four great powers. The numerical strength of his army has been variously stated. Krishnaji Anant Sabhasad puts it well above 100,000. But the causes of his military success are not far to seek. Superior discipline, superior leadership and the unquestioning confidence of his men account for the brilliant

48. J. Fryer—*A New Account of East India and Persia*, p.175.
49. *A Voyage Round the World*—By Dr. John Francis Gemelli Careri, in Churchill's Voyages, (First edition, 1704) Vol. IV, p. 212.

victories which the great Maratha obtained over the Mughals, the Portuguese, the Bijapuris and the Haidrabadis, not to mention the petty poligars who acknowledged his suzerainty. But the main question yet remains to be answered. Why did the self-seeking, watan loving Maratha submit to Shivaji's leadership? Their devotion no doubt was due to the personal magnetism of the leader, but what first caught their imagination and made them forget their age long policy of blood feud and personal aggrandisement? In that age the idea of nationality was yet unborn; but race and religion still stirred the deepest chord in the sentiment of the rude Maratha peasant soldiery. It was to these feelings that Shivaji appealed. The ideal he set forward before his people was a *Hindvi Swarajya* (Hindu empire), a *Maharashtra Padshahi* (Maratha kingdom)[50], but above all a *Dharma Rajya*, a kingdom of righteousness. He assumed the title of *Go Brahman pratipalak*, and the protection of the cow and the priestly caste was considered the paramount duty of every Hindu[51]. For this cause the Brahman could fight shoulder to shoulder with the meanest of the untouchables, the Mahar, who is not allowed to live within the village walls. And Shivaji excluded none from his army, not even the Mahar. In India religious intolerance has been very rare and Shivaji's conception of a Hindu empire was in no way identified with religious persecution. He enlisted in his army seven hundred Pathan deserters from Bijapur, at least three of his naval commanders were Muslims by faith, and he venerated the Muhammadan saint Sheikh Muhammad as he venerated the Hindu saints

50. The term "*Hindvi Swarajya*" is used by Shivaji in a letter to Dadaji Naras Prabhu. See Rajwade, *Marathyanchya Itihasachin Sadhanen*, Vol. 15, p. 272. The term *Marhasta Rajya* occurs in *Jedhe Yancha Karina* published in *Shiva Charitra Pradip*, p. 43.

51. When Chhatrasal the Bundela chief waited on Shivaji, the Maratha King urged him, in an inspiring speech, to return to his own principality and fight the Mughals there. Lal Kavi, who must have heard an account of this meeting from Chhatrasal himself, says that Shivaji addressed the Bundela prince thus: "Does not the Chuttree faith consist in protecting the cow and the Brahmuns, in guarding the Veda, in showing skill and valor in battle? and if you lose your life, will you not through the solar orb enter the mansion of bliss, enjoying plentitude of happiness and repose?" W. R. Pogson, *A History of the Boondelas*, pp. 52—53.

Tukaram and Ramdas. He granted *inam* lands for " the illumination of, and food offerings to, the shrines of Muhammadan saints, and Muslim mosques were maintained by state allowance "[52]. Only once in his eventful career did he fail to respect the asylum given by a Muhammadan saint to some fugitives[53], but he never failed to show due respect to the holy scriptures of the Muslim. And Khafi Khan who delights in showering the most opprobrious epithets (e.g. the reprobate, the sharp son of the devil, the father of fraud, that dog, hell dog, evil malicious fellow)[54] on him is yet constrained to admit that, " he made it a rule that whenever his followers went plundering, they should do no harm to the mosques, the Book of God, or the women of any one. Whenever a copy of the sacred Kurán came into his hands, he treated it with respect, and gave it to some of his Musalmán followers. When the women of any Hindu or Muhammadan were taken prisoners by his men, and they had no friend to protect them, he watched over them until their relations came with a suitable ransom to buy their liberty "[55]. The ideal of a Maratha kingdom when preached by such a man made an irresistible appeal to the Marathas and they saw in him the long expected and long prophesied deliverer of the land that had once belonged to their ancestors. A grand son of Lukhji Jadhav, Shivaji could claim to be a descendant of the hero of the *Mahabharata*, while his father claimed the hero of the *Ramayana* for his ancestor[56]. Shivaji was himself popularly regarded as an incarnation of the god Shiva[57].

The old aristocracy did not respond to his call. Though the Mores of Jawli were broken, they would not bend the

52. *Sabhasad bakhar*, p. 33, Sen, *Siva Chhatrapati* pp. 38—39.

53. This saint was Jan Muhammad. See Scott, *History of the Dekkan*, Vol. II, p. 54.

54. Elliot and Dowson, *History of India*, Vol. VII, pp. 254, 256, 262 and 269.

55. Elliot and Dowson, *History of India*, Vol. VII, p. 260.

56. The Bhonslas claim to be a younger branch of the Udaipur family who in their turn asserted that they were descendants of Rama, the hero of the *Ramayana*.

57. *Sabhasad bakhar*, p. 6.

knee before the man of yesterday. The Ghorpades of Mudhol positively identified themselves with the Bijapur Government, and so did the Manes of Mhasvad. The Savants of Wari yielded to superior force but did so with reluctance and were never reconciled to their new lot. Even the Nimbalkars, near relations of Shivaji, could not be accounted steadfast friends. Thus Shivaji could not win to his side the landowning interests, but the masses flocked to him, they hailed him as their King and leader, and it was the tillers of the soil, the hewers of wood and drawers of water, who formed the mainstay of the new movement[58].

Religion has now lost the influence it once exercised over politics and it is not easy to realise to-day how Shivaji's message stirred his co-religionists outside Maharashtra. That it touched a few responsive hearts, there is no doubt at all. Did not Bhushan[59] travel all the way from Etawa to Raigad to sing the glories of the new champion of Hinduism? Were not the same notes echoed by Lalkavi[60]? Did not Chhatrasal, the renowned Bundela chief, look to Shivaji as his ideal[61]? To a Frenchman[62] he was a second Julius Cæsar, a second

58. Even in the closing years of the 18th century a Muhammadan writer, the author of *Tarikh-i-Ibrahim Khan*, remarked that most of the men in the Maratha army were husbandmen, carpenters and shopkeepers, men of mean birth. See Elliot and Dowson, *History of India*, Vol. VIII, p. 262.

59. Bhushan wrote *Shiva Raja Bhushan*, a series of laudatory verses in which he compared Shivaji with the legendary heroes of India and observed that but for him Hinduism would have vanished from Hindustan.

60. Lal Kavi wrote of Shivaji in the following terms :—"From the time that Ourungzeb ascended the throne, a great persecution of the Hindoos commenced; their temples were pulled down; their places of religious resort destroyed; their images mutilated; and a tax was levied on every house. The Rajpoots of the adjacent country were conquered, made obedient to the Emperor, and powerful armies were sent against those who resisted his commands. All were reduced to submission except one Raja, named Sheo Raj, who set a noble example of heroism and independence, overran eleven provinces, levied contributions, seized the Soo-bahdars, and destroyed the imperial troops, whose efforts he successfully continued to repel." *Chhatra Prakash*, Canto XI. Pogson, *A History of the Boondelas*, pp. 51—52.

61. Pogson, *A History of the Boondelas*, p. 52.

62. Carré, See Orme, Historical Fragment, p. 174. Carrê's "Histoire de Seva-gy" has been translated into English by the present writer and published in the *Calcutta Review*, February, 1928, pp. 222—244.

Gustavus Adolphus. Is it any wonder that the Hindus burning with the shame of their degradation should admire and worship him?

But the new ideal died with Shivaji. His successors were impelled by other motives and guided by other principles. There was a sure but not a slow reversion to the ancestral type, and feudal institutions were revived on a larger scale and with renewed vigour. The effect was disastrous; the common ideal was lost sight of and with it disappeared for ever unity of purpose. As its former ideal grew dim, the once notable discipline of the army degenerated, and in the end the only feature common to the military excursions of Shivaji and Balaji Baji Rao was the collection of *Chauth*.

CHAPTER II.

CHAUTH AND SARDESHMUKHI.

The term *chauth* has been invariably associated with the Marathas as an appropriate expression of their predatory genius. About its character there has been some difference of opinion; but its origin has been unanimously attributed to the resourceful mind of Shivaji. Shivaji, however, did not invent this ingenious method of raising revenue nor was the system by any means confined to the Marathas. Its character, which varied according to circumstances, may be likened to the variations of the chameleon's skin, which are frequently only skin-deep.

Long before Shivaji and his Marathas were heard of, a petty Rajput chief, the ancestor of the present Raja of Dharampur, used to exact *chauth* from the Portuguese subjects of Daman. His territories were first raided and then conquered by Shivaji and as all the rights and prerogatives of the conquered were held to have automatically passed to his conqueror, he demanded *chauth* from the Portuguese as a matter of course. The demand, however, was extended to Bassein, another Portuguese possession, and in the closing month of 1677 Pitambar Shenvi[1] was sent as an envoy from the Maratha court to the Portuguese capital to settle the question, if possible, by peaceful negotiations. The relations between the two powers were not uniformly friendly, and how the negotiations ultimately terminated we are unaware. But a few letters on the subject have come down to us, which, while representing the views of one party only, are conclusive evidence of the pre-Maratha origin of *chauth*.

The first of these letters was addressed to Shivaji by Pedro d'Almeida, Conde de Assumar, Viceroy of the Portuguese state in India, on the 10th January, 1678. It runs as follows :—" Pitambar Shenvi, the envoy of Your Highness, gave me a memorial on certain negotiations that speaks of

1 Sen, *Historical Records at Goa*, pp. 12—13.

some letters delivered to the Viceroy my predecessor, to which he had given no reply, for he was at that time occupied with some business. I immediately ordered a diligent search for them in the secretariat and I shall try to ascertain the particulars of which they treated, so that I may negotiate with Your Highness (on the subject). The envoy has delivered to me the much esteemed letter of Your Highness, in which Your Highness expresses satisfaction at my arrival, informing me of your health and the progress of your arms, which delighted me much, (for) it is in accord with the excellent friendship that Your Highness always had with this state, and Your Highness may be assured of the continuation of the good relation between us without any failure on my part as the Prince my master recommended to me. Your Highness asks me to write to the captains of the fortresses of Bassein and Daman that they should pay to Your Highness the *chauth* that has been always paid to the Chauthia, as Your Highness is now in possession of his territories, I order the said captains to inform me (about it), for having arrived here only a few days ago, I have till now got little information on this subject, and with their reply I shall advise Your Highness to send a person with powers to make a settlement with the people I nominate, and after an examination of the terms of the contract by which the said *chauth* was settled and the conditions with which it was conceded. Your Highness may be certain that when it is proved that Your Highness is the absolute master of the said territories, there will remain no doubt about paying to Your Highness what has been paid to the said Chauthia. As to the rest of what Your Highness tells me in your letter, I observe to Your Highness that the Portuguese are better as friends than as enemies, and as Your Highness is so wise, you should consider these things with care, that our amity may be preserved and augmented, and Your Highness will always find in me a faithful friend. May God illuminate the person of Your Highness in His Grace[2]." Two other letters were addressed on the same

2. *Livros dos Reis Visinhos* (Goa Archives), Vol. I, fol. 2. Sen, *Historical Records at Goa*, pp. 14—15.

date to Annaji Datto and Moropant Pingle. The letter written to Annaji could not be deciphered; but in the epistle addressed to the Peshwa, reference is made to his demand for *chauth*, and the answer is exactly similar to that in the letter quoted above[3]. The Viceroy, being a recent arrival in India, was bound to enquire into the justice of the Maratha claims.

On the 15th of January the Viceroy wrote a second letter to Shivaji: "I have already written to Your Highness another letter, in response to two of yours, which I delivered to Pitambar Shenvi, Your Highness's envoy. And I thought (it proper) to write this letter to renew my thanks to Your Highness for the demonstrations with which Your Highness welcomed my arrival which I shall reciprocate with loyal friendship, preserving for ever (the good relation) that Your Highness has with this state, as Your Highness will experience throughout the whole period of my administration, for I have conceived special affection for Your Highness, as I had already heard much about your great qualities while yet in Portugal, and also because the Prince, my master, had also charged me with all possible earnestness (to that effect). As regards the business on which the above mentioned envoy came I shall send an answer to Your Highness with all possible speed as Your Highness (may perceive) in this letter. The above mentioned envoy will be able to assure Your Highness of the good will that he finds in me and the expedition that I have given to the letters. I have ordered (letters) to be written to Moro Pandit and Annaji Pandit in reply to those of theirs, and to the captains of the fortresses of the North to inform them truthfully about the particulars of which I asked them to make enquiry regarding the *chauth*, and their answer I shall send to Your Highness; and in the said letters I have charged them to maintain good relations and amity with the Subedars of Your Highness, and not to suffer in our lands the malefactors of the Kolis and the Chauthia, so that they may not create disturbance or commit

3. Reis Visinhos, Vol. 1, fol. 2.

robberies in the territories of Your Highness. I expect Your Highness will also on your part require the said Subedars to keep the same relations and friendship with the said captains, so that there may not be between us any occasion for resentment or grievance. May God illumine the person of Your Highness in His Grace[4]."

Within a fortnight of the despatch of this letter the Count of Assumar left India for Mozambique, where he died fourteen months later. And the departure of the Viceroy, naturally caused some delay in the enquiry instituted by him, as is clear from a letter addressed to Pitambar, the Maratha envoy, by Antonio Paes de Sande, one of the two Commissioners in charge of the Portuguese Government in India during the absence of the Viceroy. The letter is dated the 12th July, 1678, and runs as follows:—" We have received the letters that Pitambar Shenvi wrote to me and the Arch-Bishop Primate, in which he represented to me that he came to this city in connection with the subject of the payment of *chauth* of the territories of Daman, which used to be paid to the King Chauthia. The Viceroy Dom Pedro d'Almeida replied that he would send for information (on this subject) from the Captain General of the North and from the commandant of the fortress of Daman, and when the said information came he would advise Shivaji Raze to send a person with authority to settle this business with the said captains, after examining the terms under which the said *chauth* was created; but the said advice had not come and the decision that was expected has been delayed. To this my answer is that the cause of the delay arose from the embarkation of the said Viceroy for Mozambique and on that account the said captains neglected to send the information he asked of them. It was not therefore possible to inform you that this state is not tributary to any neighbouring king. As however I desire to preserve peace and amity with Shivaji, I do not take any notice and pretend to be ignorant of the information that the said captains gave me. From that information it is clear that the said

4. Reis Visinhos, Vol. I, fol. 3.

chauth had its origin in the covenant that the village-managers (varadores das aldeas)[5] of the district of Daman made of their own initiative with the King Chauthia, without informing the past Viceroys and Governors, in order to avoid the loss and robbery that his subjects used to commit in those villages. From that covenant a contract has been solemnly drawn up with various conditions which were to be operative between them, and I have no doubt that in conformity with them the said *chauth* will be paid to Shivaji Raze, as I am told in his letters that Shivaji is in possession of his (Chauthia's) kingdom. To settle this business Pitambar Shenvi may advise Shivaji Raze to send on his behalf a person with proper authority. I write on this subject after consulting the captain of the fortress of Daman and examining the terms under which the agents of the said villages subjected them to the payment of the said *chauth*. The consideration of this affair is entrusted to the judges deputed for it, so that after the said villagers have been heard and the common law and the known custom relating to the *chauth* have been considered, the final decision on this matter may be made with justice. Shivaji Raze may be informed that I, on my part, do not lack the desire of seeing his claim decided so that our friendship may continue to increase[6]."

The last letter bequeathed to us on this subject bears the signature of Antonio Paes de Sande and was addressed to Shivaji on the 20th of March, 1679. As it deals with other subjects besides the Maratha claim of *chauth*, I quote here only the portion relevant to that matter. "Received the letter of Your Highness, delivered by Ganu Chaty, on the subject of sending Your Highness the *chauth* that some villages under the jurisdiction of Daman used to pay to the King Chauthia, as Your Highness is now in possession of those territories. Pitambar Shenvi, the envoy of Your Highness, discussed this subject in this city with the Viceroy

5. Varadores are frequently mentioned in the *Bombay Public Consultations* as assessors of rent.

6. Reis Visinhos, Vol. I, fol. 12. Sen, *Historical Records at Goa*, pp. 17—18.

Pedro d'Almeida, and after his departure and after I had succeeded him in this Government, I solicited Your Highness as a friend to settle (this question) and to send to that end a person on your behalf with all necessary power to treat of the form and conditions of payment. For this contribution was paid by some villages of the said (district of) Daman under certain conditions to be observed by the two parties in which this state did not otherwise participate, except in the matter of giving them that permission. All these have been shown in the letter I wrote to the said envoy to be presented to Your Highness. I now remit to Your Highness a copy of that letter, so that it may be clear that I have not in any way failed in the observance and preservation of peace and amity and in offering good will to Your Highness "[7].

These letters clearly prove that the Portuguese subjects of Daman used to pay a contribution called *chauth* to the Raja Chauthia as the price of his friendship; and this arrangement had been concluded sometime prior to 1677 with or without the knowledge of the Portuguese Government who were evidently not in a position to stop the depredations and the plundering raids of the Chauthia's subjects. But as Shivaji had demanded *chauth* from the people of Surat as early as 1664, the pre-Maratha origin of this contribution cannot be satisfactorily established unless it is proved that the mutual arrangement between the villagers of Daman and the Raja Chauthia, mentioned in Antonio Paes de Sande's letter, was concluded before that date. Fortunately, other Portuguese documents conclusively prove that this was the case.

On the 12th of March, 1635, a treaty on the subject of the payment of *chauth* was concluded between the King of Asarceta and the Captain of Daman. This treaty was ratified in 1670 and 1719 and it mentions in the preamble another treaty concluded as early as 1579[8], dealing with the same subject and the relation between the Portuguese Government

7. Reis Visinhos, Vol. I, fol. 29. Sen, *Historical Records at Goa*, p 21.

8. Biker, *Tratados da India e concertos de Pazes*, Vol. II, pp. 61—85.

and the Raja of Sarceta or Asarceta in the dominion of Ramnagar. In 1617 Jaeda Rana, King of Sarceta, sent two envoys for the conclusion of a defensive alliance as well as for the regular payment and correct assessment of *chauth*[9], and in 1604 a royal *alvara* was issued on the subject[10]. This *chauth*, therefore, came into existence as early as 1579, if not earlier, and continued to be paid by the villagers of Daman and collected by the Raja of Ramnagar until 1719[11]. Let us now determine what was exactly the relation between this Raja and his Portuguese neighbours, in what form this contribution was paid, and by whose agents it was collected.

In a letter to His Majesty the King of Portugal, dated the 11th September, 1638, the Viceroy, Pedro da Silva, defined *chauth*, which was paid by the inhabitants of Daman to the Raja of Sarceta, as " a kind of impost which obliges the said King not to harbour robbers in his dominions and to refrain from capturing men and cattle belonging to the farmers of the province of Daman[12]." The royal *alvara* or letter patent of 1604 states that the King has been informed that the captains of Daman do not treat the King Chauthia fairly, but pay his *chauth* in the form of overpriced old horses and other similar things. The King forbids this unfair practice on pain of severe penalties, and orders all persons concerned to pay *chauth* in cash[13].

Of more interest is the paper recounting the favours which Jaeda Rana of Sarceta solicited through his envoys in 1617. In the first place he was anxious to secure military help from the Portuguese in case of foreign invasion. Then he goes on to ask that the *chauth* belonging to one Berba may be paid to him, as the said Berba was his uncle, to whom the *chauth* had been given by the Raja's ancestors, and the sons and

9. Biker, *Tratados da India*, Vol. II, pp. 197—203.
10. Biker, *Tratados da India*, Vol. II, pp. 81—83.
11. See footnote No. 8.
12. Biker, *Tratados da India*, Vol. II, p. 101.
13. Biker, *Tratados da India*, Vol. II, p. 82.

wife of Berba had now transferred to the Raja the *chauth* originally belonging to Berba by a deed of gift, of which a copy was sent by the King for the Viceroy's perusal and examination. In this paper Berba's sons describe the *chauth* as their "grasso," a word derived from Sanskrit "grasa" meaning "maintenance allowance," and therefore somewhat analogous to the Maratha *watan*. The King further prayed that his *chauth* should be paid in *Mahmudi Chalanis* and not in *Mahmudi Chaparis*, as was then the practice, and suggested that as the Portuguese inhabitants of Daman did not return a correct statement of the revenue of their villages and the Raja was thereby defrauded of his income, the Viceroy should send an honest and conscientious Portuguese to make an enquiry in the matter[14]. The reply of the Portuguese Government and the observations made on the subject by Doctor Goncalo Pinto da Fonseca may be passed over, for a subsequent document informs us that the arrangement made on this occasion did not take effect. It is, however, worth remarking that when the King Chauthia had declared war against the Portuguese state in 1614, the Viceroy Dom Jeronymo de Azevedo had ordered the collection of *chauth* as usual by a commission of three, especially appointed on that occasion, to meet the expenses of maintaining a small force of fifty footmen for the defence of the *chauth*-paying territories out of the fund collected which was not otherwise to be interfered with[15].

But the most interesting document is the treaty of 1635. The word *chauth* really signifies "a quarter," but the first Article of this treaty definitely laid down that the Chauthia should in no case receive a quarter of the total revenue collected[16]. In some *parganas* his share amounted to 17 per cent, while in others he was entitled to no more than 14 and 12½ per cent of the revenue. To avoid misunderstanding, these *parganas* were clearly mentioned in the text of the treaty, and Article II debarred him from making any further demands

14. Biker, *Tratados da India*, Vol. I, pp. 197—200.
15. Biker, *Tratados da India*, Vol. II, pp. 83—85.
16. Biker, *Tratados da India*, Vol. II, p. 63.

from the peasants and landholders of these *parganas*, all his claims having been included in the above mentioned 17, 14 and 12½ per cent of the revenue[17]. It was settled by Article III that *chauth* should be collected annually in the month of October in the city of Daman and its sub-divisions, and not in the villages. According to Article IV the Raja Chauthia was expected to send his *Pradhan* and receiver at the appointed time of collection to collect and receive *chauth*, and two persons of noble birth and acknowledged honesty were to be elected by the officers and people of Daman to act as assessors of *chauth*. In return for the *chauth* which he received the Raja and his people were expected to refrain from doing any injury to the *chauth*-paying districts; and if any robbery or theft was committed in the district of Daman by any of the Raja's subjects, he was to hand over the culprits to receive condign punishment, failing which he would be obliged to pay compensation for the losses caused by his people. He was not to allow the Kolis and other predatory tribes to pass through his lands. The Raja of Sarceta was also required to serve His Majesty the King of Portugal with his army, whenever he was called upon to do so by the Governor and captains of the fortress of Daman. He was to be a true and honest friend of the city and province of Daman, as his grandfather and father before him had undertaken to be. This treaty was with certain modifications renewed and reconfirmed in 1670; but the first five articles which regulated the payment and collection of *chauth* remained unaltered, and from a letter of the Viceroy in 1719 it appears that the annual *chauth* (which no longer fulfilled the conditions implied in the term) amounted to 18,000 Xerafins[18].

Despite the protest of Antonio Paes de Sande, the payment of *chauth* cannot be regarded as a private arrangement of the villagers of Daman, when it formed the subject matter of so many treaties from 1579 to 1719; nor could the Portuguese Government have been so ignorant of this system in 1678,

17. Ibid.

18. Biker, *Tratados da India*, Vol. VI, pp. 6—7.

since one of the treaties had been renewed in 1670. It is equally clear that when the Portuguese Government conceded this impost to the King of Ramnagar, otherwise called the Chauthia, they did not in any way acknowledge his supremacy or suzerainty. On the contrary, from the language of the letter patent and the treaties already discussed, he seems to have been in the position of a vassal of the Portuguese. He received the *chauth* as a sort of remuneration for the performance of certain police duties[19]. It is noteworthy that in the viceregal letter of 1638 *chauth* is described as an impost, and in another viceregal letter of 1719 it is called a pension. Professor Pissurlencar, Curator of the Records at Goa, says in a paper recently published (May, 1926) that in the old Portuguese records the *chauth* is never styled a tribute. (Tanto isto é verdade que nos antigos documentos o chouto é designado como uma pensao ou foro e nunca como um tributo), and he quotes Antonio Bocarro, who wrote in 1634 that the Raja Chauthia had enjoyed this pension even in pre-Portuguese times[20]. This may or may not be accurate; but the *chauth* which he enjoyed in Portuguese times was hardly different from the perquisites granted in the period of the Peshwas to the Koli and Bhil Naiks for keeping their disorderly bands in check and maintaining peace and order throughout the countryside[20a].

The *chauth* that Shivaji demanded from his enemies and neighbours was quite different from a pension paid by a superior power in consideration of his services. Yet it is not difficult to see how the practice prevailing in the Portuguese province of the North must have suggested to the quick mind of the great Maratha leader the idea of exacting a regular contribution from his wealthy enemies to replenish his war chest. He often passed through the principalities of Jawhar and Ramnagar on his way to Surat, the richest emporium of

19. See Foot Note No. 12.

20. P. Pissurlencar, *Portugueses e Maratas*, pp. 40—41.

20a. It may not be an accidental coincidence that the perquisite granted to the Bhils for maintaining peace and order was also called *chauth*. See *Peshwa's Diaries*, Vol. III, pp. 162—163.

trade in the east, and he was served by a very efficient intelligence department. When he learnt how a petty chief like the Raja of Ramnagar had succeeded in securing a permanent and certain income, he decided to try an experiment on similar lines for his own advantage. But until he had conquered and annexed Ramnagar, he could not claim this impost as his "grasso" or "watan"; and even that conquest afforded little validity to his claim in the eyes of his Muhammadan neighbours. But he realised that similar evils demanded similar remedies, and that if the Chauthia could by his robberies and depredations compel the Portuguese to make financial concessions to his power, he might also extort similar tribute from the harassed villagers and townsmen of Mughal India. He in no way acknowledged the supremacy of the Emperor of Delhi when he demanded *chauth* from his subjects of Surat, nor did he undertake to render any service whatever to the Rajas of Sunda and Bednore, when they were compelled at the point of sword to pay *chauth* which in this instance may be styled a tribute, or more accurately, satisfaction for refraining from plundering their territories.

Shivaji was in urgent need of money. War required funds for its prosecution, even in those medieval days; and he was fighting simultaneously against two powerful enemies. He had done all that he could to develop the natural resources of his territories; but his normal income was hardly adequate for the incessant hostilities involved in the foundation of a new kingdom and the creation of a nation. He had therefore no alternative but to make war pay for war. The Muhammadan kings of India had set an example which he now emulated with rapid effect. He sent his army on *mulk-giri*, which connoted its existence at other people's expense for eight months out of the twelve. This was obviously a clumsy way of maintaining a standing army, for the material advantage accruing to the invading force was bound to be far less than the loss it inflicted on the invaded country. Shivaji realised that it would be far more profitable and convenient to exact a regular contribution from his enemies in return for an undertaking to refrain from plunder; and this was in fact the salient feature of his subsequent demand for *chauth*. Shivaji made his position quite clear in a letter to the Governor of Surat and Mirza Mosum to which reference is made in a letter written from Surat to Bombay on the 25th of June, 1672 (fol. 47, F. R. Surat. Vol. 87): "The same day also were brought letters from Sevage to the Governor and Mirza Mosum demanding the third time (which he wrote should be the last) the Couty or ¼ part of the king's revenues under this Government, declaring that as their king had forced him to keep an army, for defence of his people, and countrey so that army must be payed and if they sent him not the money speedily, he bid them make ready a large house for him, for he would come, and sitt downe here, and receive the rents and customs; for there was none now to stop his passage." Those who condemn Shivaji as an enemy of trade and commerce forget that no belligerent power can afford to foster trade and commerce in an enemy country, nor was it to his interest to constitute himself the guardian of peace and order in Mughal provinces. It was the business of the Mughal Government to provide for the security of life and property in their dominions. How sadly they had failed in this primary duty is evident from the account of their defenceless condition as conveyed by the Surat factors to their friends at Bombay on the 26th May, 1677. (F. R. Surat. Vol. 89, fol. 40 and 41). "This citty of Surat and the countreys adjacent have for this four years been under a continuall feare of being surprized by Sevagees army, for his soldiers are loged and garrisoned securely in Nunsaree and Gundavee and the chief officers taken up the Desy's owne houses who with their family and the Cozzy's and the chiefe men are all fled to Suratt, and Sevagees men do not only force contribution from the country but come boldly into this towne with forty or fifty horse att a time and publiquely demand provisions, and contributions from the Governor and the Kings officers, and tis confidently affirmed that Sevagees army increases daily more and more, and that many of his souldiers are lodged privately in the very town of Surat upon some designe, which hath caused the captain of the castle to raise 500 souldiers more for his defence, and to keep an extraordinary strict watch day and night and you may conceive that our French and Dutch neighbours, as well as ourselves, have the same apprehension for their masters' estates, and our own libertys, but should Sevagee surprize the towne, there is no possibility for us to oppose them, but must keep as fair termes with them as wee can." In demanding and exacting *chauth* from Mughal subjects Shivaji did nothing more than the primary duty of every soldier, which consists in taking every advantage of an enemy's weakness and unpreparedness.

Although Shivaji demanded $\frac{1}{4}$ of the total revenue collected by the government of the day from a district, it is quite possible that in actual practice he was contented with much less. In a letter from Rajapore, dated 6th February, 1674/75 (F. R. Surat. Vol. 88, fols. 15-20) we read " that some of Sevagees forces have bin att Callapore which redeemed itselfe from their fury by a present-giving of 1500 pagodas, thence they went to a place called Songam which gave them 500 pagodas." The total revenue of Kolhapur must have largely exceeded 6,000 pagodas. It must also be recorded to his credit that he did not in any way molest the towns and villages which paid *chauth*; and the foreign merchants at Surat suffered comparatively little annoyance from him. Whenever he annexed a town or a district, he took all possible care to protect the population from the military license of his soldiery[21].

21. In a letter from Chupra dated the 24th February, 1679-80, (Factory Records, Surat, Vol. 108, fol. 53) we read : " As to Sevagees forces they have plundered and burnt most of these parts, excepting the townes which pays him ¼ part, those he meddles not." It can be safely inferred that this was his uniform practice, for in a Surat letter dated the 19th December, 1670, (Factory Records, Surat, Vol. 105, fol. 93) we find that while he plundered Karanja, he spared the villages about Nandurbar, from which, " he hath taken writings that they will pay him ¼ per cent. (probably a clerical mistake) of the revenues thereof." In 1678 the Governor of Hubli purchased the forbearance of Shivaji's army by payment of *chauth* as the Carwar merchants wrote on the 5th May, 1678, " this hee sayes was partely (due) to the payment of Sevagee's ¼ part of the revenue of Hubely veliott, having made peace with him upon those termes "—(Factory Records, Surat, Vol. 107, fols. 91—92). Also see another Carwar letter dated 24th August, 1678, Factory Records, Surat, Vol. 107, fols. 135—136. The successors of Shivaji also conformed to the same practice

The *chauth* in Shivaji's time was, therefore, a military contribution paid by the defenceless subjects of enemy kingdoms and territories, for the protection of their lives and property from the invading Maratha army, which held them completely at its mercy. Shivaji did not claim it as a hereditary pension, to which he was legally entitled, nor did he base his claim on an imperial *farman*, his claim rested on a basis of might, and in cases where he failed to enforce his demand, he could not resort to the issue of a royal letter patent for the prosecution of his claim, as the Chauthia had done. Sambhaji and Rajaram in turn followed in the footsteps of their father, and the character of *chauth* remained unaltered and unaffected. During the twenty years of their reign the contribution, while continuing to bear the name of its Ramnagar prototype, did not properly conform to the characteristics of that payment, and it was not until the reign of their successor, Shahu, that a reversion to the ancestral type occurred.

Shahu received as a pension what Shivaji had demanded as a tribute, and what Shivaji had offered as a favour Shahu undertook as an obligation. To the Mughal Government *chauth* still remained what it had originally been *viz.*, the purchase price of peace and security; but while in Aurangzib's time its demand indicated defiance of imperial authority, in Bahadur Shah's time it connoted unquestioned acknowledgement of the Emperor's suzerainty. Since Shivaji's time the Marathas had never once renounced their claim to the *chauth*

as in 1704 they ravaged the greater part of Berar but desisted from doing any harm to the districts which were regular in the payment of *chauth*. See J. Scott, *History of the Dekkan*, Vol. II, p. 105. As for his treatment of the foreign merchants the Dutch Resident at Surat writes on the 14th November, 1670: "A messenger had come from the invader (Shivaji) to assure us that no harm would befall us if we remained quiet." (India office transcripts of Dutch Records, English Translation, Vol. 29, No. D C C LXIII). About his attitude towards the populace of a conquered city we have the following evidence of John Child and Thomas Michell who wrote from Raibag on the 7th August, 1675—"Newes was brought us early in the morning (of the 30th July), that Sevajees party in Callapore had seized the Governor there for the King; many of the inhabitants were leaving the towne but Sevajees souldiers kept all in with promise of faire usage; soe that the townes people are preserved in quiet and some security." Factory Records, Surat, Vol. 88, fol. 95.

of the Deccan, and whenever occasion offered they enforced their claim, as can be gathered from the pages of Khafi Khan; "With large armies they invaded the *Subas* of the Dakhin, and Ahmadabad, and Malwa, for the purpose of collecting the *chauth*. To cities and large towns they sent messengers and letters demanding payment of the *chauth* from the governor or *zamindar*. Or the *mukkaddams* and *zamindars* of the towns and villages hastened out to meet the Mahratta army, undertaking to pay the *chauth*, and begged for protection. Taking back with them a messenger and a horseman to protect the village and the cultivation, instead of showing their total rent to be one or two thousand (rupees) they made it out to be four or five hundred. But whatever sum was settled, they promised payment, and gave sureties, called *ol* in the language of India. They thus saved themselves from violence and plunder[22]." Shahu might have carried on this practice for the rest of his life without any reference to the Mughal Government, but he had spent his boyhood in the Mughal camp and had learnt to regard the Emperor of Delhi as the rightful sovereign of the whole of India. Moreover, both he and his cousin of Kolhapur were eager to strengthen his cause by enlisting on his side the moral support of the Mughal power, the visible sign of which was to be an imperial *farman* for the *chauth* and *sardeshmukhi* of the six *subhas* (provinces) of the Deccan, which the Maratha prince might then regard and cherish as his "*watan*". The ministers at Delhi were eager to take full advantage of the internal dissension existing among the Marathas by procrastinating and postponing the issue of the *farman* sought by the rival parties; but the men on the spot found it difficult to maintain peace and order and to protect the peasant on whose labours the state revenues mainly depended, without coming to some sort of understanding with the Marathas. Daud Khan, therefore, consented to pay *chauth* to the Maratha Chhatrapati with one important proviso —the *chauth* was to be collected for the Marathas by the Mughal revenue officers. By this arrangement the Marathas

22. Elliot and Dowson, *History of India*, Vol. VII, pp. 464-465.

would be unable to interfere with the peasantry or the internal administration of Mughal territory. This proposal, so necessary in the circumstances, did not meet with the approval of the Emperor and his ministers, and Chinkulich Khan, the next governor, was not disposed to accept the policy laid down by his predecessor in the office. Syed Hussain Ali, who replaced Chinkulich, at first made a determined but ineffectual effort to check Maratha depredations, and shortly afterwards political events at Delhi, which need no reference here, compelled him to purchase Maratha alliance at any price. Khafi Khan says that Hussain Ali came to an understanding with " Balaji Bishwanath and Jamnaji " (Chimnaji?) through the mediation of Shankraji Malhar, a Maharashtra Brahman, who had once held an important office under Rajaram Chhatrapati. " There was to be paid to the officers of Raja Shahu," says Khafi Khan, " a fourth of what *amins*, *kroris* and *shikkdars* collected as land revenue, and as *sair* from the government lands and from *jagirdars*. It was also settled that, in addition to the fourth share which they were to get from the receipts of the *jagirdars*, they were to receive from the *raiyats* ten per cent. as *sar-deshmukhi*. Altogether they were to receive thirty-five per cent upon the total collections, (and also) upon the *abwabs* called *faujdari*, *shikkdari*, *ziyafat*, and other charges, as shown in the gross account of the collections. According to this account they were to receive nearly half the total revenue recorded in the government rent-roll, and (the collections) thus shared by the domineering collectors of Raja Shahu. This arrangement, by which they were to collect all taxes, fell very hard upon the *raiyats*, and the government officers and *jagirdars*; for in every district there were two collectors—one called the *kamaishdar*, the other the *gumashta* of *sar-deshmukhi*. On the roll of the collection the signature of the *sarristadar* of the *sar-deshmukhi* was first placed, and what was required by the rules on that account was to be taken separately[23]." Thus the Marathas obtained their desire, the right of collecting *chauth* on their own account and by their

23. Elliot and Dowson, *History of India*, Vol. VII, p. 467.

own agents; and although their demand was sometimes excessive, the arrangement, as Khafi Khan shows, had certain redeeming features. "In some places, e.g., Berar and Khandesh, the Marathas took one third leaving one third to the raiyat and one third to the *jagirdars* and villages formerly rendered desolate were now restored to cultivation[24]." But if this purchase of Maratha protection was to the advantage of the cultivator the presence of the Maratha tax collector in the Mūghal provinces was incompatible with the sovereign rights of an independent power. It inevitably led to the further expansion of Maratha territory by the gradual absorption of the *chauth*-paying districts. It was on this account that Nizam-ul-Mulk found it necessary to purchase their departure from his immediate neighbourhood. "Nizam-ul-Mulk so arranged that instead of the *chauth* of the *suba* of Haidarabad, a sum of money should be paid from his treasury; and that the *sar-deshmukhi*, which was levied from the *raiyats* at the rate of ten per cent should be abandoned. He thus got rid of the presence of the *kamaish-dars* of the *chauth*, and the *gumashtas* of the *sar-deshmukhi* and the *rahdari*, from which latter impost great annoyance had fallen upon traders and travellers "[25].

But the concession of *chauth* was by no means unconditional. A Maratha force under the personal command of Balaji Vishwanath went to Delhi in the train of Syed Hussain Ali; and the grant of *chauth* and *sardeshmukhi* made by the Viceroy was confirmed by the puppet Emperor. One of these imperial *farmans* has come down to us; its terms are clear, definite and unambiguous. As a good and loyal vassal, Shahu undertook to serve the Viceroy of the Deccan with 15,000 men; as a wellwisher of the empire, he offered to restore the deserted and devastated villages to their former prosperity within a period of three years; as a good baron, he was to devote himself to the maintenance of peace and order in the imperial provinces of the south, and prevent miscreants and evil-doers from creating troubles and disorder. If a theft was

24. Elliot and Dowson, *History of India*, Vol. VII, p. 468.
25. Elliot and Dowson, *History of India*, Vol. VII, pp. 530-531.

committed in the imperial provinces, it was Shahu's business to detect the thief and punish him; if he failed to recover the stolen property, it was obligatory on him to pay compensation for the loss out of his own coffers[26]. Shahu by his acceptance of *chauth* and *sardeshmukhi* on these terms became for all practical purposes what Shivaji never agreed to be—viz., a servant of the Emperor of Delhi. Thus both in its character and in the method of collection *chauth* became in Shahu's time a pension, exactly as the Portuguese regarded it in their relations with the Raja Chauthia of Ramnagar. From this position neither Shahu nor any of his successors openly receded, though in their practice they seldom, if ever, performed their obligations. But if the Emperor could not enforce the terms of his *farman* on the Marathas, neither could he make his powerful governors respect it. This led to constant mutual recriminations; the Marathas could never rely on the punctual payment of *chauth*; while the contribution by no means always represented a quarter of the entire revenue. The Maratha chiefs would often compound their claim for a lower sum, as they did with Hyder; for the financial results of a campaign of depredation did not always come up to their expectations, as has been pointed out by two writers of different age and different nationality. Khafi Khan states that the Maratha leaders were always eager to settle the amount of *chauth* to be paid and were not willing to indulge in pillage and loot. "Their men, on the contrary, strove to prevent any arrangement of the *chauth*, so that they might be free to plunder[27]." We hear almost an echo of this in the words of the Dutch Admiral, John Splinter Stavorinus:—"It will naturally be asked, why do the opulent states submit to be tributary? and what security have they that these licentious plunderers will abide by their agreements, and not continually encroach upon them, and raise their demands. The reason is plain; it is less expensive, and a lighter tax upon trade, to

26. P. V. Mawjee and D. B. Parasnis, *Treaties, Agreements and Sanads*, pp. 1—4.

27. Elliot and Dowson, *History of India*, Vol. VII, p. 465.

agree to some certain payment, than to engage in the unknown expense of armies, to free themselves from so irregular a foe; and as to greater exactions, if the chief have once settled the Chout, he will hardly, venture to struggle for more, as the money agreed on goes to his own pocket; and were he to proceed to the more violent method of compulsion, by invading the country, the spoil would all become the property of his troops, under the articles of plunder, and his own share would come very short of the sum stipulated; besides they have the prudence to consider, that a country ravaged by their troops, will produce neither tribute nor plunder for a time "[28].

Only one question now remains to be answered, did the Marathas ever undertake to protect the *chauth*-paying countries from external aggression other than their own? Ranade says they did so. He writes: " In 1668, the Bijapur Adilshahi kings agreed to pay three lakhs of rupees on account of *chauth* and *sardeshmukhi*, and the Golconda ruler agreed to pay five lakhs about the same time. In 1671 *chauth* and *sardeshmukhi* levies were recovered from the Moghul province of Khandesh. In 1674, the Portuguese possessions in the Konkan were made to pay tribute by way of *chouth* and *sardeshmukhi* for that part of the country. In return for the tributes paid by the Bijapur and Golconda rulers, Shivaji undertook to protect them from the aggressions of the Moghuls, and this protection was found very effective in the wars which took place about that time. Before his death in 1680 Shivaji had thus established his system of subsidiary and tributary alliances with the consent of the Mahomedan and Hindu rulers in Southern India whom he protected, and he enforced his demand on some of the Moghul provinces also. The demand for *chouth* was subsequently added with the consent of the powers whose protection was undertaken against foreign aggression, on payment of fixed sums for the support of the troops maintained for such service. This was the original idea as worked out by Shivaji, and it was this same idea which in

28. John Splinter Stavorinus, *Voyages to the East Indies*, Vol. III, pp. 140—141.

the Marquis of Wellesley's hand bore such fruit a hundred and twenty-five years late "[29].

This ingenious explanation, however, will not bear close scrutiny. In the first place Ranade forgot that whatever might have been the nature of the agreement made between Shivaji and the Sultans of Bijapur and Golkonda in 1668, the actual treaties have not come down to us. We know, however, that Shivaji did not cease to harass the provinces of Bijapur and Golkonda during the last twelve years of his life. So far as the Portuguese were concerned, it is not clear whether they ever actually paid *chauth* and *sardeshmukhi*[30], but we have already seen on what terms they were prepared to allow Shivaji to collect *chauth* (and not *sardeshmukhi*) from villages under the jurisdiction of Daman. Shivaji exacted *chauth* from Mughal provinces without the consent of the ruling power. It is, therefore, needless to point out that " the original idea as worked out by Shivaji " bore no resemblance whatever to the " idea which in the Marquis of Wellesley's hand bore such fruit a hundred and twenty-five years later." The main features of the policy of subsidiary alliance as pursued by Wellesley was the surrender of the diplomatic independence on the part of the allied states on the one hand, and on the

29. Ranade, *Rise of the Maratha Power*, pp. 223-225.

30. According to a manuscript chronicle entitled *Rellacao da guerra que o Inimigo Marata fes no Estado da India, e dos progrecos della desde o dia seis de abril de 1737 the os primeiros de janerio de 1741 com algua's noticias das antecedencias e principios que teve origem a mesma guerra* (Archivo Ultramarino of Lisbon, fundo geral, No. 1605), the Marathas began to demand *sardeshmukhi* (or as the Portuguese writer calls it, " a decima parte de rendimento) from the Portuguese Province of the North as early as 1718, but it was not until 1739 that the Viceroy Conde de Sandomil agreed to pay 40 per cent. of the revenue. Vyankat Rao, the Marathas General, had penetrated into the Portuguese territories as far as Margao and his retreat had to be purchased at any price. And besides the 40 per cent. of the revenue the Viceroy further agreed to pay an indemnity of 20 lakhs of Rupees. The 40 per cent. probably consisted of 25 per cent. *chauth*, 10 per cent. *sardeshmukhi* and five per cent. *ghasdana*. Only one instalment of the indemnity was paid but when a Maratha General entered into the Portuguese territories to realise the promised tribute during the second viceroyalty of Marquez do Lourical, he was expelled by force of arms. See *Relacam das victorias alcancadas na India contra o inimigo Marata sendo Viceroy daquelle Estado o Illustrissimo e Excellentissimo D. Luiz Carlos Ignacio Xavier de Meneses V. Conde da Ericeira e 1° Marquez do Lourical*, pp. 9-15.

other, assumption by the East India Company of the responsibility for their defence against foreign aggression. With the internal affairs of their allies the East India Company's Government had nothing to do. Shahu, on the other hand, made himself responsible for the maintenance of peace and order in the six imperial provinces of the Deccan; and although he undertook to serve the Viceroy with 15,000 men, he could not expect the Mughal Government, which certainly did not agree, to surrender their diplomatic independence or to shape their foreign policy according to dictation from Satara or Poona. During the Peshwaship of Balaji Baji Rao and Madhav Rao I, we read more often of *khandani* and *mamlat*, under which terms were included all Maratha claims for the time being. The term *mamlat* was used in relation to the less powerful principalities like the Rajput states of Udaipur, Jodhpur and Jaipur, who were expected to pay their contribution with more regularity and without much resistance. It was never applied in relation to more powerful states like those of the Nizam and Mysore under Hyder Ali and Tipu, and the Maratha Government never concluded anything approaching a subsidiary alliance in their political relation with them. But the weaker states probably did expect some protection against foreign aggression as we may infer from a Hindi *sanad* granted to the Chief of Bhandawar by Balaji Baji Rao in the year 1746-47. The Chief ceded half his territories to the Peshwa, who in his turn undertook to defend his territories against all aggression[31]. Be it remarked, however, that protection was not purchased by the payment of *chauth* or any other contribution, but by territorial concessions, which are the usual accompaniment of a subsidiary alliance. By an agreement made with Rao Raja Umed Sing of Bundi in the year 1769-70, he was required to pay his *khandani* (tribute or contribution) punctually to the Peshwa's agent and to refrain from allying himself with any enemy of the Maratha state. The Peshwa offered to protect the Rao Raja "according to the agreement" if he behaved loyally to the Maratha state;

31. *Peshwa's Diaries*, Vol. III, p. 21.

but the nature and extent of this protection are in no way indicated in the above mentioned agreement[32].

While the Marathas exacted *chauth* on an extensive scale, the practice was not confined to them alone. According to Lal Kavi, the author of *Chhatra Prakash*, "Raja Chumput levied the chouth from all the neighbouring Umeers and Soobahdars, who hastened to transmit it to his camp in order to avert the impending calamity. On receiving that tribute from every contiguous country, province and city, he discontinued hostilities, and granted them peace and protection"[33]. When Chhatrasal resolved to wage war against the Emperor, he decided, as Lal tells us, to levy *chauth* on the Emperor's subjects. "Thus at the head of a powerful army, I shall wage war, levy contributions, and grant no respite till the enemy consents to pay the chouth. He may then remain unmolested." This was the plan disclosed by Chhatrasal to his brother Ratan Shah[34]. The Sikhs in the cis-Sutlej provinces also maintained themselves at the expense of their less warlike neighbours, and the reports of Maratha envoys at the court of Delhi show that Mahadaji Sindhia scarcely knew how to shield the imperial districts from their depredations. They demanded a contribution called *rakhi* which formed a proportion of the revenue of the district. At first it was two annas in the Rupee or 12½ per cent of the entire revenue; but with the growth of their power their demand increased, and they sometimes demanded as much as eight annas in the Rupee or 50 per cent of the revenue. In one letter we read that the Sikhs also claimed *chauth* from their victims[35].

Such contributions naturally appealed to the imagination of predatory people like the Bundelas and the Sikhs in their early days but it is not generally known that the English also

32. *Peshwa's Diaries*, Vol. IX, pp. 280—282.

33. Pogson, *A History of the Boondelas*, p. 23.

34. Pogson, *A History of the Boondelas*, p. 57.

35. Many letters published in *Delhi Yethil Marathyanchin Rajkaranen* refer to *rakhi* levied by the Sikhs. See Vol. I, pp. 112, 135, 156 and 164; for *chauth* levied by them see Vol. I, p. 181 and for their demand of fifty per cent of the revenue, see Vol. I, pp. 206—207.

on one occasion received *chauth* from two petty chiefs of the Bombay Presidency. It is needless to add that in this case *chauth* was not obtained by military expeditions or plundering raids; but the Maratha rights were by a peaceful agreement transferred to the English in 1802. Baji Rao II sought English assistance after his flight from Poona and signed the treaty of Bassein, which practically marks the end of the Maratha imperial power. Among the territorial and other rights which he conceded are mentioned "Waunsda Choute," which amounted to 7,000 Rupees, "Durumpoory Choute" 9,000 Rupees, and "Surat Choute" 4,21,000 Rupees[36]. Surat now forms an integral part of British India, and *chauth* no longer constitutes any part of its revenue; but the Raja of Dharampur still pays *chauth* to his British suzerain. The English took good care to include the *chauth* in all the territorial cessions obtained from the Peshwa's Government[37], for they knew that so long as the Marathas retained the right of collecting this contribution from the ceded districts, the English would never be secure from their interference. But the cession of the Dharampur *chauth* could not cause them any inconvenience, while the cession of the Surat *chauth* was doubly welcome, as it gave them in practice, if not in theory, full and undisputed dominion over that district of South Gujarat.

Lastly it may be noted that the Marathas once paid this humiliating impost to their hated enemy of Janjira, as is shown by the treaty of 1755 (concluded between the Peshwa Balaji Baji Rao and the English East India Company). Article IV of that treaty runs as follows: "It having been a custom, during the Government of Angria and the Mahrattas at Bancote that the Seeddees received a chouth or quarter part of the customs, the Mahrattas engage to satisfy the Seeddee in this particular, and that the Honourable Company do not meet with any embarrassment concerning it, nor concerning the

36. Aitchison, *Treaties Engagements and Sanads*, (1909 edition), Vol. VI, p. 59.

37. This is apparent from the treaty of 1755 and those of Salbye and Bassein.

royalty of this river, which is hereby given and made over to them for ever "[38].

In its origin and character *sardeshmukhi* differed widely from *chauth*. While the latter was based openly on might and could be exacted from any province of India, the former was based on a legal fiction and was expected to be limited in its application to the Deccan. Shivaji claimed to be the hereditary *sardeshmukh* of Maharashtra and *sardeshmukhi* was supposed to be his *watan*. In theory this claim did not conflict with the sovereign rights of the existing Governments and could be conceded by them with better grace and less loss of prestige. According to Ranade, Shivaji first claimed *sardeshmukhi* for Junnar and Ahmadnagar in 1650. In a letter dated the 1st of July, 1675, the Factors of Bombay wrote to their friends at Surat (F. R. Surat, Vol. 107, fol. 109): " Here hath been a very great report of peace settled between the Mogoll and Sevagee and it continues still much creditted and it is said that Sevagee is to deliver up all his castles and country which hee hath taken from the Mogoll reserving only Sallera and Mawlee and that hee is to be the King's Desy of all the countreys and that the present Governour of Junear is to come downe to be Governour of Cullian Brimberly but to this wee give noe certain creditt till wee heare further of it." Both Khafi Khan[39] and Bhimsen[40] inform us that Tara Bai offered to conclude peace with Aurangzib, if *sardeshmukhi* were granted her; or in other words she offered to serve the Emperor of Delhi as his Desai in the Deccan. But the Emperor's sense of prestige did not allow him to conclude peace on such terms. At last Daud Khan granted *sardeshmukhi* and *chauth* with the wise reservation that the collection of the two contributions should be left in the hands of Mughal agents. This arrangement, as has already been pointed out, did not meet with the Emperor's approval; and nothing but the imperial sanction could implement the fiction

38. Aitchison, *Treaties*, Vol. VI, p. 15.
39. Elliot and Dowson, *History of India*, Vol. VII, p. 409. According to Khafi Khan, Tara Bai demanded 9 per cent of the revenue.
40. Scott, *History of the Dekkan*, Vol. II, p. 151.

on which the demand for *sardeshmukhi* was based. Legal validity was eventually secured when Balaji Vishwanath obtained for Shahu imperial *farmans* for *chauth* and *sardeshmukhi*. The terms on which the grant was made were the same as in the case of *chauth*; but for the *sardeshmukhi* Shahu had to promise a *Peshkash* of one crore seventeen lakhs nineteen thousand three hundred and ninety Rupees twelve annas, a quarter of which was to be paid immediately and the remaining three quarters by instalments[41]. As a result of this arrangement, says Bhimsen, "for a time the calamities of war and its attendant famine, which had vexed Dekkan for a long series of years, subsided, and the people began to taste repose; but the governors of districts and farmers of revenue were more distressed than ever, as they had now three collectors, one from the presence, one for the choute, and a third for the deesmukkee[42]."

To the *chauth* and *sardeshmukhi* the Marathas added later another demand, viz., the *ghasdana*, or fodder money, a military contribution amounting to five per cent of the revenue. This contribution was specially associated with the Bhonslas of Nagpur and was sometimes levied even in the Peshwa's territories[43].

We have now examined at some length the origin and character of *chauth* and *sardeshmukhi*. The first grew out of a precedent found in the Portuguese province of the North, and the second was based on a legal fiction suggested by the prevailing revenue system of the country. Shivaji needed a strong army for his wars, and a strong army demands a long purse. To meet this demand he adopted these ingenious methods for raising funds. His aim was twofold. While he was fighting for his race and religion, he was also fighting to subdue the disruptive forces of feudalism. That was the reason why he could not follow his neighbours' custom of paying his men by grants of land or *jahgirs*, and was obliged

41. Mawjee and Parasnis, *Treaties, Agreements and Sanads*, pp. 3—4.
42. Scott, *History of the Dekkan*, Vol. II, p. 152.

43. It should not be supposed that the Bhonsla alone levied this contribution. It was levied by almost all the principal chiefs.

to find ready money by other means. Unfortunately for the future of the Maratha empire, the system which he devised for replenishing the exchequer of a militant national monarchy was subsequently employed to revive and extend that very feudalism, against which he had so wisely set his face, and which ultimately wrecked Maratha dominion.

CHAPTER III.

REVIVAL OF FEUDALISM.

Tradition dies hard. Reformers in every country and in every age have an uphill task. They are often far in advance of their contemporaries and the final success and ultimate acceptance of their ideals do not depend wholly on themselves. The gospel of Christ, the inspired utterances of Muhammad needed the Apostles and the Khalifas respectively for their dissemination and acceptance by the world. The ardent loyalty to the king which Shivaji had inspired in his people, the iron discipline which he had enforced in his army, the subordination of the military to the civil authority which he had striven to secure, were not in any way the result of orderly evolution from historic precedent, but were essentially new revolutionary ideas conceived by the mind of a born leader of men. Novel though his ideas were, they failed to shake the implicit trust of the people in him or to arouse their doubts as to the soundness of his policy. His successors, unfortunately, had neither the foresight nor the ability to carry on his unfinished work, and when the moral impetus which he had given to it was spent, old ideas regained their ascendancy and feudalism entered upon a new and vigorous life.

Sambhaji has been blamed for undoing his father's work, but for the revival of feudalism he was not responsible. He was a good soldier but he did not possess his father's statesmanship, vision and idealism. With his troops he was immensely popular and although his personal example was hardly calculated to improve discipline, he did nothing to encourage hereditary appointments in the army. His financial difficulties were great and punctual payment was impossible. This led him to relax the military code of his father; and spoils of war which in Shivaji's time had formed the property of the State were now left entirely to the army. This no doubt impaired discipline, but Sambhaji went no further. He did not try to solve his financial difficulties by creation of fiefs in favour of his military officers, and the inspiration which he failed to give during his life time he supplied by his death. For though he lived a rake, he died a martyr and for a time at least his demoralised followers were fired with a religious enthusiasm that Sambhaji's death had kindled.

The period succeeding Sambhaji's death, though decidedly critical, was not wholly destitute of hope for the Marathas. It is true they were losing fort after fort, and that Rajaram, their new king, had to seek safety in distant Jinji, leaving the defence of Maharashtra in other hands. It is true that Maratha officers, like Suryaji Pisar, did not hesitate, as in the days of old, to sacrifice the interests of the State to their own. Yet, thanks to Aurangzib, a new spirit was engendered among the Marathas and the triple barrier, which divided them politically so long, was demolished by the Mughal conquest of Bijapur and Golkonda. Moreover, the imposition of *jiziya* was not calculated to conciliate a warlike people who had long been unfamiliar with religious intolerance. Unfortunately Rajaram, who did not possess the magnetic personality of his father, permitted himself to delegate his authority to two Brahman officers, and thereby lowered the prestige of the kingly office in an epoch when the ruler had perforce to be either the supreme war-lord of the State, or, failing that, a nonentity. The task which he had thus delegated to Pralhad Niraji and Ramchandra Pant Hukmatpanha was unusually arduous, for with an empty war-chest, they were expected to repel an attack backed by the whole weight of the Mughal empire. Aurangzib's errors of policy had disposed the majority of the Marathas to support their cause; but despite this fact, their inability to command the same devotion that was shown to Shivaji or that would have been shown to Rajaram, if he had inherited his father's qualities, obliged them to purchase the loyalty of their adherents by concessions of the type most appreciated by the Marathas. Hereditary fiefs were created in favour of successful warriors and fresh services were rewarded with fresh *jahgirs*. In fact the *jahgir* was often granted in districts still in Mughal possession and the favoured *jahgirdar* had frequently to kill the bear before he could own the skin. The old discipline fell rapidly out of date, and Shantaji Ghorpade, the only officer who adhered to it[1], was weakly sacrificed by the impotent King to the fury of his discontented soldiers. Within twenty years of his death Shivaji's military reforms were relegated to the scrap-heap, though the kingdom he had founded still survived.

The decline of the monarchy steadily continued after Rajaram's death, for the long minority of his two sons offered excellent opportunities to the fief-holders of consolidating their power and extending their prerogatives. The advent of Shahu still further improved their chances. Shahu's claim to the throne of Satara was hotly contested by Tara Bai and her partisans, and this led to a long civil war by which the Mughals alone profited. The feudal chiefs made the best use of the monarchy's need and weakness, and Damaji Thorat, Udaji Chauhan and Kanhoji Angria began to ravage Shahu's territories and to exact *chauth* from his partisans. These powerful chiefs have been described as robbers and miscreants by Grant Duff, for he derived his information from the Satara records. But in theory they regarded themselves as vassals of the rival house of Kolhapur and considered the persons and property of Shahu's followers as their rightful prize. Ultimately Shahu's party emerged victorious and the power of his Kolhapur cousin was limited to a small principality, with option to extend towards the south and with free communication with the sea through the old naval port at Malwan. Shahu's success, however, far from restoring the power of the royal house of Satara, was merely symptomatic of the complete revival of feudalism.

Balaji Vishwanath, who contributed more than anybody else to Shahu's success, found it beyond his power to reduce

1. Khafi Khan says that Shantaji used to inflict very severe punishment for the slightest offence. See Elliot and Dowson, *History of India*, Vol. VII, p. 359. Rajaram did nothing to compose the differences between Shantaji and Dhanaji, the unpopular general was deserted by his followers and when the death hunt was being vigorously made the weak Raja remained an indifferent and impotent spectator.

Kanhoji Angria, but managed to achieve by diplomacy what he could not obtain by war. Kanhoji offered allegiance to Shahu, but retained his fief and naval command. Probably this suggested to Balaji a new method of conciliating other military chiefs and restoring internal peace and order by directing their attention abroad. When he obtained the imperial *farmans* for *chauth* and *sardeshmukhi* for his master, he had some thing tempting and some thing definite to offer to those who would loyally serve Shahu and acknowledge his authority. The *sardeshmukhi* was the Raja's *watan* and could not be alienated; but only a quarter of the *chauth* was retained for the Raja and was henceforth styled *Rajbabti* or royal perquisite. The remaining three fourth of the *chauth* was available for distribution among Shahu's followers, six per cent of the total *chauth*, called in Marathi *sahotra*, was set apart for the Sachiv; another three per cent was denominated *nadgaundi*, while the balance called *mokasa* was granted to different military leaders, in return for their maintenance of a fixed military contingent and an undertaking to perform military service on behalf of the State, whenever occasion so demanded. Balaji Vishwanath's arrangement, however, did not end here. Lest the interests of the different chiefs should in any way clash and lead to hostilities, he clearly defined their "spheres of activity." Thus Khandesh and some part of Balaghat were reserved for the Peshwa; the Senapati received Baglan and Gujarat; to the Sena Saheb Subha was assigned Berar and Gondwana and all the territories to the east; the Sarlaskar was in charge of Gangthadi and the province of Aurangabad; while the districts between the Nira and the Warna were left to the Pratinidhi's care[2]. These chiefs were to collect *chauth* from the territories assigned to them; they could if they liked extend their activities further in their immediate neighbourhood. They were to make a stipulated contribution to the royal treasury and to meet the expenses of some of the *karkhanas* or royal establishments; within their fiefs they were to exercise

2. Malhar Ram Rao Chitnis, *Thorle Shahu Maharaj Yanche Charitra*, ed. Sane, 3rd edition, p. 47.

sovereign authority without any interference from the Raja. Thus peace at home and expansion abroad were at once provided for. As some checks on these feudal chiefs, who for all practical purposes became independent princes, their civil establishments were appointed from head quarters. The Raja's Chitnis sent his agent for similar work with a *jahgirdar*, as also did the Fadnis and the Potnis. The King was henceforth not to trouble himself about financing military expeditions or the payment of the army. The *sardeshmukhi* and *babti* were expected to meet all his personal needs. Thus the feudalisation of the army and the State was complete.

Spain had recourse to a somewhat analogous arrangement when adventurers like Cortes and Pizzaro were authorised to equip military expeditions on their own account. The King was occupied with matters nearer home and had neither the time nor the means to undertake distant conquests and private enterprise was encouraged where the State was unwilling to risk men and money on expeditions of doubtful character. The leaders of such expeditions naturally demanded dictatorial powers and were rewarded with rich grants in the newly conquered lands. The State profited without running any risk. But here the Spanish analogy ends; for the extraordinary authority and special powers conceded to the first "conquistadores" were not hereditary, and the Spanish Government took good care to curb their power by sending special commissions to the newly conquered kingdoms. It may also be added here that the Portuguese followed a similar policy in India, most of the lands in Bassein and Bombay having been granted in the first instance to deserving military officials and others, who in return were bound to furnish military service to the King of Portugal. Subsequently, the obligation to perform military service was exchanged for a "quit-rent." The defects of the Maratha system were obvious. It made unity of command impossible and created hereditary commands by postulating hereditary genius. It transferred civil administration to military officers who were not necessarily qualified for such works, and as a result even military efficiency suffered.

In theory the Senapati still continued to be the Commander-in-Chief, but in practice he was supplanted by the Peshwa. Under Shivaji's scheme the Peshwa had to lead expeditions and to render military service like the Dalwai[3] of the old Vijayanagar kingdom; but during the reign of Rajaram the chief command was conferred on able generals, such as Shantaji Ghorpade and Dhanaji Jadhav, whose military reputation was so high that no Peshwa could think of disputing their authority. Shahu appointed Chandrasen Jadhav to the office of Senapati on his father's death; but when Chandrasen joined the Nizam, the office was conferred on Khande Rao Dabhade[4]. His son Trimbak Rao, a military officer of high reputation, was defeated and killed by Baji Rao at Dubhoi, and thereafter the Senapati hardly played any part in Maratha history, although the Dabhades still continued to enjoy their *jahgir*. When the family was at last deprived of its hereditary office and *jahgir*, the Peshwa simply legitimised an accomplished fact by granting Gujarat to the Gaikwads with the office of Sena Khaskhel. The office of Senapati was on different occasions offered to Ramchandra Jadhav and Murar Rao Ghorpade, both of whom had hereditary connection with the office; but by that date it had become an empty honour.

In rank the Sarlaskar, the Sena Saheb Subha and the Sena Khaskhel were below the Senapati, but it is difficult to say which of these officers had precedence over the others. The office of Sarlaskar was older than the other two and the office of Sena Khaskhel was originally conferred on a junior member of the Senapati's family, just as the posts of Sena Dhurandhar and Sena Bahadur[5] afterwards served to console the junior

3. It is worth noting that Dalwai and Peshwa are synonymous terms, and both the officers exercised almost the same functions. I am inclined to think that the Peshwa's office was created after the model of that of the Dalwai rather than that of the Vizier.

4. Khande Rao's immediate predecessors were Chandrasen's step-brother Santaji Jadhav, and Man Sing More. See *Itihas Sangraha, Peshave Daftarantil Sanadpatranil Mahiti*, p. 349.

5. The Sena Dhurandhar's office was certainly older than that of the Sena Saheb Subha, for it is mentioned in the memorandum drawn in the first year of the coronation era. See Sane, *Patre Yadi Bagaire*, p. 358.

members of the Bhonsle family, the eldest branch alone being entitled to the higher office of Sena Saheb Subha. To each of these offices was attached a *jahgir* in return for which the holder was expected to maintain a stipulated force. These honours, it appears, were confined only to the older families who had risen to prominence under Rajaram or Shahu.

This system did not work well, and led to conflict which it was expected to obviate. The Peshwa fought with the Senapati, the Dabhades rendered no service to the State as genius was not hereditary, the Gaikwad and the Bhonsla were not very favourably disposed towards the Peshwa and the Peshwa found it necessary to trespass on their special reserves. But the lesson of this failure was absolutely lost on the Peshwas, who, as their empire expanded, continued to create new fiefs more or less on the old lines.

In the new scheme the King's perquisites, *sardeshmukhi* and *babti*, naturally found no place. The revenue, whether collected in the annexed territories or exacted in the shape of contributions in the neighbouring dominions, was divided between the Peshwa and his Sardars. The Sardar obtained a *saranjam* or fief in lieu of his stipulated service; and although the Peshwas did not look upon the old chiefs, who held their fiefs directly from the King, with a kindly eye, the number of *saranjams* they created was enormous. These varied in size and character as well as in importance, as the stipulated quota, for which they were granted, ranged from one to twenty-two thousand *sawars* or horsemen. A list, drawn up in the year 1811-12, enumerates no less than sixty *saranjamdars*, exclusive of the powerful Sardars of Central India like the Sindhia, the Holkar, the Pawars and the Bundele[6]. They did not all get equally favourable terms. In the paper, mentioned above, we find that Nilkantha Mahadev Purandare enjoyed a *saranjam* of 2,00,000 Rupees for a body of 500 horse, while Sadashiv

The duties assigned to this office were similar to those of the Biniwala or Quarter Master General in the Peshwa period. For a *sanad* granted to Khandoji Bhonsle, Sena Bahadur, see *Itihas Sangraha, Peshave Daftarantil Sanadapatrantil Mahiti*, pp. 183-184.

6. *Itihas Sangraha, Peshave Dafatarantil Nivadak Kagadpatra*, pp. 44-46.

Mankeshwar obtained, for an equal force, a *saranjam* of 2,50,000 Rupees. Chhatra Sing Toke's *saranjam* amounted to 20,000 Rupees for a quota of 30 horses; for a similar quota Ananda Rao Thorat got no more than 14,000 Rupees. The *saranjam* figures of Raghuji Angria (60,000 Rupees for one horseman) and the Panshes (40,000 Rupees for two horsemen) are rather misleading; for Angria was the hereditary Lord High Admiral (" wajarat mav ") and the Panshes were in charge of the artillery and were not expected to serve the State at the head of a body of cavalry. The difference in the value of the *saranjam* is to be attributed to the difference in the personal allowance granted to each chief, which was settled on the merit of each case; and this principle (or want of it) prevailed as much in Central India as in the Deccan. Malhar Rao Holkar was granted a *saranjam* of ninety-five lakhs of Rupees for maintaining a cavalry force of 22,000 but Ananda Rao Pawar received no more than forty-five lakhs for a force of 15,000[7].

On paper the scheme looked quite simple and eminently practical. The burden of the civil administration and the military defence of the major portion of the empire was thrown on these *saranjam*-holders. Their interest thus became or was expected to be strictly identified with the interests of the State. They were to work a ready made and clearly defined scheme and a number of civil officers whom they could not dismiss were deputed to assist them or see that they did not in any way deviate from the line laid down by the Peshwa's Government. As under the earlier scheme of Balaji Vishwanath, the chief Sardars could (with the Peshwa's permission) lead expeditions of conquest and annexation, which would at once enhance their own importance and contribute to the expansion of the empire. The terms were generally precise and unambiguous, as we find in the *sanad* granted to Mahipat Rao Kavde in 1762-63. Mahipat Rao had previously obtained a *saranjam* for 2,500 horse. Under the terms of the new grant he was expected to maintain an additional force of 1,000. Each horseman was to receive a

7. Sane, *Patre Yadi Bagaire*, pp. 547-548.

salary of 250 Rupees a year, all charges included. And out of the income of his fief Mahipat Rao was to maintain the following civil staff on an annual salary indicated below:—

Diwan	... ...	Rs. 5,000
Khasnis	... ...	,, 5,000
Fadnis	... ...	,, 950
Sabnis	... ...	,, 400
Daftardar	... ...	,, 350
Chitnis	... ...	,, 400
Parasnis	... ...	,, 250
Jamdar	... ...	,, 300

These were the *darakhadars* or feemen designed as a check on the *saranjamdar*, who was expected to keep an additional staff of three clerks at an annual salary of 350, 300, and 250 Rupees each. As he was a chief of some importance, it was rightly surmised that he would have some *saranjamdars* of his own; and as he would have to make provision for their civil staff, an extra sum of 2,000 Rupees was granted for this purpose[8].

The *saranjamdar* himself obtained a village for the residence of his family. He was to allow the muster of his stipulated quota and receive an acknowledgement after the muster had been taken. Then he had to deduct from the revenue the sum due for the civil staff and the cavalry force in his employ, as well as his personal allowance, which was fixed at 25,000 Rupees. The balance was to be paid to the Government treasury.

In practice, however, these Sardars failed to identify their interests with those of the State. They did not maintain the stipulated force. They did not always pay their men according to the scale laid down by the Peshwa[9] and the number and value of their horses were generally below the required standard.

The Peshwas had their own method of classifying horses as first class, second class, third class and useless. We read

8. *Peshwa's Diaries*, Vol. IX, pp. 310-314.

9. See *Harivamshachi Bakhari*, p. 88.

in a paper[10] of Balaji Baji Rao's time that, "A horse worth Rs. 400 should be classed as superior, that worth Rs. 200 as middling and that worth Rs. 100 as inferior. Any horse worth less than Rs. 100 should not be counted in the muster. A horse classed as superior but having a bad rider should not be counted in the muster." The standard was obviously lowered in Baji Rao's time, for we find in the *sanad* granted to Bapuji Ganesh Gokhle[11] in 1813-14 that a horse worth Rs. 300 was to be regarded as first class and a horse worth Rs. 150 as second class, and it is clear from the few papers that have come down to us that in a *saranjamdar's* force first class animals formed a small proportion, and third class mounts largely preponderated though they were often expressly forbidden to employ third class and useless horses. In 1764-65, during the Karnatak expedition a muster of Khande Rao Pawar's cavalry was taken at Galagnath on the banks of the Tungabhadra and out of the 963 horses of his forces :—

221 were found first class,
350 ,, ,, second class,
238 ,, ,, third class,
154 ,, ,, useless.

Or in other words only 25 per cent of the animals came up to the required standard[12]. Nor was this an exceptional case; for three years later a muster was taken of the cavalry force under Gopal Govinda Patwardhan[13] and the figures given below show that the majority of the animals were below standard. The total strength of his cavalry was 11,525 and of these :—

2,950 horses were first class,
5,653 ,, ,, second class,
2,566 ,, ,, third class,
356 ,, ,, useless.

10. *Peshwa's Diaries*, Vol. III, p. 183.
11. *Itihas Sangraha, Peshave Daftarantil Nivandak Kagadpatra*, p. 88.
12. *Itihas Sangraha, P. D. Nivadak Kagadpatra*, p. 61.
13. Ibid, p. 72.

In 1784-85 Chintaman Panduranga Patwardhan[14] attended the muster with 1,283 *sawars* or horsemen, of these :—

133 rode first class horses.
1,088 ,, second ,, ,,
and 62 ,, third ,, ,,

In this instance the number of third class animals employed was negligible but the proportion of first class horses was by no means high.

If the horses were bad, the riders could not be expected to be much better; for they were seldom regularly paid. The salary of a horseman in the Peshwa days generally varied from 250 to 300 Rupees a year. In 1802-3 Baji Rao II authorised one Muhammad Jamaluddin to raise a force of 2,000 Pathans at 600 Rupees per annum per man[15], and although this sum included compensation for fallen animals and allowance for wounds incurred in action, as well as the cost of ammunition, it must be regarded as unusually high. The Peshwa found himself compelled to raise forces on any terms and probably conceded whatever was demanded by the Pathan officer, for in a paper dated 1804-5 we find that 38 Rupees per month was considered an exceptional salary for a horseman[16]. But whatever the salary allotted in the *sanad*, the ordinary soldier seldom expected to draw it regularly. We read in the *Harivamshachi Bakhar* that one of the Patwardhan chiefs deducted one month's salary every year and he should be considered very moderate[17], when the Peshwa's agent at Maheshwar writes that Holkar had failed to pay his soldiers regularly for five consecutive years. They were at last content to write off a part of their arrears, while the remainder was paid partly in cash, partly in kind and partly by *varat* or assignment[18]. Even this settlement was

14. Ibid, p. 72.
15. Ibid, p. 75.
16. Ibid, p. 75.

17. The chief used to draw from the State 11 month's pay, so his men were actually expected to serve for twelve months and were paid for ten months.

18. *Itihas Sangraha, Maheshwar Darbarchin Batmi Patren*, Vol. II, p. 225.

only made after Holkar had been subjected to a rigorous *dharna*[19].

The reason was obvious. The *saranjam*-holder had a twofold duty to perform. He was not only a military commander, but also a civil governor and in this latter capacity he had to finance the army under his command. Whenever he was called upon to lead or take part in an expedition, he mobilised his army, enlisted new recruits if necessary, and took the field as early as possible. Before, however, he could leave his headquarters, he had to advance his *Silhedars* a part of their pay under the style of *nalbandi*. He had to purchase arms and ammunition and cattle for transport purposes. The Peshwa's Government did not advance the necessary funds and the *saranjam*-holder had generally to raise it as best as he could. As a rule he contracted a loan which he expected to pay out of the proceeds of war; but all campaigns were not equally profitable, and, when the campaign was concluded, he had to submit his accounts to the examination of the Peshwa's accounts department. But even when it was clearly established that he was entitled to financial relief, the *saranjamdar* could not hope for anything but an addition to his *jahgir*. He was by the terms of his appointment bound to render an account of his civil stewardship as regularly as possible and to give a muster of his forces; but this was done at long intervals. Thus was created a vicious circle whereby military needs affected the efficiency of the civil administration and the inefficiency of the civil government reacted

19. *Dharna* was an extreme form of dunning. "The person who adopts this expedient for the purpose mentioned, proceeds to the door or house of the person against whom it is directed, or wherever he may most conveniently intercept him; he there sits down in *dherna*, with poison, or a poignard, or some other instrument of suicide, in his hand; and threatening to use it if his adversary should attempt to molest or pass him. In this situation the Brahmin fasts; and by the rigour of the etiquette, which is rarely infringed, the unfortunate object of his arrest ought also to fast; and thus they both remain until the institutor of the *dherna* obtains satisfaction." Lord Teignmouth, quoted by Forbes, *Oriental Memoirs*, Vol. II, p. 24-25. On the occasion alluded to above, Holkar was compelled by his creditors to abstain from food and drink for three consecutive days.

disastrously upon military efficiency. Both Sindhia and Holkar found it necessary to raise money by mortgaging the future revenue of their provinces and selling governorships to their creditors[20]. But even these makeshifts could not indefinitely postpone the final disaster and there came a day when the great chiefs found themselves unable to meet the just demands of their soldiers on the one hand and to render any satisfactory account of their revenue to the supreme Government on the other. On one occasion Sindhia had to submit seven years' accounts at one time, when it was found that the papers had not been properly kept[21]. The financial difficulties of Holkar led to the gradual dissolution of his forces, so that in September, 1785, he had only fifteen hundred men for four thousand horses shown on paper[22]. Some of the chiefs tried to solve the difficulty by employing only a small force in times of peace and raising fresh levies when called upon to join the Peshwa's banner. The Government often encouraged this practice, as the Peshwa on his part wanted to save the revenue by the reduction of the standing army which the fief-holder was expected to maintain. The Government at the same time expected the fief-holders to credit to its coffers the monetary equivalent for the services of which it was thus deprived. In extreme cases an indigent chief sometimes failed to render any military service or to compensate for it in cash and such failure or delinquency often escaped the stern punishment it deserved. In 1768 the Peshwa Madhav Rao ordered the confiscation of the fief of Maloji Ghorpade of Mudhol[23], as he had failed either to render military service or in the alternative to pay compensation therefor. But it does not appear that the order was executed; for a year later we find him still in possession of a large fief with an income of 1,73,900 Rupees and in 1794 he served with a cavalry force of 775 men against the Nizam at

20. Several instances of this practice are given in *Itihas Sangraha, Maheshwar Darbarchin Batmi Patren.* See Vol. II, p. 110 and 240.

21. Sane, *Patre Yadi Bagaire*, p. 318.

22. *Itihas Sangraha, Maheshwar Darbarchin Batmi Patren*, Vol. II, p. 84.

23. *Itihas Sangraha, Peshave Daftarantil Nivadak Kagadpatra*, p. 60.

Kurdla. Once feudalism was re-established, the Maratha tradition concerning the sanctity of *watan* stood in the way of any effective military reform. In February, 1787, Murar Rao Jadhav was deprived of his fief and command, as being of no use to the State[24]; but his sister-in-law was permitted to adopt a young man of the family whom she had brought up from childhood, and this youth was invested with the command of which his uncle had been deprived. It is needless to remark that such a shifting of command in itself could hardly improve the state of affairs, but as the Peshwa derived his authority from feudal customs, he could not abolish them when they happened to militate against his personal wishes and plans.

More than once attempts were made to reduce recalcitrant chiefs to submission, but beyond obviating one or two more salient shortcomings, they failed of effect and tended rather to establish more firmly the fundamental error of the system. Baji Rao I fought against Trimbak Rao Dabhade and defeated him, thus affording the strange spectacle of two servants of the same master engaged in mutual hostilities. The Senapati's power collapsed not so much by reason of that single defeat as from the fact that he had no able successor. Yet it was not possible to take full advantage of the victory, by depriving the Dabhades of their extensive fiefs immediately after the battle of Dubhoi. Similarly Damaji Gaikwad was defeated by the Peshwa's forces when he hastened to the support of Tarabai; yet it was found impracticable to crush the Gaikwads as the Dabhades had been. In his conflict with these old Sardars or military chiefs the Peshwa relied on the support of his own adherents. These in their turn were rewarded with rich fiefs and became the founders of new families. At first their gratitude held them steadfastly to their master's side, but the baneful example of the master himself was too tempting for the next generation. The Peshwa continued to multiply fiefs unchecked, and fired by his example, the rulers of various

24. Ibid, p. 92.

Maratha principalities introduced wide-spread sub-infeudation by rewarding their own immediate adherents and followers in the same manner.

But the Peshwas were not altogether blind to the possibility of the sons and grandsons of their loyal vassals growing weary of their allegiance. This they tried to prevent by playing on their mutual jealousy. Sindhia and Holkar were designed to be the two stout pillars of the Maratha empire in the north; but not infrequently they failed to agree with one another, and a day came when they became openly hostile and turned their arms against one another. The policy of the Poona Government was to effect a breach and to keep it open, not merely between two neighbouring chiefs but even between brothers of the same family. Thus they exploited the differences between Manaji and Sambhaji Angria, Govinda Rao and Fatte Sing Gaikwad, Sabaji and Mudhoji Bhonsla. But a military power based on suspicion and jealousy cannot last long; the policy recoiled against its originators when the feudal chiefs on their part exploited the dissension and disunion in the Peshwa's family. When the State, weakened by civil war, was threatened by a foreign power, Sindhia and Holkar did not fail to increase their power at its expense and Bhonsla confined himself to a policy of prevarication at a moment when active co-operation in a concerted scheme of defence and offence was imperatively required.

Feudalism was not the only evil from which the Marathas suffered. With the expansion of their empire they gradually but completely lost the early impulse, the original idea which had converted a disunited race into an imperial power. Shivaji had given the Marathas a common cry; and none appreciated the potency of that cry more clearly than Peshwa Baji Rao I. Shivaji's military reforms he would not or could not revive, but he stood forth, as Shivaji had done, as champion of Hinduism. Circumstances had suffered considerable change since Shivaji's days. The Marathas were no longer confined within their own province; they had crossed the Narbada and the whole of Hindustan stretched before them. Baji Rao, therefore, declared that his aim was to found a Hindu empire or *Hindupad Padshahi*, as he called it. It was a Hindu empire that Shivaji also wished to establish; but it was to be a Maratha empire as well, for he appealed not merely to the religious feelings but also to the racial sentiments of the Marathas. Baji Rao, on the other hand, had to win the sympathies of Hindus outside Maharashtra, and he wisely forebore to emphasise the racial character of his mission. The Hindus of Central and Northern India saw in him a new deliverer. They had not forgotten the humiliations imposed upon them by Aurangzib's religious intolerance, and they willingly ranged themselves on Baji Rao's side at considerable sacrifice. Raja Jai Sing Sawai of Jaipur secretly favoured Baji Rao's cause and influential Zemindars like Nandalal Mandloi[25] openly joined him. The Mughal Government had the wisdom to send two Hindu Viceroys to Malwa, Girdhar Bahadur and Daya Bahadur at the time when Baji Rao was gradually accomplishing its conquest and annexation. The two Viceroys did their utmost to win the Hindu nobles of Malwa back to the Mughal side. But the latter were inspired by a new spirit, which finds expression in a letter addressed by Sawai Raja Jai Sing to Nandalal Mandloi on the 26th of October, 1731[26]. "News of Malwa affairs, written on your behalf, have reached me and I have taken note of them. And Baji Rao Ballal Peshwa Pradhan of the Deccan has written on 29th Rabilakhar that, as desired by you, victory has been won in Malwa on the 21st (12-10-1731) and Viceroy Daya Bahadur fell in action. On that occasion Rao Sahebji, Thakur Narhardasji and Mayaramji Vakil, had voluntarily assisted with their own person, wealth, brothers, sons and officers but the Emperor's Subha had made such (excellent) arrangements on the pass of Mandava, three mines had been run across the route and 25,000 soldiers were stationed there and the casualty among the Marathas as they attempted to ascend the pass was very great and if they had ascended a few steps more, the defenders of Mandave would have fired the mines and the

25. For Daya Bahadur's letters to Nandalal Mandloi, see G. S. Sardesai, *Marathi Riyasat, Madhya bibhag*, Vol. I, pp. 325—327.

26. G. S. Sardesai, *Marathi Riyasat, Madhya bibhag*, Vol. I, p. 328.

entire army would have been lost. At such a crisis Rao Saheb sent us information and changing the route of Mandave he got the army safely across another route, that of Bheron Ghat, and his own people, son, brothers and officers were blown by mines on the ghat and were killed before his eyes. I am unable to describe what assistance he rendered. Such is the information I have received, but you had not given me these details. Thousand praises to you that relying on my words alone you chiefs of Malwa have ousted the Muhammadans from Malwa so that the welfare and the prosperity of our religion may be secured."

It may be noted here that most of Baji Rao's wars could be imbued with a religious character. In the conquest of Malwa he had secured the alliance of the Hindus, in his war against the Sidis he was taking revenge for the desecration of Hindu temples; in his war against the Portuguese he was undoubtedly fighting for Hinduism, in as much as the Inquisition in Portuguese India made it impossible for Hindus to profess their faith in peace. And when the Bundela chief Chhatrasal found his principality threatened by the Pathan Nawab of Farrukhabad, he turned for protection to Baji Rao as the acknowledged leader of the Hindus in India. The lover of Mastani knew well how to appeal to the religious sentiments of his co-religionists although he could scarcely be considered an orthodox Brahman.

Balaji Baji Rao was perhaps a better Brahman than his father, but as a statesman and soldier he was much inferior to Baji Rao I. The Pan-Hindu policy of the second founder of the Maratha empire was deliberately abandoned by his son. Baji Rao had pursued both in Malwa and in the Konkan a policy of conquest and annexation. A policy of annexation is at the beginning expensive and does not yield immediate financial profit. Mill had no difficulty in proving that the annexations of Wellesley were financially unprofitable, and the same criticism could be levelled against Baji Rao's progressive and aggressive campaigns. The Marathas, however, unlike the English, looked upon war as a normal source of revenue and Baji Rao suffered from a chronic lack of funds. Perpetually harassed by his creditors, he hardly knew any peace and his anxieties have often found expression in his letters to Brahmendra Swami[27]. Balaji Baji Rao, therefore, decided to abandon his father's policy and to make war profitable. In one letter he styled himself a disciple of Shivaji Maharaj, apparently because he thought he was treading in the footsteps of the great Maratha in making war pay for war. But he forgot that while Shivaji had no alternative but to foster his annual *mulukhgiri* expeditions as a normal and regular source of revenue, he himself might very well have improved his finances by developing the natural resources of the tolerably large dominions bequeathed to him by his father. The policy of annexation, which Baji Rao systematically pursued both in the north and in the west, was abandoned by his son, nor did the excellent idea of rallying the Hindus against the Muhammadan rulers of India appeal to him. When he sought an interview with Sawai Jai Sing, it was to extort money from that friendly potentate; and the main, if not the sole, purpose of his numerous expeditions was the recuperation of his exhausted coffers. This fact is clearly indicated in the following lines written by him to Nana Purandhare[28]. " My father, like Bhagirath made a stream of gold flow from the north to the south for twenty four years. Thanks to his blessings, that stream is still in ever increasing flow and has completely satisfied the rulers of the provinces, the leaders of the army and my sincere friends. The golden stream has added to thirst only. Raghuji and Fatte Sing Baba had in the past brought a golden stream from the south but its flow was interrupted at places. For many days in the interval the stream from the south did not flow. By God's grace the stream of wealth is flowing well in this army this year but there are many dry lands on the way to Poona and it will be entirely absorbed (in transit) on that account. If the northern and the southern streams could in their high flood be united at Poona without any absorption on their way, then I could get rid of

27. Rajwade, *Marathyanchya Itihasachin Sadhanen*, Vol. III, pp. 20-21.

28. Sardesai, *Marathi Riyasat, Madhya-bibhag*, Vol. II, pp. 59-60.

my debts and secure rewards of my labour both in this world and the next. The Ganges flows to the sea but saves the whole world; in the like manner do these northern and southern rivers flow in the present age and benefit many people. All rivers and streams flow to the ocean, the Kaveri alone has been brought to the service of men. So do these rivers of wealth render but little service to the main interest, though they do immense good to other people. It is proper that people with an insight should take into consideration the rights and the wrongs of this matter and so act that the sterility of Poona may be removed." The Peshwa's meaning is quite transparent, and the policy adumbrated in the letter was bound, when followed to its logical end, to produce one result only—namely, the wholesale alienation of his father's Hindu allies and the complete denationalisation of the Maratha army.

Balaji Baji Rao like his predecessors still professed to be a champion of Hinduism. He wrote respectful letters to Brahmans of known sanctity, granted them pensions and allowances, and sometimes remitted their rent, and in his letters he often expressed an ardent desire to recover from the Muhammadans the holy places of Benares and Muttra. But Brahmans and holy men were not the only Hindus; and while they might shower their blessings on the Peshwa and his family, the Hindu princes alone could assist him in his wars against the Muhammadans. Evidently Balaji Baji Rao cared more for their money than for their armed forces, for it is during his regime that the Maratha arms fell heavily on their Rajput co-religionists. Hitherto the Rajputs had welcomed this new power from the south as the avenger of Hindu wrongs in the north; but Balaji and his principal Sardars, Sindhia and Holkar, made the Rajput princes realise that Maratha supremacy meant for them nothing but a change of masters, and the change was by no means for the better. So when the Marathas stood in urgent need of men and money in 1760 and 1761 the Rajputs remained sternly aloof, while all the Muhammadan princes and nobles of Northern India, including the Nawab of Oudh whom the Marathas had done their utmost to draw to their side, rallied to the Afghan banner. Nor were these the only evil effects of the selfish policy of plunder and raid. It caused disunion and dissension within the Maratha empire. The Peshwa, in want of money, did not hesitate to sell his assistance to the Nawab of Bengal against Raghuji Bhonsla of Nagpur. Raghuji, indeed, was not well-disposed towards Balaji; but the moral effect of fighting a Maratha Sardar, while employed in a Muhammadan province, was simply disastrous. Baji Rao did not seek foreign aid in his fight against the Senapati; but Balaji extended his protection to Bengal against a Sardar of the Empire; he joined the English in order to bring about the destruction of the Angria; and his son simply emulated his example when he coalesced with Nizam Ali against Janoji Bhonsla. Thus the unhappy Raghoba certainly committed no unprecedented offence when he sought foreign military aid to secure the *musnad* of Poona. Balaji lamented the difference between Sindhia and Holkar and earnestly urged them to pursue a common policy in Rajputana, but he conveniently forgot that with the example he had set in Bengal the only common policy they could be expected to adopt was one of self aggrandisement.

It is needless to remark that although the bulk of the Maratha army consisted of feudal levies, the Peshwa had an additional force of his own. The composition of this personal force was naturally affected by the change of political ideal and political outlook. Shivaji aimed at the foundation of a Maratha empire, and his army was mainly, if not wholly, composed of Marathas. The Pathan regiment, he enlisted, probably consisted of Deccani Musulmans, who were for all practical purposes children of the soil and were by no means favourably inclined towards the Mughal empire. It is noteworthy that on one occasion Shivaji politely rejected the services of a Bundela chief. Baji Rao's proclaimed ambition was the restoration of Hindu supremacy in India and he naturally tried his best to win the moral and material support of Hindus all over India for military purposes; but we have no documentary evidence that the non-Maratha elements formed by any means the majority of his army. Balaji's sole aim was to cause the two rivers of gold from the north and the south to unite and flow into the lake of Poona, and this policy required constant fighting and a vast army. The Marathas were not very eager to spend the whole year away from their home provinces and Balaji enlisted mercenaries from all parts of India and outside India. Sikhs, Rajputs, Sindhis and Karnatakis on the one hand, and Rohillas, Arabs, Abyssynians and Portuguese of pure or mixed birth and even the so called Portuguese[29], or the native converts from Goa were welcomed in his army. They were by no means better soldiers, and were certainly more unscrupulous and less faithful. Yet they obtained from the Peshwa and his feudal chiefs better pay and better treatment than the Marathas proper. Consequently the Maratha army was now gradually, but completely denationalised. In the Peshwa's personal force[30] the Arabs and other foreigners outnumbered the Marathas; in Holkar's army the Pendharis[31] preponderated over the paid mercenaries; and in Sindhia's forces there were

29. Robert Orme had a very poor opinion of their fighting qualities. See his *Military Transactions in Indostan* (1763 edition), Vol. I, p. 81.

30. Tone says :—" In the various Mahratta services there are very little more than a bare majority who are Mahrattas by caste; and very few instances occur of their ever entering into the infantry at all." *Illustrations of some Institutions of the Mahratta People*. (1818), p. 44. We get the following significant figures about the army that opposed Colonel Munro near Sholapore.

Arabs	2,000
Mohillas (Rohillas)	1,500
Sindees	1,000
Gosaens	700
Major Pinto's infantry	1,000
Hindostani and Deccan infantry	4,000
Total ...	10,200
Cavalry	1,500
Grand Total ...	11,700

The Life of Sir Thomas Munro, by G. R. Gleig, Vol. I, p. 494. F. N.

31. An expeditionary force, sent by Holkar, under an officer name Chimaji Rao Bule, in 1783 consisted of 1,000 to 1,500 gardis, 2,000 to 2,500 cavalry and 6,000 Pendharis. See *Maheshwar Darbarchin Batmi Patren*, Vol. II, p. 40.

In 1787 Sindhia requested Holkar to send a reinforcement of 1,000 *sawars* and 10,000 Pendharis. (Ibid, p. 121). This gives a general indication of the preponderance of the Pendharis in Holkar's army.

more Purvias than Maratha soldiers[32]. They were bound by no common ideals or common interests and were utterly ruthless in their methods. It was these non-Maratha mercenaries who made the Maratha name dreaded and hated throughout the length and the breadth of the Indian sub-continent. Briefly, then, it may be said that Shivaji had organised a national army; in Rajaram's time the army was feudalised; and it was left to Balaji Baji Rao to denationalise it. This denationalisation with its consequent demoralisation inevitably led to the final overthrow of the Maratha empire. Feudalism in itself was bad, but the employment of foreign mercenaries was, as we shall see, even more disastrous.

32. *Maheshwar Darbarchin Batmi Patren*, Vol. I, pp. 10-11 and Vol II, p. 117.

CHAPTER IV.

INFANTRY AND CAVALRY.

Krishnaji Anant Sabhasad says that Shivaji had 45,000 cavalry and only 10,000 Mawle infantry in his army.[1] But the few figures that we have of his expeditionary forces at different dates contradict this estimate. A cavalry trooper was necessarily more expensive. He needed a good horse, better equipment and therefore a higher salary. Shivaji's military operations were often confined to hilly regions where horses would be of little or no use. He frequently led his men through unfrequented mountain tracks where the sure-footed Mawle alone could go, and the accuracy of Krishnaji Anant's account is, therefore, more than doubtful. From the few figures available in the contemporary correspondence of the English factors it appears that during Shivaji's time the infantry preponderated over the cavalry. On the 12th November, 1668, the Carwar factors informed their countrymen at Surat of a report that Shivaji contemplated an expedition against Goa and had with that intent assembled an army of 2,000 horse and 8,000 or 10,000 foot[2]. The army that appeared near Hubly in 1673 consisted, according to a report current at Carwar of 2,000 horse and 4,000 foot[3]. In 1675 Shivaji laid siege to the fortress of the Phonda and in the besieging force, as we learn from a Carwar letter, dated 14th April, the cavalry was far outnumbered by infantry, their respective strength being 2,000 and 7,000[4]. On the 19th November, 1678, the Rajapore factors wrote to their friends at Bombay that the Bijapur generals dared not attack Shivaji who had 15,000 horse and 20,000 foot at Panhala[5]. Even in the small force,

1. Sen, *Siva Chhatrapati*, pp. 136—139.
2. Factory Records, Surat, Vol. 105, fol. 72.
3. Factory Records, Surat, Vol. 88, fol. 32.
4. Factory Records, Surat, Vol. 88, fols. 36-37.
5. Factory Records, Surat, Vol. 107, fol. 177.

that had joined Sambhaji in his foolish rebellion, the cavalry formed the minority, for, when the prodigal son returned to his father's castle at Panhala, he was accompanied, according to an English report, by 300 horse and 1,000 foot.[6]. The infantry continued to maintain its majority in the Maratha army even after Shivaji's death, for in 1707 Dhanaji Jadhav, as we are told by the Bundela chronicler, had under his command a strong infantry force of 25,000, while his cavalry numbered 5,000 only[7].

In the Peshwa period, however, the position was reversed. The Marathas were no longer compelled to defend their hearth and home. Secure in their native territories, they were now in a position to carry war into their enemies' land, and in these distant expeditions, designed mainly for plunder, a cavalry force was far more useful than infantry. In a Portuguese report, dated June 1787, therefore, we read that the Peshwa could bring in the field 80,000 to 100,000 horse, 10,000 foot and 40 to 50 pieces of artillery[8]. In the few lists of military *saranjams* of the later Peshwa period that have come down to us, we find no mention of infantry at all, and Tone[9] tells us that in his days the Maratha did not care to enlist as a foot soldier and the infantry consisted almost entirely of foreigners. The Maratha footmen were employed mainly for the suppression of disturbances by the Bhils, Kolis and other turbulent tribes.

The first official mention of the employment of soldiers from other parts of India we find in a brief paper, dated 1734—35, which announced the appointment of Tryambak Rao

6. Factory Records, Surat, Vol. 108, fols. 34-35.

7. Scot, *History of the Dekkan*, Vol. II, p. 116.

8. Biker, *Tradatos da India*, Vol. VIII, p. 269. We also come across similar figures in Bombay Public Consultation that shows the steady numerical decline of infantry in the Peshwa's army, *e.g.*, B. P. C. Range CCCXLI, No. 9, 25th February, 1737-38, p. 51—"the notice we have received of Chimnajee's arrival at Tannah with seven thousand horse and five thousand foot;" and in Range CCCXLI, No. 11, a postscript in Captain Inchbird's letter from Kolaba, dated 10th April, 1740, says that Nana had with him, when he went to assist Manaji against his brother Sambhaji, three thousand cavalry and only fifteen hundred infantry.

9. *Illustrations of some Institutions of the Mahratta People*, p. 44.

Somvanshi as Sarlaskar and the enlistment of a number of Rajputs who had come from Jai Sing[10]. Whether these men were admitted to the infantry, and if so, on what terms, we do not know. It is also not stated whether Jai Sing had been asked to send them or whether they had voluntarily come in search of employment in the Maratha army. Seven years later two Arabs were employed by Balaji Baji Rao at a monthly salary of 11 Rupees each[11]. In 1750 one Raje Muhammad, a Jamadar of infantry, was sent to Khandesh to get fifty recruits for the Peshwa's force, but the salary, it seems, was to be fixed after a personal inspection, and probably after haggling with each man, the rate suggested varied from seven to eight and a half Rupees[12]. In a document, dated 1753—54, we find the name of Muzaffarzung[13], the *gardi* officer[14], mentioned for the first time. About this time the Peshwa had probably organised the trained battalions of his army and this necessitated the further employment of non-Marathas. The published records, however, throw no light on the condition of their service during the Peshwaship of Balaji Baji Rao.

During the administration of the next Peshwa, however, we find a deliberate attempt to strengthen the new infantry force by recruiting a large number of Sikhs, Arabs, Abyssinians, Sidis and other non-Marathas. In 1770-71 Sumer Sing, a *gardi* officer, was commissioned to enlist 400 men at a monthly salary of 12 or 13 Rupees, but it was laid down that the men would be paid for ten months only though they were expected to serve throughout the year[15]. Ali Mardan Khan, another *gardi* Jamadar, was asked to recruit another body of 400 men at a monthly salary of 16 Rupees but these men were expected to find their own muskets (Banduk). Sher Sing, a Sikh officer,

10. *Peshwas' Diaries*, Vol. I, p. 124.

11. *Peshwas' Diaries*, Vol. III, p. 165.

12. *Peshwas' Diaries*, Vol. III, p. 176.

13. *Peshwas' Diaries*, Vol. III, p. 178.

14. The word *gardi* was applied to sepoys trained in the European fashion. It was derived from the word "guard" in its English, French or Portuguese form. See Elliot and Dowson, *History of India*, Vol. VIII, p. 155, foot-note.

15. *Peshwas' Diaries*, Vol. IX, p. 336.

was ordered to engage 2 Jamadars and 198 sepoys of his persuasion, at a salary of 25 and 12 Rupees respectively[16]. And Apaji Ganesh of Ahmadabad was required to find 400 able-bodied Arabs at a salary of 15 to 16 Rupees per month; 100 good Abyssinians at a salary of 15 Rupees per man and one thousand Sidis at a salary of 15 to 16 Rupees[17]. These men were to be inspected by one Debi Sing, a Jamadar, sent from the headquarters, and Apaji Ganesh was urged not to employ men of other races or light armed men. These were not the only foreigners employed in the Peshwa's service. Goddard tells us that there was a number of Sindhis among the garrison of Ahmadabad[18], while a Portuguese writer asserts that Negro deserters[18a] from Goa were readily employed in the frontier force of the Marathas; but the terms of their employment we do not know. It is needless to say that Indian Christians and Portuguese of pure or mixed origin were also welcomed in the new regiments. In 1789-90 four Portuguese soldiers were employed in the Poona infantry at a monthly salary of 25 Rupees; their Christian comrades were paid 15 Rupees per month, while the Indian footmen in the same regiment got no more than 9 Rupees each[19].

Of all these foreigners the Arabs enjoyed the highest reputation for valour and intrepidity, and Blacker tells us that "Every substantive Native Power had a portion of these troops"[20]. Prinsep confirms this statement when he writes: "It may be proper to mention, as a proof of the estimation in which the Arabs are held as soldiers by the native powers, the rate of pay they received in the Peshwa's army in comparison with natives of other countries. "Arabs, natives of Arabia," according to this authority, got 15 Rupees a

16. Ibid.

17. *Peshwas' Diaries*, Vol. IX, p. 337.

18. G. W. Forrest, *Selections from State Papers*, Maratha series, p. 397.

18a. Joseph Roger, *Relacao dos successos prosperos e infelices do illust, e excellent, Senhor D Luiz Mascarenhas, Conde de Alva*, p. 16.

19. *Peshwas' Diaries*, Vol. VI, p. 193.

20. Blacker, *Memoir of the Operations of the British Army in India during the Mahratta War of 1817, 1818 and 1819*, p. 21.

month, their descendants born in the country got 10 Rupees, the Hindustani sepoy was paid 8 Rupees, while the lowest salary, that of 6 Rupees a month, was allotted to the Maratha and his fellow Dakshinis in the infantry service[21].

But the foreigners in the Maratha army were not always better soldiers than the country recruit. Robert Orme wrote very disparagingly of the Christian recruits from Goa serving not only in the Maratha infantry but also in the trained battalions of the English East India Company. He says: "They are little superior in courage to the lower castes of Indians, and greatly inferior to the higher castes, as well as the Northern Moors of Indostan; but because they learn the manual exercise and the duties of a parade with sufficient readiness, and are clad like Europeans they are incorporated with the European troops"[22].

The Arab, Abyssinian, Sindhi, Sikh and other non-Maratha recruits in the Peshwa's army were enlisted by their own Jamadars, commissioned for the purpose, and were either equipped by these recruiting officers, or had to find their own arms. This partly explains the difference of pay alluded above, but the custom naturally led them to identify their interests with those of their Jamadars, and their loyalty to the Peshwa was, at the best, uncertain.

The cavalry of the Peshwa consisted of four classes, (1) the *Khasgi paga*, (2) the *Silhedars*, (3) the *Ekas or Ekandas* and (4) the *Pendharis*.

Of these the *Khasgi paga* or the Peshwa's private cavalry were by far the best. They formed a choice body armed, equipped and paid directly by the State; but their number was very small. According to Kasiraj Pandit, the *Khase paga* at Panipat did not number more than 6,000 out of a total of 38,000 cavalry under different chiefs[23].

21. H. T. Prinsep, *History of the Political and Military Transactions*, Vol. II, p. 160.

22. Orme, *Military Transactions in Indostan*, (1763 edition), Vol. I, p. 81.

23 *Asiatic Researches*, Vol. III, p. 106.

Maratha Cavalry.

(By Courtesy of the Calcutta University Press.)

A document, dated 1744-45, gives details about the composition of a cavalry force in the Peshwa's service and the terms of its payment[24]. The commander of this force was Ranoji Bhonsla and its fighting strength was 700, but of these only 90 were *Bargirs* of the *Khase paga* or men equipped by the State; forty-four of these *Bargirs* were musketeers and the rest spearsmen. The remaining 610 seem to have belonged to the ordinary *Silhedar* type. These men were to be paid 2 Rupees per head per week, but it was laid down that as soon as the plundering raids began, their allowance was to be entirely stopped, with the exception of that of 124 musketeers who were granted a reduced allowance of Rupees 2 and 8 as. to be paid every six weeks. This shows a direct and important departure from Shivaji's rule of not permitting his soldiers to have any share in the spoils of the war. The 90 *Bargirs* were to be paid Rupees 413 only every six weeks, but it seems that their *rojmura* or allowance was not to be stopped even when the campaign began and their saddle bags were full of loot.

The number of non-combatants attached to a cavalry regiment was generally very large. Ranoji Bhonsla had with him no less than five clerks and 181 attendants. There were in his regiment 9 stirrup holders, 5 farriers, 8 camel drivers, 4 khijmatgars, 3 musicians, 2 scouts, 5 store keepers, 2 wardrobe keepers, 13 palanquin bearers, 2 saddlers, 1 washerman, 2 macebearers, 1 leather worker, 1 sweeper, 2 drummers, 4 messengers, 1 torchbearer, 1 barber, 1 tailor, 7 water-carriers, 2 sunshade bearers, 2 trumpeters, 4 elephant drivers, 1 potdar and 99 grooms. These non-combatants cost the Peshwa's Government very little. Most of them did not get more than 3 Rupees in six weeks and they were very lucky if this small sum was punctually paid[25].

Besides their ordinary wages the soldiers of the Maratha army of all classes and descriptions could expect a reward or compensation if they were wounded in action. After the battle

24. *Peshwas' Diaries*, Vol. III, pp. 166-167.

25. Ibid.

of Rakisbone in 1663-64 such rewards were awarded to 29 wounded *Silhedars* and *Bargirs* of different races and nationalities. The allowance granted on this occasion varied from Rupees 5 for a wound caused by a rocket to Rupees 100 for a grievous swordcut, and five persons received compensation for the injuries their horses had received in action, while funeral expenses were granted to the relatives of three persons killed on that day. The Marathas, however shy of risking their own person and that of their charger, defied all dangers to remove a wounded friend or the dead body of a comrade from the field[26], and the Government did not leave the orphans of a dead trooper uncared for. They could be fairly sure of a state pension called *Balparveshi*, and, as soon as these orphans came of age, they were admitted to the military service of the State.

The State had its own grass lands or *Kurans* for the fodder of the horses of the cavalry while stationed in the country, and compulsory free labour was often employed for the service of the cavalry. Thus in 1775 the services of 323 Mahars, 54 Mangs, 52 cobblers and 10 saddlers were requisitioned from the districts of Poona, Sangamner, Parner, Rahuri, Khed, Junnar, Nevase, Karde, Gandapur and Belapur for such petty works as making ropes and repairing the saddles and bridles for the private cavalry of the Peshwa[27].

The *Silhedars* expected a portion of their stipulated pay in advance under the style of *nalbandi* or shoeing expenses, but such payment did not always ensure their attendance at the mobilisation camp.

The third class of horsemen employed by the Peshwa were single volunteers known as *Ekas* or *Ekandas*. Tone

26. Keating says : "It is a business I cannot account for that in spite of every annoyance these people always carry off the dead." Forrest, *Selection from State Papers, Maratha Series*, p. 228. Forbes observes—" Many of the Mahrattas fell in attempting to carry off the killed and wounded, an act of humanity to which they pay the greatest attention. They seldom leave a body on the field, and venture almost to the cannon's mouth, rather than suffer the remains of a friend to be exposed; out of the number killed in this action only seven bodies were found after their retreat." *Oriental Memoirs*, 2nd edition, Vol. I, p. 385.

27. *Peshwas' Diaries*, Vol. VI, pp. 185-186.

says: "The third and the most numerous description are volunteers who join the camp, bringing with them their own horse and accoutrements: their pay is generally from forty to fifty rupees per month, mostly in proportion to the value of their horse "[28].

These troops were generally armed with muskets and matchlocks, swords and targets, spears and lances, daggers and clubs and bows and arrows. John Henry Grose says that the muskets and matchlocks were used "chiefly in bush-fighting where when they have made a discharge, they retreat in a hurry to their main body. But their chief dependence is on their swords and targets. Their swords are, generally speaking, of an admirable temper, and they are well trained up to the exercise of them; so that on all occasions in battle, they quite their musket, and betake themselves to them with great success." "As to their targets, they are exactly round, convexing almost to a point on the outside, light and covered with so smooth and hard a varnish or lacquer, that if tolerably good, they will easily turn a pistol-ball, and at some little distance a musket one. They also have among them excellent slingers and archers; but of these they make lately less account since the introduction of fire-arms; though considering their imperfection in the management of these last, it is a query whether they are much gainers by the change "[29]. Nearly forty years later when William Henry Tone wrote his Letters, the Marathas, or rather their foreign employees, had learnt to make a better use of their firearms, but in the cavalry charge they still relied more upon their swords than on their bandooks or muskets. Says Tone—"The bandook takes a longer time to load than the firelock, as it is chambered, but then it carries a ball much farther and infinitely truer; and long practice

28. Tone, *Illustrations of some Institutions of the Mahratta People* (1818), p. 37.

29. John Henry Grose—*Voyage to the East Indies*, pp. 124-125. This account of the arms and weapons used by the Marathas is corroborated by the Marquis of Alorna and Padre Francisco Alvares. See *Instruccao do Exmo Vice-Rei Marquez de Alorna ao seu successor*, ed F. N. Xavier, 3d edicao, pp. 49-50 and *Relacao da guerra que fizerao os Maratas no reyno de Carnate e Madure desde o anno de 1740 athe ode 1745.* (Archivo Ultramarino of Lisbon. Fundo geral 4179).

enabled the *nujeebs* to load with a readiness sufficiently applicable to ordinary service; they are also excellent swordsmen and are usually employed in making a charge upon any appearance of confusion in the enemy "[30].

We may here mention another offensive weapon, a projectile that was commonly used by the Muhammadans and the Marathas alike. It was still in use during the Sepoy mutiny, as we learn from the late Field Marshal Earl Roberts, but has now become obsolete owing to the rapid progress of science. This was the war rocket manufactured by private contract for the Peshwa's army, and the average price of one of these curious weapons was 5 Rupees each. The rockets were carried by camels, and probably the rocketeers were also mounted on them.

Colonel Wilks gives the following description of an Indian rocket—" This Indian instrument receives its projectile force from the same composition which is used in the rockets of ordinary fire-works; the cylinder which contains it, is of iron, and sometimes gunpowder, at its extremity, causes it to explode when it has reached its object, a straight sword blade is also not unfrequently fixed to the rocket; an attached bamboo or reed steadies its flight; the rocket men are trained to give them an elevation proportioned to the varying dimensions of the cylinder, and the distance of the object to be struck. As those projected to any distance describe a parabola of considerable height, a single rocket is easily avoided, but when the flight is numerous, the attempt would be useless and their momentum is always sufficient to destroy a man or horse. Such was the ancient Indian instrument, so inferior to the Congreve rocket of modern European warfare "[31].

A rocket was most effective in frightening away the war elephant largely employed in the Mughal army in India. In 1687 during the expedition against Golkonda, " Eeruch Khan's

30. Tone, *Illustrations of some Institutions of the Mahratta People* (1818), pp. 47-48.

31. Wilks, *Historical Sketches of the South of India*, Vol. II, p. 27. Footnote. Also see William Irvine, *The Army of the Indian Moghuls*, pp. 147-150.

elephant, frightened at the noise of a rocket, ran away. The driver used every endeavour to turn him, but in vain; so that the Khan was taken prisoner "[32]. The greatest injury was effected by a rocket when it chanced to light on the enemy's magazine, but generally an Indian soldier was much more afraid of a rocket than of a musket ball, as Muhammad Ja'far Shamlu says of Abdali's followers fighting at Panipat—" As for a musket bullet, the heroes cared not what it might do, and in that scene of carnage and slaughter the only dread entertained by the renowned and gallant combatants was for a cannon-ball, or the flight of a rocket "[33].

The Maratha horseman as well as his comrade in the infantry was very lightly and scantily clad. Grose wrote in 1757—" A roll of coarse muslin round their heads, to which they give the name of puckery, or turbant, or perhaps a bit of cloth, or striped calico, or cuttance-cap; a lungee or clout, barely to cover their nakedness, and a pamree or loose mantle to throw over their shoulders, or to lye on upon the ground, composes the whole of their wardrobe. This however is only to be understood of their common men, though the officers do not much out-figure them: so that nothing can present a more rag-a-muffin appearance than these troops, together with their little ill-favored horses, the furniture of which is in a stile answerable to the rest "[34]. This continued to be the usual dress of the ordinary Maratha trooper throughout the eighteenth century, for the author of *Tarikh-i-Ibrahimkhan*, who wrote during the Governor Generalship of Lord Cornwallis, also says that " the ordinary dress worn by these people comprises a turban, tunic, selah (loose mantle) and janghiah (short drawers) "[35]. But the *gardis*, who accompanied Parashram Bhau Patwardhan in his Mysore expedition, were better dressed. " Their coats," says Lt. Moor, " are of red serge with a blue collar and cuff cut in the country taste to

32. Scott, *History of the Dekkan*, Vol. II, p. 66.
33. Elliot and Dowson, *History of India*, Vol. VIII, p. 153.
34. Grose, *Voyage to the East Indies*, p. 126.
35. Elliot and Dowson, *History of India*, Vol. VIII, p. 263.

lap over before and tie with strings "[36]; but the fire arms used by them were as usual defective; we are informed by the same authority—" their arms are for the most part English, and out of twenty, two will be found without locks, six without cocks and perhaps not a flint among the remaining twelve "[37].

As the Maratha needed very little provision for his subsistence, he was not encumbered with much baggage and, before the introduction of the heavy field artillery, could move very swiftly. The English and Portuguese observers who wrote about the middle of the eighteenth century were all impressed with their celerity, but there was very little discipline among them. The Marquis of Alorna was of opinion that they were no better than a rabble. " I would have no hesitation," wrote he, " with a corps of five thousand regular soldiers to attack such an army though fifty thousand strong"[38]. Tone and Moor also adversely commented on the little discipline that they found in the Maratha army. The former observed: " That every man in a Mahratta camp is totally independent; he is the proprietor of the horse he rides which he is never inclinable to risk, since without it he can get no service "[39].

Another defect in the Maratha army was that it was in a state of unpreparedness for a period of four months in the year, when the privates dispersed and returned to their respective homes, and, even after the expiry of the usual period of inaction, at least six weeks elapsed before they could be reassembled.

The Pendharis formed a source of income to the Maratha generals. These predatory hordes accompanied the Maratha

36. Moor, *A Narrative of the Operations of Captain Little's Detachment*, p. 83.
37. Ibid.
38. *Instruccao do Exmo Vice-Rei Marquez de Alorna ao seu successor*, p. 49.

39. *Illustrations of some Institutions of the Maharatta People*, p. 40. Sir Thomas Munro, however, goes further, and says that the majority of the horses employed in the Maratha army belonged to non-combatant business men who hired them to the *Jahgirdars* and the Government. See Gleig's *Life of Sir Thomas Munro*, Vol. II, pp. 269-270.

army in its expeditions and were employed not so much for fighting as for plundering the country through which they passed. They received no pay from the Peshwa or his principal chiefs, but, on the contrary, paid to the general, to whose army they were attached, a tax, called *Palpatti*, in return for the protection which they received from him. Though the Pendharis became most numerous towards the close of the Maratha period, they were, by no means, the peculiar product of the Maratha method of warfare. The employment of trained robbers to harass an enemy was the time honoured custom among the ancient Hindu princes. Kautilya recommended the employment of " brave thieves and wild tribes who make no distinction between friend and foe," and Brihaspati and the author of Shukra's polity lay down rules about the division of spoils brought by such authorised robbers. " When anything has been brought from a hostile country by freebooters," says Brihaspati, " with the permission of their lord, they shall give a sixth part to the King and share (the remainder) in due proportion "[40]. The same principle is also advocated by the *Shukranitisara*[41]. It lays down—" if thieves steal something from other's kingdom by the King's order, they should first give one-sixth to the King and then divide the rest among themselves." This proves beyond doubt the employment by belligerent powers of licensed robbers similar to the Pendharis, who shared their spoil with the State employing and protecting them, as did the Pendharis during the Peshwa period.

This military custom prevailed also during the Mughal period as Manucci says, " Along with the armies there marched privileged and recognised thieves called Bederia (Bidari); these are the first to invade the enemy's territory, where they plunder everything they find. The handsomest items are reserved for the general; the rest they sell on their own account. Prince Shah Alam, when he was within the territories of Shivaji, near Goa, had in his army seven thousand such, whose orders were to ravage the lands of

40. *Sacred Books of the East*, Vol. XXXIII, p. 241.

41. *Shukraniti*, (Sacred Books of the Hindus), p. 211.

Bardes "[42]. Irvine is unwilling to identify these Bidaris with the Pendharis but the Maratha chroniclers mention the presence of the latter in the Mughal armies operating against Shivaji. Moreover the Pendharis did not belong to any particular race, caste or creed. They drew their recruits from all parts of India without any distinction of race and religion and it is no wonder that the criminal tribe of Bedars should preponderate in their ranks. We find in a contemporary ballad that a number of Bedars was employed by the Maratha generals exactly for the same purpose for which the professed Pendharis were usually engaged at the time of the battle of Kurdla[43].

When the Pendharis were for the first time associated with the Marathas is not exactly known. From the account available in the Maratha chronicles it does not appear that Shivaji ever employed these marauders like his Mughal adversaries. But by the time of Balaji Baji Rao the Pendharis had become a common feature of the Maratha force. In a letter addressed to Dattaji Sindhia in 1753-54 the name of a Pendhari leader Dost Muhammad is mentioned[44]. It appears from two letters of the time of the first Madhav Rao that sometimes a few enterprising men sought the Peshwa's permission for adoption of this lucrative profession, and the number of Pendharis attached to each military officer was strictly limited. The first of these letters runs as follows:—" Shivchand, Pem Sing, Mohan Sing, Hiraman and Bhopat Beldar represented that if permission were given them to plunder in foreign territories and to reside without molestation in the Peshwa's camp, they would collect some Lugare and Beldar families for the purpose, and prayed that a *kaul* to that effect might be issued. Having taken into consideration this petition, a new *dhal* has been given, and permission has been granted for your residence in the camp, on condition that you should

42. Manucci, *Storia do Mogor*, Vol. II, p. 459.

43. Sane *Patre Yadi Bagaire*, pp. 55-56—" Bedadyasi hukum taka raste band karun."

44. *Peshwas' Diaries*, Vol. III, p. 178. Jonathan Scott mentions an earlier Pendhari chief, but on reference to the Persian manuscript, on which he relied, it was found to be an error of reading, see *Hobson Jobson*, ed. Crooke, p. 713.

pay five Rupees for each tent of the Beldars resident in the army and you should render to the State any elephant, palanquin, drum or banner that you may obtain in your raids "[45]. The second letter was addressed to Tryambak Rao Dhamdhere, who was authorised to entertain in his camp 50 Pendhari families, " but for every Pendhari tent exceeding that number, a *Palpatti* or tent tax at the rate of three Rupees per tent would have to be paid "[46].

The Pendharis, as has been already indicated, were not employed for fighting but exclusively for plundering purposes. Their method has been described by an anonymous writer in 1819—" The climate and hardy habits of these plunderers render tents or baggage an unnecessary incumbrance; each person carries a few days' provision for himself and for his horse, and they march for weeks together, at the rate of thirty and forty miles a day over roads and countries impassable for a regular army. They exhibit striking resemblance to the Cossacks as well in their customs as in the activity of their movements. Their arms are the same, being a lance and a sword, which they use with admirable dexterity, their horses like those of the Cossacks, are small, but extremely active and they pillage without distinction, friends as well as foes. They move in bodies seldom exceeding two or three thousand men, and hold a direct undeviating course until they reach their destination, when they at once divide into small parties, that they may with more facility plunder the country, and carry off a larger quantity of booty, destroying at the same time what they cannot remove. Fighting is not their object, they have seldom been known to resist the attack even of an inferior enemy; if pursued they make marches of extraordinary length, and if they should happen to be overtaken, they disperse, and reassemble at an appointed rendezvous; or if followed into their country they immediately retire to their respective homes "[47].

45. *Peshwas' Diaries*, Vol. IX, pp. 324-325.
46. *Peshwas' Diaries*, Vol. IX, p. 325.
47. *Origin of the Pindarries preceded by Historical Notices on the Rise of the Different Mahratta States*, pp. 147-149.

Among the Maratha chiefs Holkar employed the largest number of Pendharis, but as these hordes cost their employers nothing, they found their way into the service of every chief. Of their leaders, the most well known was Amir Khan, who was certainly more than a mere plunderer, and his ability rendered him a much greater nuisance to his neighbours than the average Pendhari leader.

Besides the infantry and the cavalry, the Marquis of Alorna also mentions the employment of war elephants by the Marathas. "The elephants," says he, "taught and trained for war are of the greatest value to the Hindus, when they are intrepid and not afraid of noise. Princes, generals and distinguished persons mount them; they are used to attack the enemy carrying different platoons of men armed with bow and arrow. When infuriated they cause great harm with the trunk"[48]. The Hindu princes in ancient days and their Muhammadan successors kept a large number of fighting elephants but it does not appear that they formed a prominent feature of the Maratha army. Shivaji's army was not certainly accompanied by these enormous brutes, and we have no proof of their presence in the camp of Sambhaji and Rajaram. Shahu and his principal officers were mounted on stately elephants during their slow and pompous march to Miraj and both Sadashiv Rao and Viswas Rao directed the Maratha operations at Panipat seated on caparisoned elephants. The Marathas wisely refrained from using these beasts for offensive purposes on a large scale, for it is very easy to frighten an elephant with firearms, and more often it proved a source of annoyance to its own party. Such a case has been mentioned by Gemelli Careri. "The Moghuls resolving to make the last effort to take it," (Daman) he says, "and having to this purpose placed two hundred elephants in the front with long sharp swords in their trunks, the beasts, frightened with the fire of the Portuguese muskets, ran disorderly upon the Mahomedan army cutting to pieces abundances of men, with the same weapons they were armed to destroy the Christians"[49].

48. *Instruccao do Exmo Vice-Rei Marquez de Alorna*, p. 50.

49. Churchill's *Voyages*, Vol. IV, p. 197.

The Maratha commanders can be divided into two classes. There were veterans like Malhar Rao Holkar, who had risen from the lowest rank. They could claim a wide and varied experience but were generally illiterate or ill educated even when judged by the standard of those days. But the second class, to which belonged hereditary princes like Balaji Baji Rao and Daulat Rao Sindhia, could claim men more fortunate in their birth, and therefore of a more cultured type. A Maratha has been generally represented as an uncultured barbarian, mainly because his portrait has been almost always drawn by his enemies. Wilks says that "They are well characterised by the Persian compound Muft-Khoor, eating at other people's expense." "A modern Maratha," he continues, "is utterly destitute of the generosity and point of honour which belong to a bold robber. If we should attempt to describe him by English terms, we must draw a character combined of the plausible and gentle manners of a swindler, the dexterity of a pickpocket, and the meanness of a pedlar; equally destitute of mercy and shame, he will higgle in selling the rags of a beggar whom he has plundered or overreached; and is versatile, as occasion offers, to swagger as a bully, or to cringe as a mendicant when he dares not rob"[50]. Such sweeping generalisation, it is needless to point out, is neither fair nor accurate. Moor, who could claim to know the Maratha officers much better than Wilks, deliberately exempted them from the charge of inhumanity;[51] and Skinner, who served under them, found many lovable traits in the Maratha character. "I have made myself well known among the Maratha chieftains," says he, "whom I found a good, generous hearted race of men"[52].

Nor were they devoid of culture; of Shivaji's officers, Raghunath Narayan Hanmante was a scholar of great

50. Wilks, J., *Historical Sketches of the South of India,* Vol. I, pp 252-253. Foot note.

51. Moor, *A Narrative of the Operations of Captain Little's Detachment*, p. 142.

52. Baillie Fraser, *Military Memoirs of Lt.-Col. James Skinner, C.B.,* Vol. I, pp. 141-142.

reputation, and compiled the *Raj Vyavahar Kosh*;[53] Parashram Pant, the founder of the Pratinidhi family, was a Sanskrit author; Mahadaji Sindhia employed his scanty leisure in composing devotional hymns, and in spite of all his faults, the second Baji Rao was known as a good scholar and theologian. A boy of a good family was early given a military training. He was not only taught the use of the ordinary weapons and riding, an accomplishment in which the Marathas generally excelled, but he was often sent on active service in company of his elder relatives[54]. But the education of the average chief was not limited to this practical military training. He was expected to learn Sanskrit, to know the epics and read such works as *Vidurniti*. Some of them attained some proficiency in Persian and accountancy, as it was then known. It is true that their education was very limited judged by modern standards, and they had hardly the intellectual equipment of a student of the military academies of Europe in the second half of the eighteenth century. But in their military knowledge and cultural attainments the hereditary chiefs were certainly not inferior to their contemporaries in other parts of India; and as men, if they were no better, they were not certainly worse than commanders of other nationality.

---

53. A very interesting work in Sanskrit, composed in the style of the *Amara Kosha*. Its aim was to supply Sanskrit synonyms for Persian words, then in common use.

54. The late Mr. V. K. Rajwade points out that during the Peshwa period boys of noble birth were expected to join the army at an age when they go to school to-day.

CHAPTER V.

FORTS.

Shivaji's name has been associated with almost all the old forts of his country. Some he had obtained by careful use of bribes, others by clever stratagem, and the rest by well planned assaults. Not content with the possession of the old fortresses he had built new ones and the hills of Maharashtra offered him excellent sites for them. Not a pass was left undefended, not a peak was left unfortified, and every *Taluka*[1] was provided with one or more strongholds, and the whole country was secured by a net work of forts. As one drives to-day by the high road from Poona to Satara through the pass of Katraj, through the mangoe groves of Shivapur and the ancient town of Shirwal, one sees on his right and left no less than ten famous hill forts well known to the Maratha ballad singers; Sinhgad, rendered famous by Tanaji Malsure, Purandar, and Vajragad that once witnessed the heroism of Murar Baji; Sajjangad, hallowed by the memory of Saint Ramdas, and Satara, once the capital of the Maratha empire. Shivaji was famous for his forts, as a popular Maratha writer informs us, and well did he deserve his fame. The military architecture of the Marathas had not attained a high standard in Shivaji's time, and he does not seem to have made any attempt to improve it. Indeed, no such effort was called for. His enemies possessed but poor artillery, their knowledge of mining did not go very far, an inaccessible site and a massive wall defended by a few resolute men even with primitive arms and crude missiles could defy for months the utmost efforts of the strongest besieging force. Only hunger and bribe could reduce a fort. All that was needed therefore was a good site, a strong rampart, sufficient provision, and plenty of military stores.

1. A. Taluka is a sub-division of a district.

The sites were generally well selected. Raigad could be reached by one narrow steep and difficult foot path that zigzagged along an inaccessible precipice and every care had been taken to provide for its defence. No less strong was the site of Lohagad. In fact Lord Valentia was of opinion that defective knowledge of fortification had considerably impaired its natural strength[2]. "We examined," he says, "the gateways as we came down, and I am quite convinced, that the whole of the artificial works much lessen the natural strength of the place. Each high side of the way forms a sheltering place, secure against all attacks from the top, whether of musquetry or their more usual weapons, large stones rolled down from above. The gateway and the parapets have the same effect. Had the whole been scalped off, and only a strong work at the top, I believe no earthly power could have taken it." But progress in military engineering as in everything else is also influenced by the laws of demand and supply. Had the artillerymen and miners of the time been more efficient, there might have been a greater necessity on the part of the military architects to use their brain and improve upon the traditional scheme of fortification they had received from their ancestors.

Shivaji's forts therefore were defended by a stout stone wall. The hill side was rendered more inaccessible by the usual bush of thorny opuntia cactus that forms the common feature of the country. Besides the barracks for men and officers every fort was provided with a *Darukhana* or powder house; an *Ambarkhana* or granary and a store house for oil and *Ghi*, a necessary ingredient for the daily food of a Maratha. The water supply was not forgotten, and even a small fort like Satara can boast of more than one tank and well that yield excellent drinking water even to-day after a century of neglect. Raigad had quite a number of tanks, and Grose was told that it was "the most completely impregnable place in the universe, for the enclosure of it is large enough, independent of the stores accumulated there, to grow grain sufficient for the

2. Valentia, *Voyages and Travels to India, Ceylon, and the Red Sea, Abyssinia and Egypt*. Vol. II, pp. 168-169.

maintenance of its garrison, which, were it but a handful of men, could with pleasure defend it against the greatest armies that could be brought to take it"[3]. The Ambarkhana of Panhala with its three enormous stone and cement granaries, named after the three life giving holy streams, Ganga, Yamuna, and Saraswati, was designed to hold 25,000 *Khandis* of grain[4]. If the material needs of the garrison were thus provided for, supernatural aid, in which soldiers and civilians equally believed in that age, was not overlooked. The main gateway was defended by a miniature figure of Hanuman, the valiant monkey general, and inside the ramparts were built a temple and a mosque, and Mr. C. A. Kincaid says that below the foundation of the walls of Lohagad were found some skeletons, whose unfortunate owners were probably sacrificed to render that fortress invincible[5]. The defensive value of these forts had been amply demonstrated during Aurangzib's invasion. Each fort cost the Mughal Emperor an enormous loss of men, money and time.

If Shivaji had perceived the advantages of these strongholds he was not blind to their perils in a hilly region like Maharashtra. If they were easy of defence, they could be easily used against him by the petty chiefs as he himself had demonstrated in his war against Bijapur. He therefore demolished all the adulterine castles as soon as his authority was fairly established in the country and no private person was permitted to build a castle, or a fort, or even a house with a bastion. But this alone was not sufficient. It was necessary to guard against all risks. He wanted to be sure that his forts must always be held in his own interests and should never be used against him. The standard of public morality was not very high. He himself had often used the silver bait with success and he knew that what had happened once might happen again.

3. Grose, *A Voyage to the East Indies*, p. 137.

4. D. B. Parasnis, *Panhala*, p. 61.

5. See his article in *Ishtur Phakde*. The Peshwas never failed to perform propitiatory ceremonies whenever anything of evil omen happened in a fort. See Sen, *Administrative System of the Marathas*, p. 402.

The first precaution he took was a judicious selection of the garrison. Every man was selected after a personal examination, and a shrewd judge of man though Shivaji was, he did not rely upon his personal judgement alone. Each man must furnish a surety for his good faith before he could be enrolled, and Krishnaji Anant Sabhasad says that generally someone of the royal personal staff was expected to stand surety for the new recruit[6]. But this was not all. In the army Shivaji had aimed at unity of command: in the fort he deliberately avoided it. No single officer was entrusted with the sole charge of the fort, it was therefore impossible for any single officer to betray it.

In every fort there were three officers of the same status and conjoint authority. Of course they had their special departments and responsibilities but in everything of the least importance touching the fort they had to consult one another. The chief of these three officers was the *Havaldar*. He was the head of the garrison, the *Sabnis* was in charge of the accounts in general and the muster roll in particular and the *Karkhannis* was mainly responsible for commissariat work. But their duties were so adroitly apportioned and so cleverly adjusted that nothing could be accomplished without the knowledge of all the three. The *Havaldar* was specially entrusted with the keys of the fort. It was his personal duty to see the gates bolted and locked after nightfall and he alone could open them at daybreak. But this work could not be delegated to anybody else, and Shivaji had particularly enjoined his *Havaldars* not to open the gates at night on any account. Malhar Ramrao Chitnis says that Shivaji had put the reliability of his *Havaldars* to the severest test. He went out on a tour of inspection, approached a fort at night, and asked the commandant to admit him. Some *Havaldars* were caught unawares, they thought that the law maker was above his law and admitted Shivaji into the fort. They were sternly censured and degraded. But the *Havaldar* of Panhala successfully withstood the test. He was in turn cajoled and threatened, he was told that his master was being hotly pursued

6. Sen, *Siva Chhatrapati*, p. 29.

by his Musulman enemies, and he was in grave personal danger, but nothing could induce him to deviate from Shivaji's regulations. He would provide for the personal safety of his prince, but the gates of the fort he would not unlock before the appointed time. The next morning he threw himself on the mercy of Shivaji who applauded his sense of duty and promoted him on the spot[7].

The official duties of the *Sabnis* and the *Karkhannis* have been enumerated in a memorandum drawn up in the first year of the Coronation era. The *Sabnis* was in charge of accounts, and he was to put his signature on every order under the *Karkhannis*'s seal. All orders involving expenditure were issued by the *Sabnis*, but they were not valid without the signature of the *Havaldar* and the sign of approval of the *Karkhannis*. The daily accounts of the two departments were drawn up under the joint supervision of the two officers, but while the cash was indicated on the account by the *Sabnis*, the *Havaldar* had to put his seal and the *Karkhannis* his sign of approval on the papers. The muster roll of the garrison was taken by the *Sabnis* while the *Karkhannis*'s department verified it. Similarly, the distribution of the stores was made by the *Karkhannis* but in the presence of a clerk of the *Sabnis*'s staff. The *Sabnis* had to explain all accounts to the superior audit officers, but the *Karkhannis* had to be present on the occasion to help his colleague[8]. We need not go into further details of this arrangement. From what we have seen it is sufficiently clear that while co-operating with one another in their official duties the three officers were at the same time serving as effective checks on each other. Even in his official correspondence the *Havaldar* had to take his colleagues into his confidence, for the letters were drafted and written by the *Sabnis*, and they could not be despatched until they had been entered in the daily ledger by the *Karkhannis*.

The system of appointing three officers in a fort was neither new nor unknown in Southern India, for it had been

7. *Chitnis bakhar*, ed. Kirtane, p. 108.
8. Mawjee and Parasnis, *Sanads and Letters*, pp. 130-132.

advocated, and probably practised, by Muhammad Adil shah; but Shivaji went further. He definitely laid down that the *Havaldar* should be a Maratha of good family, the *Sabnis* should be a Brahman known to his personal staff, and the *Karkhannis* should be a Prabhu[9]. The Marathas were doubtless good soldiers and the Brahmans and the Prabhus were well versed in accounts and clerical work, but their professional proficiency alone does not explain Shivaji's reasons for making military appointments on a caste basis; for good Brahman generals were not wanting in those days, and a Prabhu could very well be expected to perform the duties of a *Sabnis* as efficiently as those of a *Karkhannis*[10]. Shivaji had clearly laid down that the three officers must be dissimilar in caste. This would at once minimise the chance of their joint action against the king and placate the three principal castes of Maharashtra by an equitable distribution of state patronage in a manner best suited to the peculiar genius and traditions of each. The Brahman was not well disposed towards the Prabhu, the Prabhu had no kindly feeling for the Brahman who had bitterly opposed his claims to Vedic rites, and a Maratha could be ordinarily expected to be more loyal to the king of his own caste than to his colleagues of superior castes. Thus Shivaji utilised the best abilities that the three castes could provide, at the same time that he exploited their dislikes and differences to his own advantage.

But he had to provide against another danger, that of vested interest. A *Havaldar* or a *Sabnis*, if posted at the same place for a sufficiently long time, could, if he was so inclined, easily form a party of his own. The Bijapur Government recognised the hereditary rights of some officers called *Naikwaris*. These often created trouble and sometimes prevented the admission of a new governor into the forts for months, if their interest was in any way adversely affected[11].

9. Sen, *Siva Chhatrapati*, pp. 29-30.

10. There are instances of Prabhu Sabnises in the Peshwa period.

11. Carwar letter dated 20th September, 1671. Factory Records, Surat, Vol. 106, fol. 14.

Shivaji, therefore, transferred his officers from one fort to another, as his civil governors were frequently transferred from one district to another, and his ministers from one office to another, and, as in the army and civil departments, he recognised no hereditary rights in the forts. Every officer was appointed by the king to serve during his pleasure and his sons or relatives had not the least claim to the office left vacant by his death.

But in spite of these elaborate precautions Shivaji could not completely prevent treason and corruption. During his absence in the camp of Jai Sing the entire charge of the fort of Raigad had for the time being fallen on Keso Narayan Sabnis, as there was no *Havaldar*; the *Sabnis* availed himself of this opportunity for misappropriating a large sum of money from the public funds[12]. In 1663 Shivaji was compelled to postpone an expedition he had planned against the Konkan by the disquieting information of a rebellion in the fort of Sinhgad. In a letter dated the 2nd April, 1663, Shivaji writes to Moro Trimbak Peshwa and Abaji Sondev that he was thinking of marching against Namdar Khan in the Konkan, but news arrived from Sinhgad that a revolt had lately taken place in the fort. He had, therefore, to give up his project of marching into the Konkan for the present. The two officers were requested to march at once to Sinhgad with their troops and militia and take charge of the fort. They were further required to make an enquiry about the rebels and report their names to the King[13].

Besides the three principal officers every fort had one or more*Tat Sarnobat* according to its size. The *Tat Sarnobat* was in charge of the defence and supervision of the rampart, or a section of it, if it was too big for a single officer. And every unit of nine soldiers in the garrison was commanded by a petty officer called *Naik*[14]. The size of the garrison varied according to the size and the importance of the fort and according to the exigencies of the times. In times of special

12. Rajwade, *Marathyanchya Itihasachin Sadhanen*, Vol. VIII, pp. 7-8.
13. Rajwade, *Marathyanchya Itihasachin Sadhanen*, Vol. VIII, p. 11.
14. Sen, *Siva Chhatrapati*, p. 29.

danger a fort was reinforced with men, provision, and stores, but the nominal strength of a garrison probably did not go above five hundred[15]. These men were armed with swords and spears, bows and arrows, matchlocks and muskets. Against their assailants they also used rockets, which probably caused little harm to men, except when they by some lucky chance set fire to their powder store, but frightened away the war elephants. A more effective missile was the bomb, which was used in the defence of Purandar. In artillery Shivaji's forces must have been very poor, for he had to depend entirely upon the European merchants for his supply of guns and ammunition, and what cannons he purchased from his French and Portuguese friends were certainly not of the best type. When a particular fort was threatened, Shivaji had to supply it with artillery from other places. But while he was weak in firearms, his enemies were not better equipped, and the garrison could often repulse an assault by rolling down huge pieces of stone as their assailants laboriously climbed up the steep hill side. Fryer saw "on the tops of the Mountains, several Fortresses of Seva Gi's, only defensible by Nature needing no other Artillery but stones, which they tumble down upon their Foes, carrying as certain destruction as Bullets where they alight"[16]. The use of stones for defensive purposes was by no means confined to Southern India or to Shivaji's times. Sir Hector Munro and his men were violently assailed by stones when they attempted to capture Chunar[17], and Lord Valentia mentions the use of stones in the first decade of the last century when he found a range of useless and decayed cannons left in neglect near the important fort of Lohagad[18]. Ten years later Fitzclarence still found stones heaped near the forts of the Deccan when he passed through the country on his way to Bombay during the Pendhari war.

15. Fryer, *A New Account of East India and Persia*, p. 127.

16. *A New Account of East India and Persia*, p. 123.

17. Caraccioli, quoted by Sir G. Forrest, *The Life of Lord Clive*, Vol. II, p. 273.

18. Valentia, *Voyages and Travels to India, Ceylon, The Red Sea, Abyssinia and Egypt*, Vol. II, pp. 166-167.

It may be mentioned here that a fort could be captured in two ways only—by effecting a breach in the walls by means of mines or cannonade and by escalading by means of rope ladders. Shivaji's men mined the ramparts of Phonda in 1675[19] and Tanaji recaptured Sinhgad by escalading its steep ramparts under the cover of darkness of night. For this purpose the Marathas sometimes employed an ingenious method. They tamed and trained the big monitor lizard or iguana, called *Ghorpad* in Marathi, and sent it to climb up the most difficult hillsides or ramparts with a rope round its body. It soon found a convenient cleft whereto it drove its nails and steadfastly clung and enabled a man to climb up the rope that hung loosely down[20]. The rest of the operation was comparatively easy unless the assailants were surprised by the watchmen of the place.

In the defence of a fort vigilance alone was greatly needed. If the enemy ran mines the garrison had to countermine, but strong hill forts could not be easily or effectively mined. The only other danger against which the commander had to be careful was surprise. An open assault he generally tried to beat back by artillery, bombs and rockets supplemented by a heavy shower of stones. Sometimes he had to make a sally, as did Murar Baji Prabhu when Dilel Khan tried to storm Purandar[21]. But, generally, a fort was reduced by a lengthy blockade, and failure of provision alone led to capitulation.

Shivaji generally had his forts well stored with provision and ammunition, but the reduction of Panhala by Sidi Johar made him more careful. In 1671-72 he decided to have a reserve fund of one lakh and twenty-five thousand Hons, or nearly five lakhs of Rupees, to meet the extraordinary needs of beleaguered forts. This reserve fund was not to be touched if money was available from the ordinary sources. The paper

19. Factory Records, Surat, Vol. 88, Part II, fols. 48-49.

20. For an instance See Acworth and Shaligram, *Aitihasik Povade*, p 44.

21. Sen, *Siva Chhatrapati*, p. 53.

that announced this decision runs as follows :—" Rajashri Chhatrapati Saheb has decided to raise money from each *mahal* in his provinces and *watans*. This money should form a (reserve) fund and should be spent only when war with the Mughals would break out, and the Mughals would lay siege to forts, and money would not be available from any other source ; otherwise this money should not be spent for any other government work. So has the Saheb (His Majesty) decided and it has been settled that a sum of one lakh and twenty-five thousand Hons should constitute the reserve fund, and should be raised from the following *mahals* and personages at the following rate :—

Kudal	20,000
Rajapur	20,000
Kolen	20,000
Dabhol	15,000
Poona	13,000
Nagoji Govind	10,000
Jawli	5,000
Kalyan	5,000
Bhiwandi	5,000
Indapur	5,000
Supa	2,000
Krishnaji Bhaskar	5,000

It has been decided that the sum of one lakh and twenty-five thousand Hons (thus raised) should be set aside as a reserve fund "[22].

If the provisioning of the forts was necessary, their repairs demanded no less care ; and in the same year another fund of one lakh and seventy-five thousand Hons was constituted for repairing his principal forts[23]. From the English factory records it appears that Shivaji often tempted workmen from

22. Rajwade, *Marathyanchya Itihasachin Sadhanen*, Vol. VIII, pp. 16-17.

23 Rajwade, *Marathyanchya Itihasachin Sadhanen*, Vol. VIII, pp. 18-19.

Bombay with offers of better wages and better lodgings[24]. A shrewd man, he knew quite well that good work cannot be obtained from discontented workmen. In the paper that announced the constitution of this fund, Shivaji observed that as the workmen did not get their wages regularly, they grew discontented and building and repair works suffered in consequence. He therefore set aside the sum of one lakh and seventy-five thousand Hons for building and repair work alone, which was allotted as follows:—

Fort	Amount
Raigad	50,000
Sinhgad	10,000
Sindhudurg	10,000
Vijaidurg	10,000
Suvarnadurg	10,000
Pratapgad	10,000
Purandar	10,000
Rajgad	10,000
Prachandagad	5,000
Prasiddhagad	5,000
Vishalgad	5,000
Mahipatgad	5,000
Sudhagad	5,000
Lohagad	5,000
Sabalgad	5,000
Shrivardhangad, Manranjan	5,000
Korigad	3,000
Sarasgad	2,000
Mahidhargad	2,000
Manohargad	1,000
Miscellaneous	7,000
Total	1,75,000

24. We read in a Bombay letter—"Sevagee being abuilding and giving great wages, hath tempted several of our workmen to run away." (February, 1671-72) Factory Records, Surat, Vol. 106, fols. 73-74.

It does not appear that this huge sum was designed to be spent in a single year, for labour in those days was cheap and Shivaji had practically finished his principal forts by the year 1671 when this fund was constituted. We shall not, therefore, be wrong if we hold that this also was somewhat like a reserve fund, as the previous one, to be used when money from the normal sources were not forthcoming to ensure regular payment of masons and artisans employed in the forts, although it is not explicitly mentioned in the paper quoted.

The men who formed the garrison and their officers were not very highly paid. Although the chronicles are silent on this point, a few figures can be compiled from some contemporary letters that have come down to us. It appears that a *Havaldar* usually enjoyed a remuneration of 125 Hons a year. One Nagoji Bhonsle was appointed *Mudradhari* or *Havaldar* of fort Utlur in 1677 on a salary of 150 Hons per year; out of this sum, however, he was expected to retain two servants on 25 Hons each[25]. Krishnaji Surevanshi was appointed *Sarnobat* of the above mentioned fort in the same year on an annual salary of 100 Hons. The *Havaldar* in charge of the buildings in the fort got the same pay as the *Mudradhari* and his *Majumdar* was paid at the rate of 36 Hons per year. Four *Tat Sarnobats* were sent by Shivaji to take charge of the ramparts of Kot Utlur and they were each engaged on an annual salary of 12 Hons (4 ordinary Hons and 8 Kaveripak Hons). Along with them had been despatched seven *Bargirs* on a yearly pay of 9 Hons (3 ordinary Hons and 6 Kaveripak Hons) per head. We can, therefore, assume that this represented the usual remuneration of a private serving in a fort. In a document dated the 26th July, 1677, we find that Timaji Narayan, a clerk, was appointed as an extra hand for the office work in fort Valgudanur, on a monthly allowance of three Hons[26]. Besides the usual remuneration, each officer got, according to his rank and the importance of his charge, an additional

25. Rajwade, *Marathyanchya Itihasachin Sadhanen*, Vol. VIII, pp. 28-31.

26. Ibid, p. 29.

allowance for palanquin, torch-bearers, personal attendants, sunshades and pages.

The outposts guarding the outskirts of a fort were left in charge of Ramoshis, Bhils and other wild tribes. Their knowledge of the jungle by-ways made them excellent watchmen, and as they were people of nocturnal habits, they were specially efficient in keeping vigilance at night. Tradition says that Shivaji was the first sovereign to employ Ramoshis as watchmen of his fortresses, and they seem to have performed their duty with loyalty and zeal[27]. Their work made it imperative on them to live outside the ramparts, and as their standard of living was abnormally low, they were contented with a small salary and some insignificant perquisites. Whether the latter was granted in Shivaji's time we do not precisely know; but these soon became the *watan* of the Ramoshis, Bhils and Kolis who kept watch around the hill forts, and, like everything else connected with the Marathas, their office also became hereditary.

The elaborate machinery designed by Shivaji to ensure his authority in the forts survived till the close of the Peshwa period, but it ceased to function with effect soon after his death. He had demolished the adulterine castles, but the new barons took possession of the very forts Shivaji had built or captured, and they served to strengthen the disintegrating forces of feudalism instead of uniting the country under a strong central government. They were no doubt still held on behalf of the King but not for him.

When Shivaji died his kingdom was defended by 240 forts and strongholds and not one of them was held by a hereditary noble. But a complicated system, such as he had adopted in the administration of forts, required constant and vigilant supervision on the part of the King, and this was not forthcoming in Sambhaji's time. He did not do away with his father's institutions; but he did not possess his father's foresight or his father's industry. After his death things became worse. It was then possible for one single officer to

27. Captain Alexander Mackintosh, *An Account of the Origin and Present Condition of the Tribe of Ramoossies*, pp. 56-57.

betray the important fortress of Rairi which could and did stand a siege for months together. With the revival of feudalism in Rajaram's time the chief officers of the State became the custodians of the forts. The celebrated fort of Purandar was held by the Sachiv; and in 1710-11 Parashram Pratinidhi was in charge of no less than thirty-five forts, of which the most important were Vishalgad, Pratapgad, Chandan, Wandan, Satara, and Kolhapur[27a]. It became customary for every military officer to secure at least one strong fort for the residence of his family, and Balaji Vishwanath pursued the same practice when he obtained from the Sachiv Shankraji Narayan the fort of Purandar. After the expansion of the Maratha empire into Malwa and Hindustan the Peshwa's officers began to garrison the fortresses of the newly conquered province on their own account, and the contamination naturally spread among their subordinates as well. Thus there arose not only a number of hereditary military officers, but they were furnished with forts and strongholds where they could with impunity defy the authority of the central government.

Under the Peshwa's Government the three old officers were not only retained but they had all become *Darakhdars* or hereditary officers. Under normal circumstances they were not only succeeded by their sons or other legal heirs but even in their lifetime they could absent themselves from the fort, while an agent nominated by them carried on the duties of the office. The pay of a *Havaldar* or *Sabnis* or *Karkhannis* would naturally vary according to the importance of his charge, but when he lived in the fort with his family he got an additional allowance. In the year 1763-64 the *Havaldar* and the *Sarnobat* of fort Bahula got Rs. 125 each per year, while the *Sabnis* and the *Fadnis* were paid at the rate of Rs. 200; the *Subhedar* got Rs. 250 per year[28]. The *Havaldars* of Chawand and Ahmadnagar, however, got Rs. 360 and 300 respectively[29]. It will, however, be a mistake to suppose that this constituted their total salary, as they received a

27a. *Peshwas' Diaries*, Vol. I, p. 54.
28. *Peshwas' Diaries*, Vol. IX, p. 347.
29. *Peshwas' Diaries*, Vol. IX, pp. 356-357.

stipulated quantity of clothes in addition, and in those days of rampant feudalism some officers, at least, preferred to be paid by hereditary *inam* lands instead of cash. The *Sabnis* of Sinhgad in 1750-51 had an annual salary of 600 Rupees besides 100 Rupees worth of clothes, but he had two rent free villages for his services, and the difference between his salary and the income derived from the two villages alone was paid in cash[30].

It is needless to say that these officers had lost under the new system much of their old importance. The expenses of a fort were paid out of the revenue of a number of villages attached to it for that purpose, and all the forts in a province were placed directly under the authority of the provincial governor. Thus we find that in 1774-75 the eighteen forts in the province of Bassein were all placed under the control of Visaji Keshav, the *Mamledar* of that province[31]. The fortress of Anjanvel, a naval station, was under the joint control of the *Havaldar* and the provincial governor, and while the latter had in his custody the key of the outer gates, that of the inner gates was in the possession of the former[32]. Such an arrangement naturally did not work satisfactorily, and in 1794-95 a dispute took place between Bapuji Shinde, the Governor of the province, and Babu Rao Salokhe, the *Havaldar* of the fort of Dharwar[33]. The *Karkhannis* was sometimes so ill-paid that he did not care to live in the fort and attend to his official duties, and the Peshwa's Government had, therefore, to send inspectors not only to examine the stores and accounts of the forts but also for the distribution of ration and the payment of the salary of the garrison[34]. In the Peshwa period forced and unpaid labour was employed for the building and repair works of the forts. Wood was supplied from the neighbouring forests and the neighbouring villages supplied the carpenters and unskilled labourers. And here again we notice a departure from Shivaji's practice.

30. *Peshwas' Diaries*, Vol. III, p. 192.
31. *Peshwas' Diaries*, Vol. VI, p. 199.
32. *Peshwas' Diaries*, Vol. VI, pp. 208-210.
33. *Peshwas' Diaries*, Vol. VI, pp. 213-214.
34. *Peshwas' Diaries*, Vol. VI, p. 211.

The numercial strength of the garrison as before varied in different forts and at different times. In 1773-74 the garrison of Satara was reinforced by an addition of fifty new men owing to the troubled state of the country[35]. The garrison of Lohagad, when that fort was held by one Dhondji in Nana Fadnavis's interest, varied from one to three thousand men according to circumstances[36]. The salary of the private serving in a fort seems to have steadily improved since Shivaji's days. During the administration of Balaji Baji Rao the payment of a private varied from three Rupees to five Rupees and eight annas a month, and when he was transferred to a new fort, an increment[37] was given, but during the regime of Madhav Rao I, a private's pay had risen as high as seven Rupees a month[38]. But it ought to be noticed here that during the Peshwa period an ordinary soldier did not get more than eleven and sometimes ten months' wage for twelve months' service, and he was generally long in arrears. From the time of Shahu Chhatrapati a new practice, that of paying the private in rent free land, had come into vogue, and in 1774-75 such soldiers were allowed to serve in the forts by rotation, for they had to look after the cultivation of their lands as well[39]. Sometimes they rendered no service to the State and had to be dismissed. In the closing years of the Peshwa period Sir Thomas Munro noticed a peculiar practice prevailing in the Southern Maratha country. Some small forts were provided with a hereditary garrison, and their commander alone with a few followers were sent from Poona[40]. This was no doubt the extreme logical result of the feudal principles then in operation.

The Peshwas not only encouraged but sometimes compelled the garrison to bring their family into the fort. This was probably a wise precaution. Shahu had compelled

35. *Peshwas' Diaries*, Vol. VI, p. 198.

36. Valentia. *Voyage and Travels to India, Ceylon, The Red Sea, Abyssinia and Egypt*, Vol. II, p. 171.

37. *Peshwas' Diaries*, Vol. III, pp. 198-200.

38. *Peshwas' Diaries*, Vol. IX, p. 358.

39. *Peshwas' Diaries*, Vol. VI, pp. 200-201.

40 Gleig. *Life of Sir Thomas Munro*, Vol. II, p. 268.

Sheikh Mira to betray his trust by putting under arrest his wife and children who were living in an unprotected village outside the fort, and the Peshwas rightly feared that such a pressure could be brought to bear upon their officers as well by an invading enemy. During the troubles created by the pretender Sadoba the Peshwa's Government therefore not only permitted the garrison in the troubled area to bring their family within the fort, but also granted them an extra allowance and exempted them from some newly imposed taxes[41].

The provisions of the forts were annually renewed. Old grain was sometimes given to the garrison in lieu of pay and sometimes sold, and new grain was bought out of the proceeds. Sometimes the Government went so far as to store in the forts ordinary spices and even tobacco[42].

In the Peshwa period the forts were well supplied with artillery so far as quantity went. The artillery men were mostly foreigners, and they were better paid than the ordinary private. Rockets were still in use and rocket men were still employed in the forts, but stone had not been discarded. Big guns in a fort were cleaned once a year and small guns and muskets once a month, but it does not appear that they were very effectively served. For, fort after fort was captured by the English in 1818 and 1819 without much difficulty.

The process of denationalisation that we have noticed in the army, did not leave the forts unaffected, and when Baji Rao II fought against the English, most of his fortresses were mainly garrisoned by Arabs and non-Maratha Indians.

What happened in the forts under the direct control of the Peshwa also happened in the forts held by his feudal subordinates. Only they were less efficiently garrisoned and provisioned when the feudal chief in question was not financially well off. In times of danger such a chief could in theory expect relief from the Peshwa; in practice the tardy arrival of reinforcement caused irreparable loss to the feudal

41. *Peshwas' Diaries*, Vol. VI, pp. 203-204.
42. *Peshwas' Diaries*, Vol. III, pp. 190-191.

baron and consequently to his master. So, in spite of the great natural strength of the country, it offered but a feeble fight when the Peshwa's territories were finally conquered by the British.

William Henry Tone reported to a Madras officer in the last decade of the 18th century that the Peshwa ruled over "a country of great natural strength, interspersed with mountains and defiles, all of which are defended by fortresses that are reserved as depots for treasure, or as retreats in the event of ill success or defeat. Perhaps no country on earth is better calculated for the purposes of defensive war; so that, whatever be the fortune of the Mahrattas in the field, we may safely pronounce, that in their own country, they will always be impregnable. I have counted in a day's march through Candeish, nearly twenty fortresses, all in sight in different directions, Chandore, Unky Tunky, Saler Rouler, Nassick Trimmuck, Golna, and Mongy Tongy are all places of this description. A country so strongly situated is unconquerable; and of this truth the Emperor Aurangzibe, who made some attempt to subjugate it appeared latterly to be convinced"[43].

But the prophecy of Tone was belied, not because he had exaggerated the natural strength of the Maratha country or over-estimated the defensive value of the Maratha forts, but because he had overlooked the primitive character of these strongholds, in architecture, in management, in their defensive and offensive arms. Since Shivaji's days no improvement had been made in the military architecture of the forts; the feudal system that had since been revived had positively undermined the efficiency of the garrison as well as of the command; the artillery was not only not improved, but in the days of Baji Rao II, hopelessly neglected in places like Lohagad, while the English were far in advance of Aurangzib in organisation, artillery and military science.

---

43. Tone, *Illustrations of some Institutions of the Mahratta People*, p. 16.

CHAPTER VI

ARTILLERY.

The Marathas, like other Indians, never excelled in artillery. Of its efficiency as an offensive weapon of long range they had early become aware. It was to his artillery tactics that Babar owed his decisive victories over his Rajput and Pathan opponents; it was their superior knowledge of artillery that had made the Portuguese so formidable in Southern India. It became, therefore, an imperative necessity for the Indian potentates of the North and the South to furnish themselves with the new arms. Portuguese and other European adventurers were on this account warmly welcomed by Indian princes, but some enterprising Hindus had also learnt the new art. A quaint account of an artillery duel between a Brahman gunner named Rama and a Portuguese artilleryman, fought as early as 1571, has come down to us. The Brahman's gun was baptised the "butcher", while the machine of his Christian rival was called the "lion", and the two men grimaced, grinned and made faces at each other before they fired[1]. There were, therefore, some Indian gunners even before the rise of the Marathas.

Shivaji had a regular artillery department called the *Tophkhana* and among his state departments is mentioned *Darukhana*[2], the exact Persian synonym of the Portuguese "Casa de Polvora." This was quite in the fitness of things, for in the Deccan the Portuguese had at one time figured as the greatest masters of the new art, and Shivaji might have been consciously copying their methods. The real or pseudo-Portuguese in his service were not improbably employed in this department. For his supply of guns and cannons, however, he was entirely dependent on the European trading companies, for it does not appear that he had any

1. R. S. Whiteway, *The Rise of the Portuguese Power in India*, p. 40.
2. Sen, *Siva Chhatrapati*, p. 133.

gun-foundry of his own. For this deficiency we need not blame him. He was a pioneer in many things. During his short but eventful life he had attempted much and he had to leave much unattempted. It was impossible for him to accomplish everything.

The European merchant companies carried on a regular trade in artillery and ammunition, and Shivaji, like his neighbours, naturally looked towards them for this much needed weapon. It was probably with this intent that he had permitted the French to build a factory at Rajapore, and this was undoubtedly one of the advantages that he expected from the settlement of an English factory at that port, for we read in a Surat letter dated the 30th September, 1671, that Mr. Stephen Ustick and Ram Sinay were instructed to let him know " if he gives us such encouragement that wee againe setle in his port he may obtain from us those advantages that other nations doe in whose ports we trade, but we would not positively have them promise him those granadoes, mortar pieces and ammunition he desires, nor absolutely deny him in regard wee do not think itt convenient to help him against Danda Rajpore which place if it were in his possession would prove a great annoyance to the port of Bombay, and on the other side our denyall is not consistent at present with our interest, in respect wee believe the keeping in suspence will bring him to a speedier conclusion of the treaty hopeing thereby to be furnish(ed) with those things he desires[3] ". From the French he purchased 2,000 maunds of lead and 88 iron guns in 1673[4], but although he approached the English with similar proposals from time to time they avoided compliance with various excuses. On the 5th September, 1670, the Bombay factors wrote to Surat—" we know that Sevagee may furnish himself with lead or guns from the French factoryes at Rajapore but wee will not bring ourselves into any intrigues, but keepe to such orders as you have and shall appoint us[5] ".

3. Factory Records, Surat, Vol. 87, fol. 1.

4. Surat Letter, dated the 12th January, 1673-74, Factory Records, Surat, Vol. 87, Part II, fol. 77.

5. Factory Records, Surat, Vol. 105, fols. 20-21.

The excuse generally offered was that the English could not afford to offend the Delhi Government by supplying their enemies with warlike stores; but Shivaji was quite willing or even anxious to keep the transactions secret. In September, 1671, Bombay informed Surat that "an Engineer, mortar piece, grandos and a great gun or two are the assistance he expects which he thinks may be privately conveyed to him "[6]. How this could be managed we learn from another Bombay letter dated 9th November, 1671, "If Your Honour, etc., approve of spareing Sevagee 3 or 4 great gunns he sayes he will finde Portugues that shall buy them of us; as if for their owne use; and soe our name not brought in question "[7]. In 1674, Shivaji again sent an envoy "with an extraordinary kinde letter from him to the President together with a present of five loads of ordinary stuffs and a confirmation of the order for the payment of the money at Rajapore and other priviledges which hath granted to the English in his country and desired to be supplyed with 60 big iron guns and two big brass guns[8] ". The English at that moment did not possess any iron gun that they could spare but the two brass guns were for sale. The Surat authorities were, however, afraid that "soe publique an action as that would be must needs provoke this King, who being already made sensible by his ministers Bauder Ckaun[9] and others as we hear, that his enemy is furnished with provissions from our island, might be incensed to ruine our trade in his dominions should wee assist him with such ammunition[10] ". In December, 1676, the Surat council again addressed a letter to their Bombay colleagues positively forbidding them to sell the two brass guns that Shivaji was anxious to purchase. "Though Sevagee should profer you ready money," the letter ran, "for your two brass gunns yet wee should not have you part with them without a positive order from us; for it is a matter of

6. Factory Records, Surat, Vol. 106, fol. 9.
7. Factory Records, Surat, Vol. 106, fols. 32-33.
8. Letter dated 8th November, 1674, Factory Records, Surat, Vol. 107, fol 6
9 Bahadur Khan, the foster brother of Emperor Aurangzib.
10. Factory Records, Surat, Vol. 88, fol. 244, letter dated 13th November, 1674.

great consequence, and we know not how farr he may be trusted "[11].

These repeated importunities on Shivaji's part clearly indicate the extent of his need, and inspite of all the caution of the English factors, the resourceful Maratha chief did, at least once, succeed in securing some of their guns. In a Bombay letter dated 7th April, 1673 (or 1671 ?) we read " the two gunns formerly mentioned, the Deputy Governor hath sold to a Frenchman, who sold them to a Fidalgo at Tannah and he sent them as wee since heare to Sevagy "[12]. These guns were sold by their weight and were naturally of very poor quality, for the English and the Portuguese would not, for very good reason, part with their best artillery. Of the two guns that Shivaji obtained from Bombay in 1671, through the assistance of his French and Portuguese agents, the English factors write: " they are very bad within, yet with their powder and stone shott they may last a good while "[13]. In a letter dated Surat, 12th November, 1672, we read of the defects of some guns disposed that year—" we have sold all the gunns sent up hither and what are not yet taken on per shoare, from the Loyall Merchant: at the price of 5¼ Rupees per maund: 4 months time, but coming to prove them there are 6 broake in the tryall; being old defective gunns, some of them with great holes in them: others that have had new mettall dopt into holes, which appeared plainly at their breaking "[14]. In another Surat letter written on the 5th February, 1673-74 some of the guns intended for sale are described as " old and defective many of them being honey combe "[15]. Yet Shivaji was not the only potentate who was eager to purchase these machines. The Governor of Surat, the Raja of Sunda, the Generals of Bijapur, all vied with each other for their possession and Prince Shah Alam

11. Factory Records, Surat, Vol. 89, fol. 90.

12. Factory Records, Surat, Vol. 105, fol. 164. The year is wrongly indicated in the manuscript: it should be 1671. The mistake is probably due to the copyist's error.

13. Factory Records, Surat, Vol. 105, fols. 20-21.

14. Factory Records, Surat, Vol. 87, fol. 90.

15. Factory Records, Surat, Vol. 87, Part II, fol. 110.

sent a *nishan* to the Bombay Government to supply ammunition to his fleet[16]. Familiar with artillery and ammunition, as Indian princes had been for more than a century, they had done very little or nothing for their improvement and manufacture. The guns of Indian manufacture were notoriously crude and clumsy[17].

Besides artillery of European manufacture, Shivaji also possessed some light pieces of Indian make called *Jejala* and *Zamburak* or *Shutarnal*. The shots were generally of stone or iron, but Shivaji did not possess a sufficient number of guns and cannons, for when he wanted to strengthen the fortress of Panhala, he had to weaken his strongholds in the Konkan by denuding them of their guns although he had purchased no less than 40 new pieces from the French that year[18]. The Carwar factors actually thought that he had decided to leave the Konkan altogether, to such an extent were his fortresses in that part depleted of their protecting artillery, as appears from their letter to Surat dated the 24th November, 1679—" there is sent by Sevagee Sumjee Punditt, Anajee's brother, for takeing of severall pieces of ordnance out of these castles as Ancholah, Carwar, Symisecre and Pundah to the amount of 30 which by the strength of men and buffaloes are to be drawne up to Pornollah, that it is supposed he intends to deliver up the Cocon[19] to the Duccanees "[20].

Though Shivaji had employed Portuguese agents for purchasing artillery and ammunition for him, there is no mention whatever of these necessary articles of war in his two

16. Surat consultation, 10th August, 1670, Factory Records, Surat. Vol. 3, fols. 79-80.

17. One type of the guns commonly used in Southern India is thus described by Phillip Baldeus, the Dutch Missionary: " they are made of long and broad Bars of Iron, joined together with Iron Hoops;" Churchill's *Voyages* Vol. III, p. 652. The other type was not much better. For a learned account of Indian cannons see Irvine, *Army of the Indian Moghuls*, pp. 113-132.

18. Rajapore letter, dated 30th December, 1679. Factory Records, Vol. 108, fol. 37.

19. The Konkan.

20. Factory Records, Surat, Vol. 108, fol. 76.

treaties with the Portuguese Government; but that does not necessarily mean that the Portuguese dealers were unwilling to supply their powerful neighbour with these requisites of war. Sambhaji, however, was at first more fortunate than his father, for both the English and the Portuguese were willing to sell these much needed commodities to him. On the 10th February, 1681-82 the Surat authorities wrote to their Bombay subordinates:—" if Sambajee Rajah should desire anything from you, wee shall not forbid you oblidging him but be cautious and private in such a case "[21]. The Portuguese Government was equally willing to oblige Sambhaji. In a letter addressed to him on the 28th July, 1682, the Viceroy informed the Maratha Prince that he could purchase his munition and arms from Portuguese territories. He wrote: " After the envoy Esaji Gambhir Rao had delivered to me Your Highness's letter, he informed me that Your Highness had ordered two farms under the jurisdiction of Bicholy and Curalle to manufacture powder and purchase artillery, sulphur, saltpetre and other things ordered to be manufactured in the ports of Canara and Malabar, requesting me to direct the Captains of the Armada of this State not to obstruct those ships (carrying munition) and to let them, and also the provision that Your Highness's subjects may take from Canara for the ports of Vingurla and Banda, pass freely. As I desire to maintain friendship with Your Highness, I have given to Your Highness's envoy the necessary order to that effect, in conformity with Your Highness's request "[22]. Sambhaji's good relations with his Portuguese neighbours did not last long, and it is needless to say that during the critical period following his death the Marathas had hardly the time or the opportunity of making their own guns, though a portion of their powder and shot had always been manufactured in the country. In the second decade of the eighteenth century the Marathas still depended on the Europeans for their supply of artillery. Early in his reign Shahu had applied to Sir Nicholas Waite, Governor of Bombay, for arms and ammunition, and in 1713

21. Factory Records, Surat, Vol. 90, Part III, fol. 51.
22. Livrts dos Reis Visinhos (Goa), Vol. II, fol. 16. Sen, *A Preliminary Report on the Historical Records at Goa*, pp. 27-28.

Kanhoji Angria had sent the following requests to Governor Aislabie :—" If I have occasion for powder and shott you shall supply on my paying for the same. I desire also a place to make powder for which I shall send saltpetre and brimstone "[23]. To both of these requests, however, an answer in the negative was returned. It is not at all difficult to understand why Kanhoji was unwilling to part with the guns of the ships he had captured, though he was willing to restore the vessels.

In the Peshwa period some efforts were made to manufacture their own artillery and ammunition. Baji Rao had his own foundry, which was visited by Captain William Gordon, the English envoy, in 1739. He wrote on the 30th June :—" I visited the foundry, where I saw many coehorns and bomb shells said to have been cast there, and a form of a thirteen inch mortar. I was told they make such with great ease, and have learned the art of running iron for making shot "[24]. During the administration of Madhav Rao I, a cannon-ball factory was established at Ambegavan near Votur in the province of Junnar in 1765-66, and another factory was established at Poona four years later for manufacturing cannons[25]. But this did not mean that they were seriously thinking of dispensing with foreign arms. On the contrary they steadily looked for such supply and provided for them in their treaties with European nations.

By the fifth Article of the treaty concluded between the Portuguese Government and the Peshwa on the 9th January, 1722, Baji Rao was entitled to purchase powder, ball, cannons and other military stores at a just price in the Portuguese territories[26]. Another treaty was concluded between Krishna Rao Mahadev, Governor of Kalyan, and Martinho da Silveira de Menezes, Captain General of the Province of the North, on 30th January, 10th February, 1731-32, and the 10th Article of this new treaty

23. Bombay Public Consultation, Range CCCXLI, No. 4 Consultation, 14th February, 1712-13.

24. Forrest, *Selections From State Papers*, Maratha Series, Vol. I, p. 79.

25. *Peshwas' Diaries*, Vol. IX, pp. 333 and 335.

26. Biker, *Tratados da India*, Vol. VI, p. 11.

again permitted the Marathas to buy, as they had always done, what powder, ball, sulphur and lead they might require in the territories of the Portuguese Government[27]. In 1786 the Poona authorities requested the Portuguese agent to furnish them with a few bronze guns of the latest type with all the necessary materials and they also wanted some powder and ball[28]. The Portuguese Government generally complied with such requests as best as they could. In 1782 they had promptly found a quantity of sulphur for Anand Rao Dhulap the Maratha Admiral[29]. While engaged in the siege of Dharwar, Parashram Bhau Patwardhan had received from Goa 500 maunds of powder, and as this quantity was supplied from Government stock no price was charged[29a]. During the first Maratha war, Mahadaji Sindhia[29b] also purchased ammunition from the Portuguese, and even in the nineties of the eighteenth century the Peshwa's army was still dependent on the English for their heavy artillery and small firearms, although Sindhia had by that time established a fairly efficient factory for such articles under European supervision.

27. Biker, *Tratados da India*, Vol. VI, p. 177.

28. Biker, *Tratados da India*, Vol. VIII, p. 236.

29. Livros dos Reis Visinhos, Vol. XI.

29a. Biker, *Tratados da India*, Vol. IX, p. 212.

29b. Livros dos Reis Visinhos, (Goa), Vol. X. It should not be supposed that the Marathas relied on the Portuguese alone for their supply of artillery and ammunition. The Government often sent their agents to purchase guns and warlike stores at Bombay, and provincial Governors also followed the example of their masters. One Balaji Mahadev was sent to Bombay to purchase guns in 1753-54 (*Peshwas' Diaries*, Vol. III, p. 179) and again in 1764-65, 36,000 balls were sought from Bombay. (*Peshwas' Diaries*, Vol. IX, p. 328). The Bombay Government were reluctant to supply their neighbours with warlike stores, as will be apparent from the folllowing extract from Bombay Public Consultation. Range CCCXLI, No. 14A, pp. 334-335, dated 23rd July, 1745). "When Mr. Sedgewicke was at Bassen in April last the Maratha Governour (Sancrajee Punt) acquainted him he should be much obliged if we would spare him about ten thousand shot of different sizes, as also some Cohorn shells and Granadoes, since when Sancrajee wrote the President to the same import. As the giving him an entire refusal may create some disgust and the sparing him large shott and * * * is by no means proper, the President proposes to the Board let him have about one hundred and fifty hundred weight of shot from 11 lb. to 4 lb. weight at the price the black * * and to write him accordingly, making a proper excuse for not assisting him with larger shott or any shells."

As usual these guns and muskets purchased from the English and the Portuguese were neither of the best type nor in a very good condition. Only arms rejected as useless were offered for sale, and when the English authorities decided to stop this practice, Colonel Tone protested against the measure in very strong terms. "The late regulations of the Company," he wrote, "respecting the return to Europe of all unserviceable arms, may for a time prevent the increase of infantry corps, but then it will drive them to the expedient of making their own firelocks, as Scindeah has done, and his are very excellent ones, far superior to the ordinary Europe arms to be met with in the bazars. I for my own part very much doubt the policy of the orders in question. In the first place, I lay it down as a postulatum, that arms will be sold while a good price is given for them in defiance of all the regulations that can be made; and if they must be disposed of, the Company had better receive the value than any individual. In the next place, the arms purchased in the interior, are of that description which is denominated unserviceable, and generally are so. In this case it is of very little consequence in whose hands they are, since if they are useless to the Company, who have excellent Karkonnas to repair them, they can be of no great use to a native power, which has not the same means of mending them"[30]. It may be asked why the Peshwas did not try to remove a deficiency, the danger of which was so obvious. Their financial difficulties do not fully explain this indifference. The feudal organisation of the army was not wholly responsible for it; the fact is that they always sought the easiest way out of every difficulty, forgetting that the easiest was not always the safest or the shortest.

"The guns" of the Maratha armies, we learn from Tone, were "tolerably well cast, but the carriages," says he, "are in general very clumsily and badly constructed. A march of a few days shakes the carriages to pieces." "The cannon," the same writer informs us, "are never made of any precise calibre, but are cast indifferently by all diameters and the ball

30. Tone, *Illustrations of some Institutions of the Maharatta People*, pp. 54-55.

afterwards adapted to the bore. They never use cast shot, but those of wrought iron, hammered to any dimensions; the many angles, consequently on the surface of the shot in a very small course of service, destroy the smoothness of the bore and they can never be fired with that precision that a cast ball can "[31].

Shivaji, as we have already seen, had a very limited supply of artillery for his forts and fleet and he had no field artillery, although he had used cannons against Janjira and Phonda. The Marathas long suffered from this want. In 1692 Dalpat Bundela defeated a numerically superior Maratha force because, as the author of *Dilkusha* suggests, he had some artillery[32]. It was the lack of field artillery again that prevented Baji Rao I from reaping the maximum advantage of his strategic victory over the Nizam's army at Tal Bhopal. It was his artillery that saved the Mughal general from utter ruin and destruction. The Maratha army was better furnished with field artillery during the Peshwaship of Balaji Baji Rao probably when the *gardi* force was organised and the necessity of the trained battalions of infantry was recognised. By the middle of the eighteenth century, the Marathas had attained some familiarity with the use of artillery, as Grose[33] tells us, but the department was still largely manned by Portuguese and Indian Christians. The pay of an ordinary Portuguese gunner varied from Rs. 12-8 to Rs. 30 per month in 1753,[34] as a letter addressed to Shripat Bapuji in that year shows. The following artillery men were sent to serve under him and he was instructed to pay them on the first of each month the salary shown against their name.

Joki (Joachim?) Rs. 30.

Manik (Manuk?) Rs. 25.

Pharasis Rudrak (Francisco Rodrigues?) Rs. 12-8.

31. Tone, *Illustrations of some Institutions of the Maharitta People*, pp. 56 and 57.

32. Scott, *History of the Dekkan*, Vol. II, p. 82.

33. Grose, *Voyage to the East Indies*, pp. 108-109.

34. *Peshwas' Diaries*, Vol. III, p. 177.

Jacob Rujel (Rozario?) Rs. 12-8.
Malak Malkar (Melchoir?) Rs. 15.
Manvel (Manoel?) Rs. 15.

In a document dated 1754-55 one Madhav Rao Shivdev is mentioned as the Chief of the Artillery department and the civil administration of the department was vested in him and the *Dewan*, *Majumdar*, *Fadnis* and *Sabnis*[35]. The *Tophkhana* like other departments must have been furnished with the usual *Darakhdar* staff of eight officers, although only four are mentioned in the document quoted above. A fifth officer, the *Potnis*, is mentioned in a letter of 1765-66, where we read that the *Potnis* of the artillery commanded by one Bhikan Khan attached to the army of Raghunath Rao had an annual salary of 150 Rs. only[36].

In 1777 a Portuguese officer named Noronha commanded part of the Peshwa's artillery and he had a number of European artillerymen under him[37]. In 1782 one Musa Naraj (Monsieur Noronha? or George?) held a similar command[38]. The most well known Maratha artillery officer was Bhim Rao Panshe. He came into prominence during the first Maratha war and in accordance with the usual Maratha custom obtained a large *saranjam*, which was held by his descendants after him.

The trained battalions in the Peshwa's service had their contingents of artillery. With the old battalions of Boyd were employed 8 Portuguese gunners, who got a monthly salary of 60 Rs. each, 2 *Jamadars* on 30 Rs. each, 2 *Havaldars* at the rate of 18 Rs. each 42 *Golandazes* or gunners at 12 Rs. each and 24 *Khalasis* on 10 Rs. each. In the artillery department there were 32 mechanics, namely, 9 carpenters, 8 blacksmiths, 10 stonecutters and 5 camp followers. This

35. *Peshwas' Diaries*, Vol. III, p. 180
36. *Peshwas' Diaries*, Vol. IX, p. 331.
37. Forrest, *Selections from State Papers*, Maratha Series, p. 294.
38. *Peshwas' Diaries*, Vol. VI, p. 190. The son of this Musa Naraj afterwards entered Holkar's army. See *Maheshwar Darbarchin Batmi Patren*, Vol. II, p. 218.

force was much increased when a new regiment was added to Boyd's two old battalions[39].

In 1812 John Ford had the following staff for the artillery of his battalions[40] :—

2	Serjeants at a monthly salary of	35 Rs. 12 annas each.
4	Gunners	25 Rs. 12 annas each.
2	Serangs	30 Rs.
2	Tandels	12 Rs.
4	Drummers	10 Rs. 4 annas.
2	Water suppliers	9 Rs. 8 annas.
60	Laskars	8 Rs. 8 annas.
1	Master Carpenter	25 Rs.
2	Carpenters	18 Rs.
1	Master Blacksmith	25 Rs.
2	Blacksmiths	18 Rs.
2	Armourers	18 Rs.
1	Hammerer	10 Rs.
1	Bellower	8 Rs.
1	Water supplier (for the smithy)	14 Rs.
3	Clerks—one for writing Marathi.	
	one for writing English.	
	one for attending the court.	
1	Shroff for testing coins.	
10	Pioneers at a monthly salary of	8 Rs. 8 annas each.
1	Havaldar	12 Rs.

It is to be noticed that the *laskars* of Ford's artillery got a lower salary than Boyd's *golandazes* and *khalasis* but the 4 gunners under Ford were much better paid, probably because they were of European origin or Indian Christians from Goa.

39. *Peshwas' Diaries*, Vol. V, pp. 184-187.
40. *Itihas Sangraha, Peshave Daftarantil Nivadak Kagad Patra*, pp. 94-95.

The record left by the Maratha artillerymen cannot be regarded as a glorious one. On their performance at Panipat, Kasiraj Pandit, an eye witness, has left the following comment :—" Mahratta guns being very large and heavy and their level not easily altered, their shot began to pass over our troops, and fell a mile in the rear "[41]. The inferiority of the Maratha artillery was responsible for the conversion of a sure victory at Arras[42] into a defeat, but Bhim Rao Panshe earned some credit by his operations in the Bhore Ghat region against the badly led army of Colonel Egerton. The operations of Parashram Bhau's artillery during the siege of Dharwar left an unfavourable impression on the mind of an English observer, Lieutenant Moor. He writes, " From the method of proceeding adopted by the Mahrattas, we are convinced they would not, with twenty guns against the present garrison, approach and breach Darwar in seven years. A gun is loaded, and the whole of the people in the battery sit down, talk, and smoke for half an hour, when it is fired, and if it knocks up a great dust it is thought sufficient; it is reloaded, and the parties resume their smoking and conversation. During two hours in the middle of the day, generally from one to three, a gun is seldom fired on either side, that time being, as it would appear, by mutual consent set apart for meals. In the night the fire from guns is slackened, but musquetry is increased on both sides, and shells are sparingly thrown into the fort with tolerable precision "[43]. This may have marked an advance from the early Mughal days, when the gunner frequently had his beard singed when he fired his gun; but such clumsy methods and slow firing could hardly be expected to secure any advantage in a battle against a European enemy, as was demonstrated in their final struggle with the English[44].

41. *Asiatic Researches*, Vol. III, p. 119.

42. Forrest, *Selections from State Papers*, Maratha Series, pp. 227-229.

43. Moor, *A Narrative of the Operations of Captain Little's Detachment*, p. 30.

44. Sindhia's artillery caused great loss to the English at Assye but it was not well supported by cavalry and infantry. See *Notes Relative to the Transactions in the Marhatta Empire*, Fort William, December 15. 1803, pp. 61-63. It should not be forgotten that Sindhia's artillery was the creation of European experts and not of the Marathas.

The Marathas had great faith in their artillery and always carried with them a large number of guns. This was supposed to add to their prestige[45] in the eyes of other Indian powers, but their artillery often proved a source of great and unmixed inconvenience. However old and useless, their honour demanded that they should not allow any of their guns to fall into the hands of their enemies or to be left behind, while the transport of heavy pieces was necessarily slow, as they were drawn by bullocks on very clumsy gun-carriages. Major Dirom, an eye witness, has left the following pen picture of the slow movement of these heavy and often useless machines :— "The park of artillery, where all their guns are collected, made an extraordinary appearance. The gun-carriages, in which they trust to the solidity of the timber, and use but little iron in their construction, are clumsy beyond belief; particularly the wheels, which are low, and formed by large solid pieces of wood united. The guns are of all sorts and dimensions; and, having the names of their gods given to them, are painted in the most fantastic manner; and many of them, held in esteem for the services they are said to have already performed for the state, cannot now be dispensed with, although in every respect unfit for use. Were the guns even serviceable, the small supply of ammunition with which they are provided, has always effectually prevented the Mahratta artillery from being formidable to their enemies. On a marching day, the guns and the infantry move off soon after daylight, * * * the guns and tumbrels, sufficiently unwieldy without further burden, are so heaped with stores and baggage, that there does not seem to be any idea of its ever being necessary to unlimber, and prepare for action on the march. As there are no pioneers attached to the Mahratta artillery to repair the roads, this deficiency is compensated by an additional number of cattle, there being sometimes a hundred or a hundred and fifty bullocks, in a string of pairs, to one gun"[46]. Lt. Moor says that "The gun is so heaped up with baggage of every description, that it could not be cleared ready to fire, under,

45. *Itihas Sangraha, Aitihasik Kirkol Prakaranen*, p. 3.
46. Dirom, *A Narrative of the Campaign in India*, 1792, pp. 10-12.

at least, half an hour; nor could anyone from its appearance, in its travelling state, were it not for the number of bullocks dragging it, conceive it to be a gun; fifty, sixty, and sometimes a hundred couple of bullocks, drag one of these guns; and in very heavy roads, where the cattle have been hard worked and ill fed, an elephant is posted in the rear, who pushes it with its head over difficult passages "[47]. Besides the heavy artillery the Peshwa's army was furnished with a large number of *Shutarnals*, small swivels mounted on swift camels[48]. These had the advantage of speed but were otherwise of little use. The Maratha chroniclers and Mannuci mention swivels mounted on elephants as commonly used by the Mughals, but this practice seems to have been unknown in the Maratha army.

Their artillery among other things ensured the supremacy of the English in India. To the Marathas it afforded little or no advantage in their final struggle for the empire. The weapon was not ineffective. It had a great future and its possibilities had not yet been exhausted. But the Marathas had borrowed a scientific weapon without mastering its science and unintelligent imitation seldom leads to success. Assimilation of new ideas is always fruitful, for assimilation signifies complete comprehension of the underlying principles and ability to make further contribution in the same line. Since the introduction of firearms in Europe immense improvement had been made in their mechanism, weight, range and frequency of firing. But the Marathas were unwilling and unable to make any improvement. They were quite satisfied with the weapons rejected by their rivals as useless, their factories turned out a number of antiquated guns of a type hopelessly out of date. The result was that the Marathas lost their speed and mobility which constituted their superiority in offensive and defensive operations without gaining any corresponding advantage. They were compelled to fight their English rivals on their own terms, in their own

47. Moor, *A Narrative of the Operations of Captain Little's Detachment*, pp. 78-79.

48. Victor de Saint-Genis, a biographer of De Boigne wrongly attributes the invention of camel swivels to that officer. See *Une Page inedite de l'histoire des Indes*, p. 203. For camel swivels before De Boigne See *Churchill's Voyages*, Vol. IV, p. 250.

fashion and with inferior weapons. This was not the only disadvantage. Their army consisted of forces of different character, with different traditions, different equipments and different methods of warfare not yet reconciled to their old tactics. Their confidence in artillery and trained infantry led the Maratha leaders to neglect their cavalry, and the result was disastrous[49]. It was like a combat of the eagle and the lion. So long as the noble bird kept in its own elements it could with safety and effect harass the mighty beast, but compelled to fight the lord of the forest in his chosen ground with wings cleft and talons shorn the eagle had no chance. It had to yield to its enemy and give up the unequal contest.

---

49. Sir Thomas Munro condemned the Marathas for neglecting their cavalry. See Gleig's *Life of Sir Thomas Munro*, Vol. I, p. 354-355.

CHAPTER VII.

EUROPEAN OFFICERS AND TRAINED BATTALIONS.

The army that had become so formidable under Shivaji and the first Baji Rao consisted entirely of light cavalry and fleet footmen, but the army that lost the battles of Assaye, Argaom and Lasswari had in it a new element,—infantry regiments armed, disciplined and trained by European officers in the western style. This improvement or innovation has been popularly attributed to Mahadaji Sindhia, the celebrated founder of a new empire in Hindustan, but it has been commonly ignored that although the popularity of trained battalions was largely due to him, the appointment of Benoit de Boigne in 1784 was the inevitable corollary of the employment of Muzaffar Khan and Ibrahim Khan nearly thirty years earlier.

Mahadaji was by no means the first Indian ruler to appreciate the superior fighting qualities of European officers. They had been welcomed by Indian princes since their first advent in the country, and Cosme da Guarda[1] tells us that in the seventeenth century every European in India was supposed to be an artillery expert, and even an apostate clergyman did not find the least difficulty in securing a lucrative office in the Mughal army without any previous military training. Gemelli Careri was asked by Rajaram's men, whom he met on his way to Goa, "whether he could shoot out of a Musket or understood the Art of Gunnery," and he further tells us what a good pay and an easy life a European in the Mughal service might expect. "Many *Frenchmen* belonging to the Army," he writes, "told me it was a Pleasure and Diversion to serve the *Mogul*, because they that will not Fight, or do not keep their Guards are Subject to no other Penalty but losing that day's pay, that they are convicted of having

1. Cosme da Guarda, *Vida e accoens do famoso e felicissimo Sevagy*, p. 109.

Transgress'd, and that they themselves did not value Honour much in the Service of a Barbarous King, who has no Hospital for the wounded Men. On the other side there being no Prince in the World that pays his Souldiers better, a Stranger that goes into his service soon grows Rich, especially an European or Persian "[2]. We are further told by the same Italian traveller that " All this Artillery, especially the heavy, is under the direction of *Franks* or Christian Gunners, who have extraordinary pay; especially the *Portuguese*, *English*, *Dutch*, *Germans*, and *French*, who go from Goa, or run away from aboard Ships. Some of them formerly had 200 *Roupies* a Month; but now the *Moguls* have learnt somewhat of the Art they have less "[2a].

The same reason that led the Mughal Emperors to offer such excellent terms to foreigners of unknown antecedents with nothing but their European origin to recommend them, had also induced the Maratha princes to employ them in their own army. Since Mahadaji's time trained battalions had become so much the rage of the day that even Bapuji Ganesh Gokhle[3] had in his army infantry regiments commanded by two European officers, and those who could not find white captains were content to engage some *gardis* led by their brown disciples. But long before the superiority of the western method of warfare was appreciated, the westeners' efficiency as sailors and artillerymen had been recognised by Indian rulers and even Shivaji had some Portuguese in his army. Their presence in the Maratha force had probably occasioned some protest from Mirza Raja Jai Sing, but in which department of the army and in which capacity they had been employed by Shivaji, we do not precisely know. In July 1686 a royal proclamation was issued requiring " all English subjects who had entered into the service of the Country Powers, particularly the Mogul, the King of Siam, the Queen of Acheen, and Sambagee Rajah, to return to the Company's settlements at Bombay or Madras, within six months of the

2. Churchill's *Voyages*, Vol. IV, p. 234.

2a. Churchill's *Voyages*, Vol. IV, p. 250.

3. Gurwood, *The Dispatches of Field Marshal The Duke of Wellington*, Vol. I, p. 93.

publication of this Proclamation in India "[4]. The English subjects in Sambhaji's army might have been Portuguese or Indian residents of Bombay, but it is not improbable that some English deserters had found employment with their nearest neighbour. English deserters continued to seek a safe refuge in the Maratha service during the Peshwa period as well, for they are specifically mentioned in the instructions framed for Captain W. A. Price, who was sent on an embassy to Poona in 1759[5]. John Henry Grose, who came to India in 1750, also says that the Marathas " encouraged deserters from European nations " and gave them " a pretty high pay," but he also adds that " no Europeans take service amongst them, but such as are of desperate fortunes, or have committed crimes that have obliged them to seek refuge amongst them "[6]. In the navy also these European deserters were warmly welcomed. Even if we leave aside the ambiguous reference to the Portuguese soldiers in connection with one of Shivaji's naval expeditions, there is conclusive evidence of the employment of European sailors and gunners by Kanhoji Angria and his sons. Clement Downing says that there were several Dutch men in Kanhoji's fleet and Plantain, a notorious pirate, also entered his service, while Kanhoji himself mentions a Portuguese officer in his letter to Governor Boone[7]. Captain Anselm of the *Derby* saw a Portuguese and a Dutch gunner in the employment of Sambhaji Angria[8].

Till 1750, therefore, the Maratha chiefs had employed in their army and navy European gunners, engineers and sailors, but in 1751 Balaji Baji Rao realised the need of going a step further. In his war against his hereditary enemy of Hyderabad he had suddenly found himself confronted with a new method

4. John Bruce, *Annals of the Honourable East India Company* Vol. II, pp. 568-569.

5. Forrest, *Selections from State Papers*, Maratha Series, p. 127.

6. Grose, *Voyage to the East Indies*, pp. 122-123.

7. Kanhoji's Letter to Boone, dated 27th April, 1718, Bombay Public Consultations, CCCXLI, No. 4, pp. 77-83.

8. *A Faithful Narrative of the Capture of the Ship Derby (belonging to the Honourable the East India Company, Abraham Anselm Commander) by Angria the Pirate*, p. 111.

of warfare hitherto unknown to him. Bussy had carried the war into the Peshwa's own territories and penetrated as far as Koregao. Balaji Baji Rao at once perceived that the superiority of the hostile army was not due entirely to their artillery, and the tactics of the French general were different from those known to his Indian opponents, although the men under his command had been recruited in this country. The Peshwa adopted the time-honoured expedient of extracting a thorn with a thorn. He would gladly employ a European officer to face this new danger, but none, it appears, were available. He seriously thought of subsidising an English force, but the Government of Bombay was not in a position to lend any[9]. But if competent French and English officers were not available, there were Muhammadan adventurers with some knowledge and experience of the new methods ready to serve the Peshwa, and first Muzaffar Khan, and later Ibrahim Khan, entered the service of Balaji Baji Rao. They had both been trained by Bussy and were more or less familiar with his military methods, but they could hardly be regarded as fit substitutes for that general, and the Peshwa tried his best to induce him to leave Hyderabad for Poona. At one time the Peshwa felt sanguine about the ultimate success of his negotiations and in 1756 he actually communicated to his Portuguese neighbours of Goa the happy news of the admission of Monsieur Bussy in his service. On the 22nd May, 1756 he addressed two letters to the Governor and the Secretary of State. The concluding paragraph of the first letter runs as follows:—"In the company of Salabat Jang, who came to assist me, was M. Bussy. He left the said Nawab owing to some difference between them. I admitted M. Bussy into my service and gave him leave to go to his house at Masulipatam. He will join me after the winter and I make this communication so that Your Excellency may be informed of this happy news." The Secretary of State was told that Bussy had expressed his willingness to enter the Peshwa's service to which he had been accordingly admitted[10]. The temporary difference between

9. Forrest, *Selection from State Papers*, Maratha Series, pp. 120-121.

10. Biker, *Tratados da India*, Vol. VII, pp. 49-51. Also see Rajwade, *Marathynchya Itihasachin Sadhanen*, Vol. III, p. 445.

the Nizam and his French protector was, however, soon composed, and Balaji Baji Rao could not procure any European expert to raise trained battalions for him. It should, however, be noted that he did not intend a wholesale military reform or the rejection of the old predatory tactics, but his old army was to be supplemented and reinforced by the new battalions as the Nizam's had been, and this was exactly what the new *gardi* force of Muzaffar and Ibrahim did. They did not replace the old predatory force but they co-operated with it. The Peshwa did not pause to enquire whether such a combination of two entirely different and irreconcilable methods was practicable.

The *gardis* have left a very bad record in the military annals of the Marathas. They were mercenaries of the worst type drawn from all parts of India and were not bound to the Maratha empire by any bond of common tradition or common interest. They had been attracted by prospects of pay and preferment and had therefore not the least hesitation in changing masters. Muzaffar Khan, one of their officers, had left the Nizam's service for that of the Peshwa. After a difference with his new master he left Poona for Shrirangapattan and then joined the Nawab of Savnur. He had taken a prominent part in the defence of that place against the allied armies of the Peshwa and the Nizam. After the fall of Savnur he had been re-admitted into the Peshwa's service in spite of the protest of Sadashiv Rao, but he plotted against the life of that prince and was executed. Ibrahim Khan, his colleague and successor in the Peshwa's new regiments, had also changed masters, but not so frequently, and he had not been disloyal to the Peshwa or his cousin, to whom he seems to have been personally attached. But the evil reputation left by Muzaffar was enhanced by the part taken by some of the *gardi* leaders in the political intrigues of Raghoba, and the murder of the young Peshwa Narayan Rao irretrievably tarnished their reputation[11].

11. The *gardis* were notorious for their unruliness and their troublesome attitude finds reference in many contemporary letters. For one such instance, see Rajwade, *Marathyanchya Itihasachin Sadhanen,* Vol. I, p. 199.

The Maratha victory at Udgir was rightly attributed to the prowess of the new force and naturally added to its prestige. But it was not long before the incompatibility of the new method with the traditional Maratha tactics was demonstrated in the fatal field of Panipat. The Maratha horseman depended less upon his arms and more upon his speed. He left the hostile army alone as long as he could, and tried to harass it by devastating the country around. But the new regiments relied for success on its superior artillery and fire arms. They sought a pitched battle, while their colleagues systematically avoided it. The conflict between the old ideas and the new was pointedly brought home to the Maratha leaders when Malhar Rao Holkar and officers of the old school advocated the use of the traditional tactics (popularly called *ganimi kava*) against the heavily armed Afghan army, and Ibrahim Khan Gardi strenuously opposed their counsel.

He knew that he and his men could not expect to keep pace with the light Maratha cavalry. In such an operation their artillery would be more of an encumbrance than an advantage and the small force would be easily annihilated by their Afghan opponents. He, therefore, not only opposed Holkar's suggestion but compelled its rejection by threats of opening his battery upon any body who dared to move away from the entrenched camp. For this obstinacy Ibrahim Khan paid with his life, but the irretrievable disaster strengthened the conservative elements in the Maratha army and they became openly hostile to the new-fangled ideas borrowed from foreigners. The Peshwa and his cousin should not be strongly blamed for their failure to find some means of reconciling the two methods. They had not much time for it, but though the trained battalions immensely gained in prestige, if not in popularity, since De Boigne demonstrated their superiority over the old armies of the country, no attempt was made to find a solution of this difficult problem during the forty years that intervened between Panipat and Assaye.

The disaster of Panipat did not lead to the disbanding of the new force, as the circumstances that had originally called it into existence still prevailed, and the Peshwa still needed a strong and well-armed infantry force to meet similar regiments in the employ of other Indian powers.

Mahadaji Sindhia simply continued the experiment begun by Balaji Baji Rao, but he was more fortunate than his master. The Peshwa failed to seduce Bussy and could not secure the service of any other competent European officer. Sindhia, however, obtained in the person of De Boigne, an expert of ability and experience, trained in the best military schools of Europe, who had served under the French and the Russian flags before his arrival in India. It was necessity and not love of innovation that compelled Mahadaji to employ this European veteran for raising trained battalions for him. Mahadaji, unlike the Peshwa, did not confine his ambition to plundering raids, but he wanted to establish his authority over the remnant of the Mughal empire in Hindustan. This brought him into direct conflict with the Rajput princes and the Muhammadan generals who were still associated with the imperial Government or what remained of it. To harass them in the open field was comparatively easy, and with reinforcement from Poona he could even beat their united army, but the predatory method of the Marathas had been found utterly useless in siege operations; and Mahadaji did not like to share his new conquests with the Government of Poona. The permanent subjugation of the imperial territories, which Mahadaji aimed at, demanded the reduction of numerous forts and strongholds held by unfriendly chiefs and the annihilation of their armies in the open field. For such a work the service of infantry regiments trained in western methods would be invaluable. He had witnessed the splendid stand made by Ibrahim Khan and his *gardis* at Panipat, and the achievements of the small English army in the first Maratha war could not but have highly impressed him. In the meantime, other Indian chiefs and princes had been enlisting European officers, and we have reason to believe that Sindhia was aware of the service rendered by such adventurers as Madec and Sombre to their Indian employers[12]. Mahadaji had obtained very convincing

12. Both Madec and Sombre were at one time in the service of the Jat Raja; Madec had some guns manufactured under his supervision. See Emile Barbe, *Le Nabab Rene Madec*, p. 30.

evidence of the Savoyard officer's military ability, and his employment was not, therefore, a leap in the dark. The achievements of the new army amply justified Sindhia's decision, and other Maratha leaders soon found themselves compelled to adopt similar methods. His nearest neighbour and rival, Holkar, was not long in following his example, and appointed a French officer, Dudrenec[12a], to command the trained battalions of his army. The Poona Government enlisted some white officers for a similar purpose, although they could not get a European of reputation before Boyd entered their service[13].

The growth of the regular army in Sindhia's service was naturally slow. Mahadaji himself was fairly well convinced of its superiority, but he had to proceed with caution and circumspection. It is needless to say that his countrymen did not approve of his military policy, and the disaster of Panipat apparently afforded considerable justification for their prejudice. In 1784 De Boigne was commissioned to raise two battalions only. The two thousand men under his command formed an insignificant fraction of the immense horde that fought at Lalsot and Chaksana. De Boigne did not as yet hold an independent command, but though the Maratha army was beaten, the two battalions of De Boigne more than vindicated their employer's confidence. When Sindhia's fortune was at low ebb, De Boigne left him, evidently because he was not content with a subordinate position and the service did not offer any bright prospect in the immediate future. But in 1790 he was recalled and asked to raise a brigade of ten battalions of infantry with a suitable complement of cavalry and artillery. The success of Patan and Merta led to the addition of a second brigade, and a third brigade was not long in coming. When Daulat Rao Sindhia challenged the

12a. This name is differently written as Du Drenec, Du Dernaig, Duderneg, Du Dernec, Dodernaigue, and Dudernek. Compton, *European Military Adventurers of Hindustan*, p. 347. The Marathas called him Jujharnag.

13. Rajwade, *Marathyanchya Itihasachin Sadhanen*, Vol. VII, p. 15, gives the following names of officers commanding a *gardi* force of 10,000 men—Musa Motro, Musa Kuras, Musa Jalle, Musa Bas, Musa Pit and Musa Joranj.

English supremacy established by the treaty of Bassein, the three principal Maratha chiefs had all a fairly strong regular army with them. The regular armies of Sindhia and Holkar were officered by European adventurers, while that of Bhonsla was led by Indian officers alone. The total numerical strength of the three regular armies has been thus estimated by Major Lewis Ferdinand Smith[14]:

	Battalions.	Guns.	Cavalry.
SINDHIA.			
Perron's 5 Brigades ...	39	225	5,000
Filoze's Brigade	8	45	500
Sombre's Brigade	6	35	500
Shepherd's Brigade under Umbajee	5	25	500
Umbajee's army	10	40	10,000
HOLKAR.			
Vicker's Brigade	6	30	500
Armstrong's Brigade	4	20	200
Dodd's Brigade	4	20	200
Under native commanders including the Park ...	10	130	30,000
BHONSLA.			
Under native commanders ...	15	60	30,000

The regulars in the Peshwa army were not so numerous and consisted of two battalions only.

"A brigade was composed of 8 battalions. Each battalion comprised within itself infantry and artillery. Each was commanded by a captain, having under him a lieutenant, either European or European by descent. A battalion had eight companies of infantry; each commanded by a subadar aided by two jemadars, one kot havildar, three havildars, four naicks and fifty-two sepoys. The artillery of the same battalion consisted of one sergeant-major (European), and five European gunners, one jemadar, one havildar, five naicks,

14. Lewis Ferdinand Smith, *A Sketch of the Rise, Progress and Termination of the Regular Corps formed and commanded by Europeans in the service of the Native Princes of India with details of the Principal events and actions of the late Marhatta War*, p. 61.

thirty-five golandaz, five tindals, thirty-five klassis, twenty bildars, thirty gariwans, four ironsmiths and four carpenters. A battalion had also a native surgeon, and a complement of matsadis, water carriers, and the like. Every battalion had 408 stand of arms, four field-pieces, one howitzer, five tumbrils, 120 bullocks, and two native carts. Every gun had constantly ready with it 300 rounds of shot and 100 rounds of grape. A howitzer had fifty stone balls shells and fifty rounds of grape. The monthly pay of the native officers and men of a battalion was about 4500 rupees." "The pay of the commissioned officers was as follows:—A colonel received 3000 rupees; a lieutenant-colonel 2000; a major 1200; a captain 400; a captain-lieutenant 300; a lieutenant 200; an ensign 150. These rates were increased fifty per cent when the officers concerned were serving in the Dekhan. The men received under the same circumstances, a proportional increase. Besides their pay, officers commanding brigades, whether colonels, lieutenant-colonels or majors received 100 rupees a month as table allowance."

"A brigade of eight battalions consisted of 6000 men. Besides the battalion complement of guns above detailed the brigade had attached to it three battering guns and two mortars with men to serve them. Each had likewise 200 irregular cavalry and 500 irregular infantry (Rohillas)."

"The battalions were named after the famous cities or forts, such as Delhi, Agra, Burhanpur. The men were disciplined according to the English regulations of 1780, then in force in the British army. The regular infantry were armed with muskets and bayonets manufactured at Agra. The irregulars with matchlocks and bayonets. The cavalry were well mounted. Seven hundred of them were armed with matchlocks and swords; 500 with carbines, pistols and swords; they were drilled in the European fashion." Such was in short the composition and constitution of the regular army under De Boigne[15].

15. For these details we are indebted to the small but valuable work of Lewis Ferdinand Smith, but the above extracts are quoted from the excellent summary of Colonel Malleson in his *Final French Struggles in India*, pp. 192-194.

Though the army was organised on the European model its Commander-in-Chief was paid, according to the current feudal ideas, by an extensive *jahgir*. While encamped near Jaipur in 1792 Mahadaji had received a letter from De Boigne. The army was in arrears for seven months and the General bitterly complained about the hardship and anxiety to which he was subjected by the irregularity of payment; and in order to avoid similar troubles in future Sindhia decided to place an extensive province entirely at the disposal of De Boigne. This decision was communicated to him in the following terms:—" You complain of the delay in sending the arrears of the army. You say that at the end of Shawal the pay will be seven months in arrear. I have got your receipt for 190 thousand Rupees that you have permitted to be paid to your soldiers and officers. On account of three months of the arrear you demand 185 thousand Rupees more and you apprehend that the money may not be sent to you."

"In reply be assured that I have personally taken notice of all your demands and find them correct. The anxiety, the disquiet, the pre-occupations that overwhelm you are even heavier and more painful in my case; my own embarrassments are greater than you can believe. It is my very keen desire and ambition, you know, to render durable these military creations which have cost us so much labour and such enormous expense and to prove my affection for an army whose services I appreciate."

" Wishing therefore to cut short these embarrasments and to put an end to the incessant complaints caused by the continual delay that my treasurers make in paying the salaries, I have decided to give my soldiers a new mark of my solicitude and you complete satisfaction by separating from my administration and confiding to your exclusive care a province of my estate having a revenue equal to the total amount of the annual pay and expenses of the army. You will have the sole control of the territory, you yourself will choose the governors and the collectors who will be your men. You will fix the extent of this district in the light of your experience, and I am confident of your discretion, and you will regularly pay the troops each month without being henceforth obliged to have recourse to my ministers for this care."

"This grant, which I make to you, of a wide stretch of country, offers me another advantage, the certainty of seeing in this province, the increase of population and the improvement of agriculture, thanks to your talents and to your sense of justice and foresight "[16].

De Boigne was an able administrator as well as a military leader and Sindhia's expectations were fully justified. Aligarh and its neighbouring districts prospered under De Boigne's Government, but luckily for Mahadaji, the Savoyard had no desire of settling in India or carving out an independent principality for himself. With a splendid army and the entire revenue of one of the richest provinces of the empire at his disposal, the Savoyard might have easily succeeded in accomplishing what an Irishman, more daring but less fortunately situated, attempted in vain. Whether the Peshwa's Government had realised the unwisdom of granting such rich *jahgirs* to strangers we do not know, but neither Boyd nor John Ford was as lucky as De Boigne and Perron. The new experiment was fraught with other dangers. The Marathas did not enter the regular army. Their tradition and habit equally disqualified them for such service, and the regular forces, whether under Sindhia or under the Peshwa, were composed entirely of non-Marathas. The Hindu privates, commonly called Telingas, were drawn mainly from Oudh and the Muhammadan contingents, called Najibs and Alygholes, consisted almost entirely of Rohillas and Pathans. William Henry Tone, who knew them well, has described them as the most unscrupulous adventurers who did not hesitate to commit the worst crimes[17]. The private in the newly raised battalions, therefore, was not morally superior to his predecessor in the old *gardi* regiment. If the men were bad, their officers were

16. Victor de Saint-Genis, *Une Page inedite de L'histoire des Indes, Le General de Boigne*, pp. 192-193.

17. Tone says of them : " They are mere soldiers of fortune and serve only for their pay : . . . . They have no idea of patriotism or love of their country, but would plunder their native village without pang."

worse. The European adventurers who sought the service of Indian princes came in pursuit of fortune. They were more daring than the old *gardi* leaders but hardly less unscrupulous. If Muzaffar Khan had been guilty of frequently changing his masters, Dudrenec behaved no better and he was by no means the only offender in this respect. Their inconstancy earned Dudrenec and his colleagues the unenviable epithet of *Daghabaz* or traitors from Jaswant Rao Holkar[18]. Moreover, these unreliable officers were hardly a match for accomplished English generals like Lake and Wellesley. Most of them had no previous military training. Perron, Borquin and George Thomas were all runaway sailors, and the French officers in Sindhia's army have been described by Lewis Ferdinand Smith as " low in every sense of the word." " Low they were in every sense of the word "—he writes— " in birth, in education and in principle. Perron's army was a minute miniature of the French Revolution—wretches were raised from cooks, bakers, and barbers, to be the Majors and Colonels, absurdly entrusted with the command of brigades and shoved into paths to acquire lacks "[19]. Michael Filoze, who made a fortune in Sindhia's service and then retired to Europe, is described by the same writer who knew him, as a " Neapolitan of mean birth, low character and illiterate "[20]. Some allowance might have been made for the natural bias of an Englishman against his French rivals in the same service, had not Smith's denunciation of the average officer been substantially confirmed by Colonel Skinner who was absolutely free from such a prejudice.

Although adventurers of all nations were equally welcome in Sindhia's army, Frenchmen and Englishmen, naturally from

18. Compton, *European Military Adventurers of Hindustan*, p. 350 for Holkar's aversion to the French, *ibid*, p. 337.

19. Lewis Ferdinand Smith, *A Sketch of the Rise, Progress and Termination of the Regular Corps*, p. 47.

20. Lewis Ferdinand Smith, *A Sketch of the Rise, Progress and Termination of the Regular Corps*, p. 55. Filoze stopped for a time at Goa after retiring from Sindhia's service and obtained a Tenente (Lt.) Colonel's commission in the Portuguese army. See Letter No. 85, Officios dos Governadores, Maco 32, (Archivo Ultramarino tf Lisbon). It is not known whether Filoze ever reached Europe. His descendants still enjoy a *jahgir* in the Gwalior State.

their long connection with and acknowledged interest in the country, formed the majority. The only result was dissension and disagreement. Sutherland could not get on with Perron and the latter's promotion as Commander-in-Chief after De Boigne's resignation did not improve their relations. Even the Savoyard Drugeon was jealous of his French superior and wrote to De Boigne on the 30th April, 1802:—"Here M. Perron, so far as concerns power, is as autocratic as the King of Prussia, and as regards money, he resembles Croesus, for it falls upon him like the most abundant rain by night and by day in the form of rupees. Courted at the same time by all the Rajas and grandees of the country, even by the Prince who fears him, as indeed do all his chiefs; for like him, they are all of them, so to speak, under Perron's orders. At the same time M. Perron must not deceive himself despite his strength (you have prepared the soup for others who to-day have only got the trouble of eating it) and imagine that he has served the Prince well"[21]. They had all dared the unknown dangers of a long journey to a fabulously rich land with the sole desire to be put on "the way to lacks," they all wanted to have a share of the excellent soup and could not brook the least disappointment.

The cupidity of the foreigners did not constitute the only danger to the State that employed them. The *gardi*, at the worst, cared for his own interest and he was not definitely identified with any power other than his master. But however ill-educated or ill-born the Frenchman or the Englishman might be, he was imbued with a certain amount of patriotism with which the average Indian in those days was unfamiliar. War with the French was a remote possibility but war against the English was a certainty, and the Marathas ought to have been prepared for such a struggle after the treaty of Salbye. But in such a war the Maratha employer could not rely on the services of his English captains. They would not and could not fight against their countrymen and in such a contingency the military secrets known to these officers were sure to be

21. Victor de Saint-Genis, *Une Page inedite de L'histoire des Indes*, p. 367.

used against their previous masters. When war broke out in 1802, not only the English but the French officers as well of the Maratha army, took advantage of the Governor General's offer. They had come to seek fortune and not to lose it. The strong fort of Aligarh was captured with incredible ease, for while the French commander of the garrison was not particularly anxious to defend, its reduction was rendered easy by the local knowledge of Lieutenant Lucan who led his countrymen to the weakest points[22]. Skinner complains that the " conduct of the Europeans in the Mahratta service totally ruined their own character and led to the destruction of their comrades who had remained stanch to their master's cause "[23]. The powerful army organised by Mahadaji and De Boigne which had served so well against Indian rivals, proved utterly useless at the moment of the greatest need, because its officers would not fight. And the Maratha empire was so easily shattered because its defence had been entrusted to foreign mercenaries.

British subjects were, as a matter of policy, encouraged to enter native service to safeguard their country's interest and to counterpoise the French influence in the Maratha army which had caused great anxiety at Calcutta and Bombay. Boyd and Tone were really serving the British Government at Hyderabad and Poona[24]. But the Marathas on the other hand did not make the least distinction of nationality in their choice of military officers. Their ignorance or indifference about the country and the nationality of their employees was apalling. To mistake Boyd for an Englishman was probably natural and immaterial, but even De Boigne has frequently been called an *Ingraz* or Englishman[25]. There was a scarcity of military experts, and when one was available the Marathas did not take the slightest trouble of making enquiries into his

22. Bailie Fraser, *Military Memoir of Lt.-Col. James Skinner*, Vol. I. pp. 262-263; 265-266, 271; and Thorn. *Memoir of the Campaigns in the Hindoostan of the Late General Lord Lake*, p. 99.

23. Bailie Fraser, *Military Memoir of Lt.-Col. James Skinner*, Vol. I. p. 303.

24. Martin, *Dispatches of Wellesley*, Vol. I. pp. 6-7.

25. *Itihas Sangraha, Hingnyanchi Vakili*, pp. 11, 13 and 26.

nationality or antecedent, while his complexion was considered enough evidence of his military knowledge. The Marathas in the Nizam's army had not the least scruple in fighting against their relatives of Poona and it was argued that an Irishman or an American might also be expected to look after the interests of his master even when they clashed with those of his country. As a result of this blind confidence or childish sense of security the military secrets of the Marathas were never safe, not even in times of peace.

In 1788 an English soldier named John procured some information sought by the Portuguese Government[26]. In 1802 Drugeon wrote to De Boigne that a European officer had been guilty of carrying treasonable correspondence with his master's enemies[27], and Colonel Close obtained valuable information about Holkar's army and military designs from a European officer in his employment[28].

With all its defects Sindhia's regular army was the best that any Indian prince had at that time. The defects were common to them all, but Sindhia's men were better armed, better paid and more efficiently trained. In theory, however, the trained battalions of Sindhia did not belong to the Maratha empire. De Boigne had his *jahgir* in Hindustan and though Perron took part in the battle of Kurdla the new army was supposed to serve the Emperor of Delhi. The Peshwa's trained battalion was never so numerous as that of Sindhia, and its first commander, of whom we know anything, was an English deserter from Madras. He was a bold man, as is testified by Lt. Moor who knew him, but he could not be expected to know much of the higher science of war that had rendered the European forces so superior to their Indian opponents. Evans had under him about fifty Europeans of diverse nationality but he was succeeded in his command by his wife, a native Christian woman[29]. Baji Rao II, however,

26. Officios dos Governadores, Maco 22, No. 35 (Archivo Ultramarino of Lisbon).

27. Victor de Saint-Genis, *Une Page inedite de L'histoire des Indes*, p. 366.

28. Forrest, *Selections from State Papers, Maratha* Series, pp. 565-566.

29. Moor, *A Narrative of the Operations of Captain Little's Detachment*, pp. 26-27.

had two battalions under the efficient command of Col. Boyd. The old battalions consisted of 677 sepoys commanded by 2 Captains, 4 Lieutenants, 3 Sergeants, 14 Subhedars, 2 Cumedans (?) 20 Jamadars, 59 Havaldars and 38 Naiks, while the new battalion of 484 Sepoys had 1 Captain, 2 Lieutenants, 1 Sergeant, 4 Subhedars, 5 Jamadars, 32 Havaldars and 7 Naiks. Both the battalions had a complement of artillery but only the new battalions had also a body of 15 horsemen commanded by a Jamadar. Colonel Boyd, who held the chief command, got a salary of 3,000 Rupees per month, the Captains under him got 400 Rs. each, a Lieutenant was paid 250 Rs. per month, while his Sergeant's monthly remuneration was 90 Rs.[30]. The scale of salary, therefore, was not higher than that in Sindhia's army; for when Sindhia's men were called upon to serve in the Deccan they got an allowance in addition to their usual pay[31]. John Ford, who commanded the Peshwa's battalions in 1812-13, got a lower salary than Colonel Boyd (2,500 Rs.), but the two Captains under him got 1,000 Rs. each, while the two Assistant Captains were paid 500 Rs. (each) per month[32].

The European soldiers in the Maratha service enjoyed many high privileges irrespective of their pay and position, as Colonel Tone informs us. "I calculate," writes he, "that there were scattered about, in the interior, in the various services, of all countries, and situations, about three hundred Europeans; of these about seven commanded tolerably large corps, and may be considered as men of fortune. There were perhaps about sixty more, in the rank of officers; the remainder were serjeants and gunners, some of whom have deserted from the settlements; others from ships, but the majority were French. Persons of this description had from thirty to sixty

30. *Peshwas' Diaries* Vol. V, pp. 184-187.

31. Lewis Ferdinand Smith, *A Sketch of the Rise, Progress and Termination of the Regular Corps*, pp. 50-52.

32. *Itihas Sangraha, Peshave Daftarantil Nivadak Kagad Patra*, pp. 93-95. The scale of salary in the service of the East India Company was as follows in 1743 (Bombay Public Consultation Range CCCXLI, No. 13, p. 172). Subedar—20 Rs., Jumbledar—13 Rs., Havaldar—6½ Rs., Naique—4-2-20, Sabnis—4-2-20, Trumpeteer—4 Rs., Colour bearer—4 Rs., Bhaldar—4 Rs. and Sepoy—4 Rs.

rupees per month; being under very little discipline, were generally of extremely irregular conduct and do but small honour to the European character, except by their extraordinary courage and intrepedity when employed on actual service; yet so great is the partiality of the Mahratta chiefs for Europeans in general, that they enjoyed many privileges in this country which the native himself does not partake of. The various European articles necessary for his consumption passed through the Mahratta territories duty free; in the native durbars, no person in the service can set up a palankeen without permission but with regard to an European, no leave is ever required. In the Mogul Government no person can make use of a yellow howda but the nabob, except Europeans, who labour under no restriction of this kind. In travelling through the interior, your baggage is transported from town to town without expence, and your person and property are perfectly secure, none of the natives, but military men, have any advantage of this nature "[33].

These concessions might have been justified if the Marathas had meant to make the fullest use of the military knowledge of the foreigners whose superiority was thus frankly acknowledged. But though the Hindu and Muhammadan soldiers of the North readily enlisted in the new battalions the Maratha scrupulously kept away. He preferred his time honoured profession of an irregular *Silhedar*, the strict discipline that the new method enjoined and the Drill Sergeant, an unfamiliar figure, did not appeal to him, and the average *saranjam* holder could not afford to have such an expensive force, while by the terms of his *saranjam* he was expected to serve the State with inexpensive cavalry regiments only. Of the numerous military leaders who were called upon to account for their rent free estates before the *Inam* Commission only one, Rupram Chaudhari, could claim to be the commander of a *paltan* or trained battalion[34]. The Europeans were employed not to teach and train the Marathas

33. Tone—*Illustrations of some Institutions of the Maharatta People*, pp 67-68.

34. Mawjee and Parasnis, *Kaifiyats Yadis*, p. 94.

for a period of transition but were expected to occupy a permanent position in the Maratha army; and as we have seen, all of them did not possess even the minimum qualification.

Such a force, though useful in a war against an Indian rival, equally or more inefficient, could not stand against the superior army of the East India Company. It did not in any way strengthen the fleet Maratha horseman, it only hampered him. Gopal Rao, a conservative officer in Sindhia's service, had once given his master a significant warning: "Our fathers," he said, "the first founders of the Mahratta power, made their houses on the backs of their horses; gradually the house came to be made of cloth; and now you are making it of mud; take care—and mark my words—take care that in a very short time it don't all turn to mud, and is never rebuilt"[35]. What was true of the barracks was equally true of the army. The main strength of the Maratha army lay in its speed and in its mobility. It was the interest of its European rival with better artillery to catch it in the open field and to force a pitched battle. It was the interest of the Maratha to elude his foe, to keep out of the range of his death scattering cannon, to ravage his country, to cut off his supplies, and to harass him. These tactics were successful against Egerton and Goddard when they tried to penetrate into the heart of Maharashtra through the Bhore Ghat. These tactics, when pursued by Jaswant Rao Holkar, caused Col. Monson much more trouble than the English generals ever suffered from the regular army of Daulat Rao Sindhia. But neither Sindhia nor Bhonsla could execute the rapid marches, the quick evolutions, the unexpected surprises in company of their artillery and musketry laden trained infantry, and their army succumbed to the superior artillery and superior generalship of Lake and Wellesley. Trained battalions had made Mahadaji the master of Delhi and Agra, and trained battalions had led his nephew to his doom and reduced him to the position of a humble feudatory of the British Government.

35. Bailie Fraser, *Military Memoir of Lt.-Col. James Skinner*, Vol. I, p 191.

CHAPTER VIII.

THE MARATHA ARMY ON THE MARCH.

Shivaji relied for his success on the secrecy and quick execution of his plans. His army was kept in constant readiness to cover the longest distance at the shortest notice. Speed and personal comfort could not very well be contrived together in those days. Shivaji and his men, therefore, had to accustom themselves to "Fare Hard and Journey Fast." They must have slept under the stars on their way to Surat in 1670, for they had no tent with them. During the Karnatak expedition the army carried only two small tents. These afforded shelter and some comfort to Shivaji and his principal officers[1], but his men must have been left to shift for themselves as best they could. They did not burden themselves with anything above the barest necessities and these were very few. But even the iron physique of the hardy Maratha leader demanded at times some relaxation, and when he was not pressed for time he would change his horse for a palanquin, in which comfortable conveyance his officers also occasionally indulged[2]. This is all that we know about his marches. Lightly equipped, without any tent, without any camp equipage, unencumbered with field artillery, he and his men moved from place to place with such incredible speed that his bewildered victims credited him with the knowledge of the black art[3].

1. *Indian Historical Records Commission, Proceedings of Meetings*, Vol. VI, p. 25. Paul Kaeppelin, *La Compagnie des Indes Orientales et Francois Martin*, p. 163.

2. Factory Records, Surat, Vol. 88, fols. 45-48. In April 1775, the English Factors met Shivaji while he was returning from one of his expeditions; he had, we are told, about 150 palanquins with him. The use of palanquin, as a more comfortable conveyance, was continued as late as 1792. See Moor, *A Narrative of the Operations of Captain Little's Detachment*, p. 81.

3. Cosme da Guarda writes, "The question is still unsolved whether he substituted others for himself, or he was a magician or the devil was in his place." (*Vida do celebre Sevagy*, p. 10.) He tries to give a rational explanation of Shivaji's supposed presence at different places at the same

From the brief account of Sambhaji's and Rajaram's campaigns, that has come down to us, it appears that they had not much deviated from their father's ways so far as personal comforts went during a military expedition. Born and bred up in the mountains of Maharashtra, they were not accustomed to the pomp and splendour of their Mughal enemies. But Shahu had cultivated different tastes. He was brought up in a Mughal camp, where not only comforts but luxuries were provided, and the grandeur of the Mughal army was reflected, though faintly, in the pomp of the only expedition that Shahu led in person. He was more accustomed to ease and comfort than his father and grandfather, and he could afford to proceed on his journey slowly. He was not in a hurry like them.

Shahu's march resembled more a ceremonial procession than a military expedition. He preferred the more stately elephant to the martial steed, and behind him followed the ladies of his seraglio, similarly mounted. Then followed forty or fifty elephants carrying the great nobles according to their official precedence. Immediately before the Raja was placed the artillery, and next came the imperial banners, surrounded by the guards, musketeers and the cavalry. In front of all marched the *Biniwala* who had charge of the van. Immediately behind the flags and the banners marched the regiments of the nobles placed in the van, behind them the attendants and the military band, followed by elephants, horses, chariots and camels. Behind these animals were placed the lancers, spearsmen and rocketeers; and between the King and the artillery were the arms bearers and mace bearers, musicians and other personal attendants. The road was carefully sprinkled with water to prevent dust. When so much care was taken to provide for their personal comforts the King and his companions could

moment. Oxinden wrote on the 26th June, 1664, "Sevagy is soe famously infamous for his notorious thefts that report hath made him an airy body and added wings; or else it were impossible hee could be at soe many places as hee is said to bee at, all at one time. Sometimes hee is certainly believed to be in one, and in a day or two in another place, and soe in half a dozen remote one from another; and there burns and plunders without controule." (Sir William Foster, *English Factories in India*, 1660-1664, p. 345.)

not expect to accomplish a long march, and it was decided that no more than three or four *Kosses*[4] should be attempted in a single day. Malhar Ramrao Chitnis hints that Shahu was deliberately copying the Mughal customs. He was accompanied by the principal officers of the State and a place was assigned to each of them according to his rank and station. The Sena Dhurandhar and the Sena Saheb Subhe were placed in the van. The Pratinidhi, the Peshwa, the Amatya, the Sachiv and the Mantri were stationed in the right wing, while the Senapati and the cavalry commanders were placed on the left. The Panditrao and the Nyayadhish, two civilians whose presence in the camp was probably demanded by the formalities of the court alone, also had their stations with the Sumanta on the left. The Chitnis, the Potnis, and the clerical staff occupied a place near the treasury as their official duties demanded. The Fadnis and the officers of the secretariat were placed on the left side near the stores. The rear was guarded by the Sarlaskar and the chiefs under his command, and every arrangement was made for the comforts of the King by the tents department in advance.

As Shahu wanted to earn the good opinion of his subjects, for it was through his own dominions that he was marching, he laid down that his soldiers should obtain all their necessities by fair purchase and should not cause the least trouble to the peasants. Any breach in this respect was to be punished with the loss of limbs. How far these orders were obeyed by the privates we do not know, but as Shahu was really making a peaceful demonstration of his power, the cultivators probably suffered less than usual on this occasion[5].

Shahu was the last King to play the military head of the State. This function after his death was invariably exercised by the Peshwa except during the minority of the second Madhav Rao. During the Peshwa period the army was divided into three great bodies during the march, as we learn from William Henry Tone. The vanguard (or *aghadi*), which included the whole infantry, was called *sadi fauj* (Tone's

4. 1 *Koss*=2 miles

5. Malhar Ramrao Chitnis, *Thorle Shahu Maharaj Hyanchen Charitra*, pp. 92-94.

' cherry fodge ') or light troops and was commanded by the holder of the *Jari Patka*, the imperial banner, a little wallow-tailed flag worked in gold and scarlet, and hoisted on a very high staff. The centre division was called the *bich laskar* and was considered as a body of reserve. It was not encumbered with any unnecessary equipage or artillery. The Peshwa himself commanded the rear, and the grand park called the *jinsa*, as well as the baggage of the whole army were placed in the rear which was called *bunga*, according to Tone[6].

It was the Biniwala or Quartermaster General who circulated the Peshwa's decision about the camping ground[7]. On his arrival at the selected site the Biniwala hoisted a little flag to indicate the place for the Peshwa's tent. In front of this tent met the *bazar* or the market of the camp. The *Banias* accompanying the army fixed their little tents or *pals*, which consisted of a single blanket supported on a few sticks. Each of the Sardars then fixed his tent according to his own convenience and hoisted his flag to indicate his whereabouts to his followers. No order was followed. Each private shifted for himself, but the different Sardars had each his own *bazar* which met in the immediate neighbourhood of his tent. While a private had often nothing better than a *pal*, and sometimes the shadow of his mount or a shrub or a tree was considered sufficient shelter for his repose[8], the officers were much better provided. The principal chiefs had not only comfortable but quite spacious and costly camp equipage. James Forbes, who accompanied Raghoba in his marches, writes : " The magnificence of the Indian tents, pavillions, and summinianas, or canopy, far exceeds anything of the kind in Europe, especially among the Moguls. These accommodations are the more necessary where their women and children

6. Tone, *Illustrations of some Institutions of the Mahratta People*, pp. 35-36.

7. The *Biniwala's* decision was circulated by beggars accompanying the army; for this service they enjoyed some small perquisites from the shop-keepers of the camp. See Moor, *A Narrative of the Operations of Captain Little's Detachment*, p. 79, and *Peshwas' Diaries*, Vol. III, p. 182.

8. *Instrucçao do Exmo Vice-Rey, Marquez de Alorna, ao seu successor*, ed F. N. Xavier, 3rd edition, p. 49.

accompany them to the field. The Mahrattas seem to prefer their tents to house , and enjoy more pleasure in a camp than in a city "[9]. In fact a Maratha camp in the later Peshwa days much resembled a city where commercial transactions of considerable volume were daily contracted.

The camp *bazars* not only supplied the needs of the army but formed a fruitful source of income to the Maratha chiefs. Every shop-keeper paid a fixed tax, and every man who plied his profession there had to pay for his license. The four *bazars* in Sindhia's camp as Major Broughton informs us[10], yielded no less than 14,000 Rupees in *palpatti* or tent tax alone. " The bajar, or market-place belongings to his (Raghoba's) own division," says Forbes, " and to the principal generals, contained many thousand tents, where every trade and profession was carried on with as much regularity as in a city. Goldsmiths, jewellers, bankers, drapers, druggists, confectioners, carpenters, tailors, tent-makers, corn-grinders, and farriers, found full employment; as did the whole rows of silver, iron, and copper-smiths; but those in the greatest and most constant requisition, seem to be cooks, confectioners and farriers "[11]. Nor was the camp unprovided with places of worship. Raghoba had a special tent for his idols, and Forbes tells us that " in the different divisions was a temporary dewal, or tent, consecrated to religious duties, where Brahmins regularly officiated, and prayer and sacrifices were offered to the deities with the same ceremonies as in the Hindoo temples "[12].

Like Shahu the Peshwas were accompanied in all their expeditions by a staff of civilian officers, and the ordinary works of administration were punctually attended to in the camp. Civil and criminal justice was daily administered, petitions were regularly heard and audience was granted to the poorest man who might seek it. The camp was provided with all the necessitities, with all the conveniences, with all the comforts of life then known in India. The days of Shivaji

9. Forbes, *Oriental Memoirs*, Vol. I, p. 341.
10. Broughton, *Letters from a Mahratta Camp*, pp. 112-113.
11. Forbes, *Oriental Memoirs*, Vol. I, p. 345.
12. Forbes, *Oriental Memoirs*, Vol. I, p. 345.

were forgotten. The Peshwas and their chiefs emulated the splendours of the Muhammadan nobility of the North, and this new taste for comfort and ease led to the slackening of the rigid discipline Shivaji had insisted on.

Shivaji did not permit any women to accompany his forces, but the Peshwa's camp was generally full of them. When exactly this innovation or lapse first occurred we do not know. Probably when Baji Rao I began to enliven the tedium of his leisure hours in the company of the fair Mastani, his followers also began to seek similar relief and similar relaxation. Gopika Bai sometimes accompanied her lord in his expeditions; and at Panipat the presence of the wives and mothers of his comrades caused Sadashiv Rao no little anxiety. Parvati Bai, his wife, was safely conducted home, but Nana Fadnavis lost his mother. The experience of Panipat, however, proved no deterrent, for Forbes, Broughton and Moor, who wrote from personal knowledge, all testify to the presence of a large number of women and non-combatants in the camps of Raghoba, Daulat Rao Sindhia and Parashram Bhau Patwardhan[13]. Moor says that "the number of women with this (Patwardhan's) army, could they be at all accurately computed, would not be believed; our estimate so far exceeds the bounds of probability, at least strangers would deem it so, that we are afraid to give it"[14].

The privates and their officers had with them their wives and concubines, and dancing girls, jugglers and other women of doubtful character frequented the camp as a place most suitable for their profession. Nor did the *bazar* lack wine stalls and *arrack* shops, so that the votaries of Comus could spend their evenings in a manner most congenial to them but not conducive to discipline in a camp where it was particularly slack[15].

13. Forbes, *Oriental Memoirs*, Vol. I, pp. 349-351; Moor, *A Narrative of the Operations of Captain Little's Detachment*, p. 87; Tone, *Illustrations of some Institutions of the Mahratta People*, p. 58.

14. Moor, *A Narrative of the Operations of Captain Little's Detachment*, p. 29.

15. Broughton, *Letters from a Mahratta Camp*, p. 21.

The private had perhaps some justification in bringing his wife with him, for the camp attendants were few and generally the halt was brief[16]. So, while he looked after the needs of his horse, his wife could cook his food and administer to his comforts. But whatever the excuse for bringing them, women and children are encumbrances, which an army can hardly afford, at least during a season of active operations.

Besides the women and children the army was further encumbered by a large number of animals. "The number and variety of cattle necessarily attendant on an Asiatic army," write Forbes, "is astonishing; the expense of feeding these animals, as also the difficulty of procuring provender, is very great; and their distress for water in a parched country and sultry climate, often fatal. Exclusive of the Mahratta cavalry trained to war, were many thousand horses belonging to the camp-followers; the bazar alone required twenty thousand bullocks to convey the commodities of the shop-keepers, besides a number of small horses and asses. Some thousand camels were employed to carry the tents and baggage; but the elephants, proud of their distinguished elevation, were appropriated to some honourable service, or, covered with caparisons of embroidered velvets and scarlet cloth, decorated with gold and silver fringe, were destined to carry the houdahs of Ragobah and his chief officers"[17].

However useful these animals might prove for transport and other services, their feeding was not the only problem with which the army was confronted. There was no separate place for herding and stabling the beasts, and sometimes lack of care and underfeeding told so heavily on their health that the poor animals proved a source of infection. Broughton says that he and his companions always camped at least a mile away from Sindhia's army to avoid the disagreeable "stench arising from carcases of horse, bullocks, and camels, which no one takes the trouble to remove"[18]. The men in

16. See the opinion of Major Dirom quoted in Moor, *A Narrative of the Operations of Captain Little's Detachment*, pp. 85-86.

17. Forbes, *Oriental Memoirs*, Vol. I, p. 351.

18. Broughton, *Letters from a Mahratta Camp*, p. 22.

the Maratha army often lived pell-mell with their mounts, and this insanitary condition sometimes led to the outbreak of epidemic when the distress of the poor sufferers knew no bounds. For although the camp was well supplied with druggists and quacks, there were but few qualified physicians, and hospital arrangements were either unknown or deemed unnecessary[19].

The Maratha generals had no commissariat department. For their supplies they depended entirely on the enterprise of their foragers and the Brinjaras. The Brinjaras were mostly Hindus by religion and Jats by race. A hardy race of nomads, they travelled in large bands termed *tandahs* and had their own headmen and peculiar organisation. They travelled throughout the country and were well capable of defending themselves in war and peace, but their service was most in demand during the wars, when they transported a large quantity of provision laden on bullocks to the war zone from peaceful settlements and trading centres. As traders they were honest, but sometimes they did not hesitate to obtain their merchandise by force. Railways and quicker methods of transport have to-day rendered it difficult for us to appreciate the service rendered by the Brinjara hordes to the belligerents in India, and their number seems almost incredible now. Wellington says that there were no less than 10,000 Brinjaras with Dundhia Vagh, the notorious robber Chief, who infested the frontier of Mysore and Southern Maratha districts[20]. Although this might have been an unusually large band, companies of 3 to 5 thousand were by no means uncommon. On the 20th August, 1800, Wellington wrote from Hubli—" I have 1200 loads in the grain departments, and 1500 full brinjarries in the camp; I am told that I have 5000 between the Werdah and Malpoorba; and as the headman has not deceived me lately, I believe it. Besides that, 3000 brinjarries left me at Kittoor on the 5th, in order to fill along the borders of Soonda, Savanore, and Darwar. There are 5000

19. *Itihas Sangraha, Aitihasik Kirkol Prakaranen*, p. 6, also *Aitihasik Tipanen*, Pt. II, pp. 94-95.

20. Gurwood, *Dispatches of Wellington*, Vol. I, p. 71.

brinjarries full, who are following Nizam's camp "[21]. Wellington regarded the Brinjaras as public servants and regulated the sale of their grains to keep his army well supplied[22], but we have no evidence of any Maratha general ever exercising such wise and farsighted control over the food supply. Besides the Brinjaras, the Marathas could count upon the Pendharis accompanying them. Those marauders and freebooters had an uncanny genius for discovering the secret stores of the villagers. Whatever they found, they brought to the camp and sold at a price much below the current rate. The lack of supervision of such sales, however, sometimes led to hardships after a few days of plenty, as the Maratha army experienced during the second Mysore war. But, generally, a Maratha private and his mount were both accustomed to subsist on very little food and fodder[23].

For their ordinary transport the Marathas employed asses, camels and bullocks, but transport across the rivers demanded other methods. While operating in Northern India this was performed by bridges and boats, as had been usual in the Mughal days. Boats were chained together and made to support a light platform of sticks and mud over which the men and the beasts passed with their arms and stores. But it does not appear that the Marathas themselves had ever undergone the trouble of constructing such bridges; they generally got some local men to build bridges for them[24], and, while operating in Southern India, they crossed the rivers in basket boats according to the custom prevailing in the locality. Lt. Moor gives the following description of these peculiar baskets: " From the month of June to October, the river is not fordable, and in that time round baskets are used to convey passengers, goods, and cattle across; these baskets are made of all sizes, from three to fifteen feet diameter, constructed with split bamboos, and covered with half dressed hides.

21. Gunwood, *Dispatches of Wellington*, Vol. I, p. 64.

22. Gurwood, *Dispatches of Wellington*, Vol. I, pp. 64-65.

23. *Instruccao do Exmo Vice-Rey Marquez de Alorna*, 3rd. edition, pp 51-52.

24. *Rajwade, Marathyanchya Itihasanchin Sadhanen*, Vol. I, p. 338, Vol. III, p. 227.

The method of constructing them is very simple: a number of pieces of split bamboo, twenty perhaps, are laid on the ground, crossing each other near the centre, and there fastened with thongs; the ends of the bamboo are raised by a proper number of people, and fixed by stakes at due distances from each other, in which situation they are bound by other long slips of bamboo, introduced alternately over and under the first crossed pieces, and tied at the intersections; this being completed, beginning from the bottom or centre, the parts above the intended height or depth of the basket are cut off, and it is liberated from the stakes, overset, and covered with hides sewed together by thongs. They are not more than three feet in depth, and will carry thirty men: we are inclined to think some of them will carry many more, for if we mistake not, the Bhow's heavy guns were transported over this river, (the Tungabhadra) and the Kristna, in these baskets. When bullocks are to cross, they are tied to the basket, goaded in the proper direction, and they tow it over the river; at other times it is rowed over with paddles, and when the water is not too deep; pushed with long bamboos "[25]. It is needless to say that the basket boat was by no means a satisfactory conveyance, for when the current was strong, it was likely to be carried away. But though clumsy, it had some special advantage, for its construction needed little time and less labour. A Maratha general was compelled to provide himself with beasts of burden before he set out on his expedition, but he did not always take the precaution of providing himself with boats or baskets in advance. He relied so much on local supply that Wellington laid down that a war against the Marathas should be commenced in June, for they would be unable to cross the rivers and harass the movements of the English army, if the baskets were properly guarded. It should be noted that during the critical days of Abdali's invasion in 1759 the Marathas relied on the local chiefs for building their bridges and the consequent delay considerably hampered their military operations.

25. Moor, *A Narrative of the Operations of Captain Little's Detachment*, p. 122.

Before he started on an expedition a Maratha chief would invariably consult an astrologer to ascertain an auspicious moment for his intended journey. With all his practical wisdom even Shivaji could not rise above this common superstition, but while his efficient financial arrangement enabled him to start at the earliest possible moment, the chronic financial difficulties of the Peshwas and their chiefs rendered it most uncertain. Their first march was therefore only a nominal one, a tent was pitched just outside their headquarters, where they would go at the time fixed for their journey, but at this place they could be detained for several days by their soldiers clamouring for pay. Tukoji Holkar had to take elaborate precautions in 1794 to avoid the undesirable attention of his creditors and narrowly escaped the inconvenience and humiliation of a *dharna*[26].

The Maratha camp was the frequent scene of this extreme form of dunning which was seldom absolutely ineffective. No man, whatever his rank and position, was immune from it. Haripant Phadke, Sindhia, Holkar, and even the Peshwa had been subjected to this last recourse of desperate creditors[27]; and, as a Maratha chief was often indefinitely detained by the *dharna* of his soldiers, it will not be irrelevant here to explain this peculiar method of realising arrears, in the words of an English observer. Major Broughton writes: This curious mode of enforcing a demand is in universal practice among the Mahrattas; Seendhiya himself not being exempt from it. The man who sits the *dhurna*, goes to the house or tent of him whom he wishes to bring to terms; and remains there till the affair is settled: during which time the one under restraint is confined to his apartment, and not suffered to communicate with any persons but those whom the other may approve of. The laws by which the *dhurna* is regulated are as well defined and understood as those of any other custom whatever. When it is meant to be very strict, the claimant carries a number of his followers, who surround the tent, sometimes even the

26. *Itihas Sangraha, Maheshwar Darbarchin Batmi Patren*, Vol. II, p. 250.

27. Many instances are given in Broughton's *Letters from a Mahratta Camp*, Khare's *Adhikar Yog*, and *Maheshwar Darbarchin Batmi Patren*.

bed. of his adversary, and deprive him altogether of food; in which case, however, etiquette prescribes the same abstinence to himself: the strongest stomach of course carries the day"[28]. Strange though it may seem, the victim, however powerful, did not dare to break the traditional rules and had to come to terms with his tormentors. Even Jaswant Rao Holkar and Amir Khan, the two most unscrupulous military leaders of their time, had to bear the penalties of this time-honoured custom with patience, though not forbearance[29]. Encumbered with innumerable women, tradesmen, children and cattle, disturbed by the constant wrangling of debtors and creditors, without order, without discipline as it was, the Maratha camp was not easy to surprise. The cavalry that furnished the picket were very alert and were kept on duty night and day. The Maratha chiefs, moreover, were served by very efficient scouts, and Colonel Tone was of opinion, that it would be next to impossible to surprise a Maratha camp [30].

The scouts formed an old institution of the country. Shivaji had a separate department of *Jasuds* or scouts, and his chief scout Bahirji Jadhav was a man of exceptional ability. It was to Bahirji's familiarity with the less known by-ways of the country that Shivaji was indebted for much of his success and not a little of his safety. The *Jasuds* maintained their reputation even during the Peshwa period, when they acted, not merely as scouts but also as mail bearers. When employed in the latter capacity, they generally went in pairs, for we always read of *Jasudjodi* and *Kasidjodi*[31]. They travelled day and night, knew all the short cuts and by-roads, and could cover the longest distance in a reasonably short time. On their way they could rely on the assistance of every village headman and district officer, and cottages and resthouses were provided

28. Broughton, *Letters from a Mahratta Camp*, pp. 31-32.

29. Prinsep, *Memoirs of the Pathan Soldier of Fortune*, p. 346 and p. 405.

30. Tone, *Illustrations of some Institutions of the Mahratta People*, p. 60.

31. *Itihas Sangraha, Maheshwar Darbarchin Batmi Patren*, Vol. I, pp. 21, 40, 47. Sometimes when they had to send an urgent message they employed camel riders. See Ibid, p. 57.

for their use on the usual main route. While employed as scouts they had to use various disguises and their knowledge of the locality stood them in good stead. It does not appear that the *Jasuds* formed a separate department during the Peshwa days, but a number of them was usually attached to each army, the trained battalions not being excepted.

The damage committed by a Maratha force, while on the march, was enormous. No distinction was made between friend and foe, and the Peshwa's Government had often to grant some remission of rent under the title of *Paymalli* to the cultivators of the district through which their army had passed. It is needless to say that this remission could not always be adequate to the loss caused by the irresponsible soldiery. Holkar's forces probably enjoyed the greatest notoriety for their destructive propensities, for in this army the professional marauders or unpaid Pendharis outnumbered the ordinary *Bargir* and *Silhedar*. Lord Valentia says that the depredations of Jaswant Rao Holkar's men caused a famine in the Peshwa's territories,[32] and a popular Maratha ballad of the time presents a most horrible picture of the misdeeds for which these covetous and cruel mercenaries were responsible[33]. It runs as follows :—

> "They stayed not to weigh or to measure their spoil,
> They stripp'd off the grain from the sheaves on the soil;
> Not Chandi was safe, nor Gunputti the wise;
> Nor Shiwa the ruler of destinies:
> His Pindi was broken, then who could expect
> That the pots of the housewife a god would protect?
> No order was left, every rank was confus'd,
> Preceptor and pupil were robb'd and abus'd;
> Every villain, and traitor, and rebel came forth,
> And stirr'd up revolt from the south to the north;
> From the south to the north, from the east to the west,
> From the sea to the Ganges the land they infest;

32. Valentia, *Voyages and Travels to India, Ceylon, the Red Sea, Abyssinia and Egypt*, Vol. II, p. 108.

33. Acworth, *Ballads of the Mahrattas*, pp. 96-98.

The gold of the rich, the rags of the poor
They strip, and the Brahmans they seize and secure;
They bind them in prison, and sentinels stand
Around them, and tramp on each road in the land.
No escape! from the wife of the peasant they tear
The pearl-studded jewel that fastens her hair;
From the peasant they wrest all his hoarded rupees,
The grain from his grain-pits, the food off his knees;
If any delays or refuses to give,
He tastes such a beating that scarce he will live."

This picture may or may not have been overdrawn, but it should be remembered that the offenders were the Pendharis and the Purvias, and not Marathas. These mercenaries were responsible for the worst crimes associated with the Maratha name. It was they who plundered and defiled the Sarada temple of Shri Shankaracharya of Shringeri during Parashram Bhau Patwardhan's campaign against Tipu Sultan [34]. It was they again who harassed the Brahmans of the South when Sindhia's trained battalions arrived in the Deccan to re-establish their master's lost influence at Poona. The mercenaries of the North were accustomed to plunder their own camp even during the Mughal days, and the Maratha leaders alone should not be held responsible for the outrages committed by these myrmidons [35]

War is normally expected to be destructive and it brings forth the worst tendencies of human nature. This is borne out by universal experience and no people and no country offers an exception. Only sixty years ago the federal army of the United States committed excesses that sound incredible even when reported in simple uncoloured prose. Mr. B. J. Hendrick, the biographer of Walter Heine Page, writes,

34. Khare, *Aitihasig Lekha Sangraha*, Vol. IX, p. 4474.

35. Scott, *History of the Dekkan*, Vol. II, p. 203, refers to the plundering propensities of the Mughal soldiery in the following manner: "The ameer-al-amra was dangerously wounded*** His remaining attendants brought him back*** to the camp*** where from a want of regularity and order, common in Hindustan, his tents, baggage and treasures had been wholly plundered by the soldiery and followers, on the supposition of his death."

"Part of the cavalry encamped in the Page yard; their horses ate the bark of the mimosa trees; an army corps built its camp fires under the great oaks, and cut their emblems on the trunks; the officers took possession of the house, a colonel making his headquarters in the parlour. Several looting cavalrymen ran their swords through the beds, probably looking for hidden silver; the hearth was torn up in the same feverish quest; angry at their failure, they emptied sacks of flour and scattered the contents in the bedrooms and on the stairs; for days the flour, intermingled with feathers from the bayonetted beds, formed a carpet all over the house"[36]. Soldiers, like children, are the same all over the world. It was not for their ruthlessness that the Marathas lost their empire. The cause must be sought elsewhere.

The Southern states soon forgot the war atrocities—"The mimosa bloomed, the cotton was planted again, and the peach trees blossomed; and the barnyard and the stable again became full of life." The same thing happened in Maharashtra when peace was re-established. The temples were repaired, the village walls were restored, the peasant again cultivated his lands and his wife became busy with her household duties. But here the parallel ends. In the meantime the Peshwa lost his empire, his feudatories acknowledged the supremacy of the British Government and the Maratha soldier changed his taste so completely that half a century later Lord Roberts classed the Marathas with the Madrasis and the Bengalees as a non-martial race.

---

36. *The Life and Letters of Walter H. Page*, Vol. I, p. 10.

CHAPTER IX.

The Third Battle of Panipat and its Lessons.

The third battle of Panipat marks a turning point in the History of India. About its ultimate result there is no difference of opinion, but its immediate effects have been variously estimated. The victor, it may be safely asserted, hardly derived any permanent gain, he had to leave Delhi shortly afterwards and he failed to consolidate his authority in the Punjab where the Sikhs were founding a new power. The powerful confederacy of the Muhammadan potentates of Hindustan dissolved even before the departure of the Afghan leader, and they had to settle their accounts with the Marathas as best they could. The vanquished were temporarily stunned but were not annihilated. Their supremacy survived for another forty years, and twenty-five years after the disaster of Panipat, Delhi again found a Maratha military dictator using its impotent Emperor as an instrument and symbol of his power. Panipat did not deal the death blow to the Maratha empire, as it is commonly suggested, it only arrested its expansion and granted the future rulers of India the respite they needed for consolidating their power in Bengal. But the campaign of Panipat might have proved a blessing in disguise to the Marathas, had they been able to profit by its lessons. It revealed the glaring defects of their military and imperial organisation that ultimately led to their overthrow.

The contest between the Marathas and the Afghans had been long impending. Ahmad Abdali made his first invasion of India in 1748. His first expedition proved a failure, but henceforth one party in the court of Delhi looked towards him for support, while the other preferred a Maratha alliance. Eventually, the Emperor, Ahmed Shah, came to an understanding with the Hindu power. The negotiation on the Maratha side was conducted by Malhar Rao Holkar and Jayappa Sindhia, and the Emperor granted the *chauth* of

Thatta, Multan, the Punjab, Rajputana and Rohilkhand to the Peshwa Balaji Baji Rao[1], who in his turn undertook to defend the Emperor against his enemies and disloyal subjects, among whom are specifically mentioned Abdali, the Rohillas, the Rajputs and the Amirs of Sindh. The document unfortunately bears no date but probably this agreement had been concluded sometime about 1750. The Peshwa had, therefore, nearly ten years for completing his military and diplomatic arrangements before his cousin met his Afghan rival on the fatal field of Panipat.

According to their agreement, the Marathas made an expedition against the Rohilla chiefs, and it was at the instance of the latter that Abdali made his second expedition to India, which resulted in the conquest of the Punjab. The Rohillas were hardly a match for the Marathas. But, while common danger cemented a union among the threatened Muhammadan chiefs, the Marathas failed to pursue a common plan, for they were more anxious to secure their personal ends than to serve the common interests of the empire. Sindhia and Holkar, the two principal chiefs who were expected to look after the Maratha interests in the North, did not always agree; Hingne, the diplomatic agent stationed at Delhi, had no confidence in his military colleague Antaji Mankeshwar; and the military force employed in Hindustan was not always adequate; the Peshwa, above all, urged his officers to turn the channel of the golden stream from the North to the South. The result was that the Marathas made many enemies, they had given offence to the Rajputs, Jats, Rohillas and other Muhammadan chiefs by their financial demands, but their military expeditions were too short and the party strife in their council was too strong and their policy consequently was too shifting to inflict a crushing blow upon any of their enemies. Raghoba's first expedition to Hindustan in 1753 did not improve matters. Sindhia opposed Holkar's resolution of exterminating the Jats; the Raja of Jodhpur was secretly encouraged by Holkar in his war against Sindhia; and Raghoba had not the

1. Rajwade, *Marathyanchya Itihasachin Sadhanen*, Vol. I, pp. 1-10.

satisfaction of bringing his brother the much needed financial relief.

But this was not all. In June 1754, Emperor Ahmad Shah was deposed and Mir Shahabuddin obtained the exalted office of the Vizier of the Empire with the help of his Maratha friends. The result was that other parties at Delhi were totally alienated from the Marathas, and the new Vizier soon gave the powerful Afghan monarch a just cause for entering India for a third time by his interference in the affairs of the Punjab.

Among the Maratha officers employed in Hindustan none, understood the complex political situation better than Govind Pant Bundele. In February, 1755 he addressed a letter to the Peshwa explaining the unsatisfactory political condition then existing and suggesting the necessary measures that it demanded. He told the Peshwa plainly that a force of at least 20,000 well trained and well disciplined men who were not given to plunder should be permanently stationed in Northern India for safeguarding the Maratha interests and securing the Maratha possessions there. He plainly told that the force under him was not at all adequate and, in view of the impending return of Raghoba to the Deccan, he urged the necessity of sending a strong army [2]. About four years earlier Bapuji Mahadev Hingne had requested his brother to explain the necessity of posting a strong force at Delhi, for the Maratha cause was by no means popular there[3]. But all these warnings from the men on the spot were left unheeded, and when in the rainy season of 1755 Raghoba left for home and Holkar accompanied him, only a small force was left with Antaji Mankeshwar to look after the Maratha interests in Northern India. Sindhia was still employed in a protracted war against the *de facto* Raja of Jodhpur.

This offered Abdali and his Indian friends an excellent opportunity of which they did not fail to take an early and quick advantage. He entered India at the head of a well

2. *Itihas Sangraha*, *Aitihasik Tipnen*, Pt. II, pp. 77-78.
3. Rajwade, *Marathyanchya Itihasachin Sadhanen*, Vol. VI, No. 556, quoted in Sardesai, *Marathi Riyasat*, Vol. IV, p. 15.

appointed army of veterans and literally swept everything before him. The small Maratha army was easily put to flight, Delhi was occupied by the Afghan and Rohilla armies and the recent political arrangements were entirely set aside.

The Peshwa again sent his brother to meet the new danger, and if he had promptly proceeded to the war-zone, Raghoba might have met the Afghan army before it left India. But he allowed himself to be diverted with some money-raising expeditions in Rajputana and lost the opportunity of overtaking a war-worn enemy not a little fatigued by his movements in the unaccustomed heat of an Indian summer. When Abdali had left and there was no formidable opponent to fear, Raghoba and Malhar Rao Holkar entered Delhi and inflicted a severe defeat upon the Rohillas. But Raghoba committeed the mistake of extending his clemency to the defeated Rohilla leader who was the staunchest supporter of Abdali in India and therefore the most irreconcilable enemy that the Marathas had. Then he went to the Punjab, drove Abdali's agent from that province and planted the ochre-coloured banner of the Maratha empire on the banks of the Indus at Attock.

Here Raghoba lost an excellent opportunity. While on the banks of the Indus, he obtained an autograph letter from the Shah of Persia proposing an alliance against the common enemy [4]. Raghoba took it lightly. He underestimated the strength of his enemy and talked of the conquest of Kabul and Kandahar, as they had once formed an integral part of the Mughal empire. But if he had been seriously thinking of further conquest and annexation, it is difficult to understand why a strong Maratha force was not permanently posted on the natural frontiers of India. It would be far more easy to prevent Abdali's aggression with the mighty Indus in front and a hostile Persian army at his flank, while his Indian co-religionists would be absolutely incapable of rendering him the least assistance, for a comparatively small force would be sufficient for keeping the Rohillas in check. But in 1758

4. *Itihas Sangraha, Aitihasik Sphuta Lekha*, Pt. IV, pp. 39-41.

Raghoba again left for home. His army had long been in arrears and probably nothing would induce a southern force to stay away in a northern province for two successive rainy seasons.

When Raghoba left Hindustan, an enormously heavy task was imposed upon Sindhia. He had to look after the extensive region from Lahore to Muttra and he was further expected to lead an expedition to Bengal, not for any political purpose but to relieve the financial difficulties of the Peshwa. It was expected that Holkar would co-operate with him, but as early as 1756 Govind Pant Bundele had informed Sadashiv Rao that the prevailing difference between the two chiefs rendered any concerted action impossible, and the situation demanded the presence of both the Peshwa and Sadashiv Rao at Delhi[5]. As before, no notice seems to have been taken of this warning.

In 1759 Ahmad Shah Abdali came to India for the fourth time. As usual he was confronted by a hopelessly inferior force. Dattaji Sindhia had allowed himself to be duped by the friendly professions of Najib Khan, and, when he was at last undeceived, lack of boats prevented him from crossing the Jumna and punishing the perfidious Rohilla. The appearance of Ahmad Shah at once turned the scales against him. Loth to leave his post, he wrote to Holkar for speedy reinforcements. The joint army of the two chiefs might probably have yet stemmed the tide of Afghan success, but Holkar, as usual, allowed himself to be engaged against a Rajput chief, while the fate of his race was being decided on the banks of the Jumna. Dattaji rashly faced a superior Afghan army and paid for his daring with his life. His nephew, the legitimate head of his family, was wounded and his army was totally routed. Then Holkar tried the traditional harassing tactics of his race against the formidable Afghan cavalry, but in vain. The Afghans were hardy mountaineers and, unlike the Mughals of the Deccan, they could move swiftly when they wanted. Holkar was defeated, the Marathas were expelled from Delhi

5. Rajwade, *Marathyanchya Itihasachin Sadhanen*, Vol. III, No. 149, pp. 137-138.

and the Afghan leader was organising a general confederacy of Muhammadan chiefs against their hated Hindu enemy, when Sadashiv Rao set on his memorable expedition.

The Maratha army was flushed with recent victory; their leader enjoyed a high reputation for his bravery and statesmanship; he had lately enlisted in his army a well known Musulman officer who had been trained by the celebrated Bussy. If he could attack Abdali before his diplomatic negotiations were concluded, there was yet hope for the Marathas.

Lack of boats had prevented Dattaji Sindhia from punishing Najib Khan; lack of boats again impeded the progress of Sadashiv Rao. He had asked Govind Pant Bundele to arrange for boats, but Govind Pant did not, or could not, comply with his order. And when the Maratha army reached the banks of the Jumna, the river was no longer fordable. The main army of Ahmad Shah Abdali was encamped at Anupshahar, while two weak detachments held Delhi and Kunjapura.

Formidable as the Maratha army was, it was faced with one supreme difficulty. It was for all practical purposes in an enemy country. In Northern India the Marathas were known by the common name of *ganim* or enemy. They had once prided themselves on this distinction, but the general ill feeling that the policy of rapacity lately initiated by Balaji Rao had roused, now proved their ruin. Sadashiv Rao had before him the difficult task of winning the alliance, or failing that, of securing the neutrality of the Northern powers. His negotiations with Shuja-ud-daula proved unsuccessful, but the Jats were won over to the Maratha side. Mr. Keene has described the campaign of Panipat as a contest between the united Hindus of India and a confederacy of Muhammadans. It was nothing of the sort. The Muhammadans, indeed, had rallied to the banner of their Afghan co-religionist, all on account of the clever propaganda of Najib Khan, but the Rajputs held sternly aloof. Sadashiv Rao had no rallying cry that would appeal to them. It was not *Hindupad Padshahi* that he was fighting for; he was, according to his own confession, fighting for the Timuride empire.

It appears that Sadashiv Rao had at first under-rated his enemy's strength. At one time he had expected that the very rumour of his approach would frighten the Afghans away. Much of his tactical and stategical mistake was due to this over-confidence. In July the Maratha army captured Delhi, the Afghans had encamped on the opposite bank but were forced to witness the fall of the imperial city without being able to help their comrades. From Delhi Sadashiv Rao proceeded to Kunjapura and reduced that place. Hitherto he had not been guilty of any tactical blunder. He was perfectly right in reducing all the Afghan stations on his side of the river and trying to cut off the enemy's retreat, but no general can be pardoned for omitting to provide for his own safety in case of an unforeseen defeat.

The greatest blunder that Sadashiv Rao committed at this stage was that he did not adequately guard the fords. On the 17th October the Maratha army reduced the Afghan garrison stationed at Kunjapura, and six days later Abdali crossed the Jumna at Bagpat without any opposition[6]. Thus the Maratha army was cut off from its base of operation.

The exact strength of the two contending forces has been variously estimated by contemporary writers. The total strength of the Marathas amounted, according to Kasiraj Pandit, to 55,000 horse, 15,000 foot, 200 cannons, rockets and *Shutarnals* without number, besides 15,000 Pendharis[7]. The allied Muhammadan army, according to the same writer, consisted of 41,800 horse, 38,000 foot and 70 to 80 cannons [8]. Muhammad Ja'far Shamlu gives a much higher figure [9]; but on the whole, the rival forces were probably equally strong. The Marathas were superior in cavalry and artillery; their opponents had a superior infantry and the greater advantage of superior generalship.

6. *Asiatic Researches*, Vol. III, p. 107.
7. *Asiatic Researches*, Vol. III, pp. 106-107.
8. *Asiatic Researches*, Vol. III, pp. 104-105.
9. Elliot and Dowson, *History of India*, Vol. VIII, pp. 146-149.

The army of Sadashiv Rao differed as much from that of Shivaji as the hardy followers of Babar differed from the ease-loving officers who accompanied Aurangzib to the Deccan. Sadashiv Rao and his principal officers had, like the Mughal grandees of Aurangzib's time, costly tents and expensive camp equipage. They had been accompanied by their wives and female attendants. Nana Fadnavis, then a young man in indifferent health, had accompanied the army with the intent to visit the holy places of Northern India; and he had with him his young wife and widowed mother. A large number of traders and shop-keepers had followed the Maratha force to supply its daily needs. Sadashiv Rao was encumbered with a huge crowd of non-combatants, and worse still, the presence of so many ladies of noble birth immensely added to his embarrassment. His army was hardly competent to carry on those harassing tactics, the success of which entirely depended on speed. He was, therefore, right in rejecting Holkar's suggestion and his decision was further justified by the failure of such tactics in the late campaign. But it is difficult to understand why he did not try to fall back on Delhi even at the risk of a battle and re-open his communication with his base of operation and his far-off native province.

Instead of that he entrenched himself strongly at Panipat. In his fortified camp defended by a deep ditch and a strong mud wall with mounted cannons he could easily beat off any attack of Abdali. And it was his plan to compel his enemies to fight the Maratha army on its own ground. Govind Pant Bundele was expected to devastate the territories of the allied princes with a flying corps of Maratha cavalry, cut off their supplies and drive Abdali to meet his destruction at Panipat. The plan looked well on paper, but its success depended mainly on the operations entrusted to Govind Pant Bundele. This officer, however, had neither the ability nor the means, as Mr. G. S. Sardesai points out, to carry out the instructions of his commander. He was by profession and training a civilian. His following consisted of the militia needed for revenue collection, and the cavalry under his command was hardly adequate for the enterprise upon which the fate of Sadashiv Rao's grand army depended so much. But Sadashiv Rao and his companions were confident of success. Their jubilant confidence found expression in a letter written by Krishna Joshi[10] on the 5th November, 1760. The Muhammadan army, he informed his correspondent, was suffering from scarcity of provisions, while there was abundance of it in the Maratha camp. He expected the Afghans to fall upon their entrenched camp in a few days and meet certain destruction from their artillery. He ascribed the inactivity of the Afghan general to his fear of Maratha prowess. He jubilantly concludes his letter with the remark that "Abdali cannot retreat to his own country as the road is blocked, he dares not fight the Marathas as defeat is certain, he cannot sit idle as he is short of provisions." The unfortunate writer died two days afterwards, and he hardly realised when he penned these lines how accurately he was describing the difficulties that awaited his own commander. Sadashiv Rao had attempted the combination of two fundamentally opposite methods, and the result was disastrous.

We need not mention here the skirmishes that at different times took place between different companies of the two armies. From the middle of November the Marathas had begun to feel the want of food and provender, but still their commander persisted in his policy of starving his enemy, blindly ignoring the fact that his enemy had much better facilities for procuring supplies than he could have, unless and until he succeeded in reopening his communications with Delhi. With the first signs of famine in his camp Sadashiv Rao ought to have attempted to force his way back to Delhi; but, after Govind Pant Bundele's death in the third week of December, he had no excuse for persisting in his original plan. Abdali could no longer be driven into the snare laid for him. It was no more possible to cut off his supplies, on the other hand, it became increasingly difficult for the Marathas to send out their foraging parties. Still the Brahman general's confidence did not forsake him and even in the face

10 Rajwade, *Marathyanchya Itihasachin Sadhanen*, Vol. I, No. 265.

of famine he persisted in the way of certain destruction and ruin.

He knew quite well that peace on honourable terms was no more possible, and Kasiraj Pandit tells us that Najib Khan was now opposed to peace on any terms. He knew that the Marathas were now completely at the mercy of the allied army; he knew that he had given them repeated offence and he dared not let them escape from their self contrived annihilation.

At last the Marathas could no longer bear the pangs of hunger. Animals began to die in large number, the privations suffered by men were enormous and they could no longer wait in their fortified camp. At this crisis it appears that Sadashiv Rao did not possess the coolness and patience that the situation demanded. He resolved to fight, but even at the last moment it was his duty to direct the battle rather than throw himself desperately among his enemies. It was his duty to think out a fairly good plan of battle, but at the last moment he wavered. It was decided, if we are to rely on a contemporary chronicle, on the previous night that the army should form a hollow square, with the women in the centre, and with the help of the artillery try to cut its way through the hostile rank[11]. But on the following morning this plan was suddenly abandoned and the whole army was ordered to fall upon the Muslim force. The Marathas advanced with their artillery in front. On their left marched the trained infantry of Ibrahim Khan, on their right rode the cavalry of Sindhia and Holkar, while Sadashiv Rao in person led the centre. No reserve was left, no strategy was tried, the artillery played no important part in this momentous battle, the contest was decided by a close hand to hand fight, and superior man power ultimately triumphed.

Ibrahim Khan Gardi was resolved to give a good account of himself and his battalion. He took a banner in his own hands and led a resolute bayonet charge against the Rohilla

11. *Bhau Sahebanchi Bakhar*, ed Sane, pp. 142-143.

divisions of Hafiz Rahamat Khan and Dundi Khan. The Rohillas were utterly routed and broken, eight thousand of them were killed and wounded and hardly one thousand were left with each chief. At the same time the Maratha centre led by Sadashiv Rao and Viswas Rao fell on the Afghan centre where the Grand Vizier commanded a compact body of ten thousand horse, seven thousand Persian musketeers and one thousand camels mounted with *Zamburaks*. Here also the resolute Marathas carried everything before them. Attai Khan, the nephew of the Grand Vizier, was killed, three thousand of his followers were slain or wounded and the demoralised Afghans began to run away. The Grand Vizier reproached them, expostulated and argued with them, but in vain. He urged Kasiraj Pandit to bring Shuja-ud-daula to his rescue. But the Chief of Oudh seems to have been an indifferent spectator; his intention, most probably, was to watch the fight and join the victors. Jankoji Sindhia, however, failed to make much impression on the division of Najib Khan. The Rohilla chief had under him eight thousand infantry and nearly six thousand horse. " They advanced slowly under cover of a kind of breast-works of sand, which were thrown up by a great number of *Bildars* who were with them, and who, having finished one, advanced the distance of half a musket shot in front of that, under cover of their own people, and threw up another; to which the troops then advanced, while a third was thrown up in the same manner." These defensive tactics saved them from the violent cavalry charge of the Marathas that had nearly broken the Afghan centre. Damaji Gaikwad, whose division, Kasiraj Pandit tells us, supported Ibrahim Khan, behaved very well and he himself received several wounds.

The Marathas fought with the courage of desperation and for a moment the Afghans lost heart. But they were led by a consummate general. Ahmad Shah had been watching the battle coolly and had kept a strong reserve ready at hand to be used at the right moment. The Marathas had been able to make no impression on the Muhammadan left, and when the fresh reserve charged the Maratha centre and reinforced

Abdali's right, the tide of battle at once turned. The Muhammadan victory was complete and a whole generation of Maratha and Brahman officers was slaughtered on that fatal field.

The defeat was due as much to bad generalship as to the inherent defects of the Maratha military system. Had there been a strong standing army to be permanently stationed in Hindustan, had Raghunath Rao held the Indus frontier, had Holkar joined Sindhia's army in time, the battle of Panipat might not have been fought at all. But the feudal organisation of the army and the chronic financial needs of the Peshwa and his Sardars frequently compelled them to divert their energy to minor expeditions, while the real source of danger was ignored. The failure of Govind Pant Bundele was due more to the system than to any remissness on his part. His districts had been for several years disturbed by hostile Rohillas. Yet he was expected to meet not only the financial demands of the grand army but to raise a sufficiently strong cavalry force to devastate Oudh and Rohilkhand and to drive the allied army upon the artillery of Ibrahim Khan at Panipat. Another lesson of Panipat that was lost upon the Marathas was the impracticability of combining two opposite methods of warfare. The experiment proved disastrous at Panipat, and Colonel Malleson says that the fatal defeat of Assaye was mainly due to its repetition. During the Panipat campaign, Sadashiv Rao had relied almost entirely on his trained infantry for victory; his successors went further; their infatuation for this new method of fighting led them to neglect their once powerful cavalry, and during the forty years that intervened between Panipat and Assaye, Maratha generalship had also hopelessly degenerated.

CHAPTER X.

THE BEGINNING OF THE MARATHA NAVY.

Shivaji's followers had inherited from their ancestors a great military tradition; but the sea was a new element to them. The western coast of India had from time immemorial been inhabited by an intrepid race of sea-farers, but no evidence can be found to support the view that any attempt had been made in the past to establish a naval power. Though the Yadava Kingdom, for example, had stretched right up to the seaboard, the ambition of the Devgiri princes seems to have been land-bound; they did not aspire to rule the waves. Shivaji may, therefore, be justly described as the father of the Maratha navy. The English factors, in their wrath, called him a robber and a pirate[1]; but he was in reality trying to create a new sea power; and it was not his fault that the Maratha fleet did not ride the sea with as much confidence as the Maratha horse scoured the land.

His policy was, however, not one of mere adventure, nor was his object by any means impracticable. The coast line of the Konkan, broken by many creeks, offered excellent shelter for ships, and the rocky islands near the coast presented excellent sites for naval strongholds. Shivaji had before his eyes the example of the Sidis and the merchant powers of Europe, and he could not have been ignorant of the exploits of the pirates known to European writers as "Malabars." Once in secure possession of the Konkan, it did not take his keen intellect long to perceive the advantages as well as the necessity of a strong fighting fleet. The peace of his country and the prosperity of his ports equally demanded it.

The peace of his country was threatened by the Abyssinian ruler of Danda Rajpuri. Secure in his island stronghold the could and did harass Shivaji's land with sword and fire. The towns and villages on the coast were burnt and plundered, children and women were kidnapped to be sold as slaves, yet

1. Factory Records, Surat, Vol. 89, fols. 69-70.

Shivaji's governors were helpless, directly the invaders betook themselves to their native element.

His ports offered Shivaji a brilliant chance of improving his finances. Foreign merchants, attracted to these new marts, would not only improve the general prosperity of the country by purchasing its products but would contribute directly to the coffers of the State in the shape of customs duties. He could also derive greater profit by embarking on commercial enterprises on his own account, in consonance with the practice of the Portuguese rulers of Goa and the English traders of Bombay. But free navigation of the sea was in those days denied to all who could not enforce their right. The sovereignty of the sea had been for many years effectively claimed and exercised by the Portuguese. No merchant dared to launch his bark on the Arabian Sea or the Indian Ocean without first purchasing the permission of the Government of Goa. Even sovereign powers like those of Golkonda and Bijapur had to undergo this humiliation[2]. It is true that they obtained Portuguese *cartazes* to a specified number merely for the asking; but these permits were accompanied in all cases by vexatious conditions. They were not to import or export certain articles mentioned in the *cartaz*, they were not to visit the ports of the Imam of Muscat and of other enemies of the Portuguese and they were not to carry with them any Christian slave. To ascertain whether these conditions were being loyally observed the Portuguese claimed and exercised the right of search[3]. In short they denied their weaker neighbours the freedom of the sea. But such was the dread of the Portuguese name in those days that even the mighty Emperor of Delhi deemed it prudent to provide for the safety of the pilgrim boats bound for Mecca by soliciting the

2. The Portuguese right to control navigation was often secured by treaties, as for instance the treaty of 1548 between Adilshah and the Portuguese, Biker, Vol. I, pp. 122-127; the treaty of 1631, between Virappa Naik, King of Canara and the Portuguese, Biker, Vol. I, pp. 270-275 and the treaty of 1645 between Jahangir and the Portuguese, Biker, Vol. I, pp. 189-192.

3. Sen, *A Preliminary Report on the Historical Records at Goa*, pp. 46-51; Biker, *Tratados da India*, Vol. IV, pp. 181-188.

cartaz of the Portuguese Viceroy. Although Indian traders and Indian rulers had accepted the Portuguese sovereignty of the sea as a settled fact, this assumption of authority had been from the very beginning disputed by the merchants of other European nations. And in Shivaji's time the English, the Dutch and the French successfully demonstrated the possibility of defying the Portuguese in their own element. Shivaji, possessed of a strong fleet, could secure for his subjects the same rights, the same immunities and the same advantages.

Moreover, a fleet in those days did not cost the State much to maintain. While protecting the mercantile fleet of the country the fighting fleet would raise a revenue by emulating the example of the European powers settled on the western coast. Like the English and the Portuguese, the Marathas could also sell their passports to alien traders if they could hold their own afloat. There was another advantage which Shivaji must have foreseen even in the earliest days of his struggle against the Muslim powers of the Deccan and Hindustan, that his enemies might try to starve him into submission by prohibiting the export of provision from their country[4] as Bahadur Khan actually did. But if the sea was open to him he could get an abundant supply from the ports of the South even when the usual trade routes of the country had all been blocked against him. Prudence therefore dictated and foresight suggested that he should equip a fighting fleet of his own to protect his people, to punish his enemies, to provide for the prosperity of his ports and to secure for himself and his subjects a share of the maritime trade. It was not his aim to secure the freedom of the sea against the world; he was quite content to share the sovereignty with his neighbours.

At what date he framed his naval programme and when he gave effect to it we do not precisely know. But this novel adventure did not fail to attract the early notice of his friends

4. Factory Records, -Surat, Vol. 88, fols. 216-217. Swally Marine, 4th October, 1674—" Bawder Ckaun hath lately sent orders that no provisions be permitted to be carried out hence or from Broach, saying that Sevagee is supplied thereby.

and foes. Khafi Khan mentions it as a new instance of his perfidy. Shivaji "had seized the ports of Jiwal, Pabal and others near Surat," he informs us, "and attacked the vessels of pilgrims bound for Mecca. He had built several forts by the seashore, and had entirely interrupted maritime intercourse "[5]. Sabhasad sounds a note of exultation when he writes of the equipment of a mighty armada by his master as an instrument of offence as well as defence[6]. But as usual neither the Muhummadan nor the Maratha gives any indication of the date of so important an event. Cosme da Guarda, the Portuguese biographer and admirer of Shivaji, was definitely of opinion that his hero turned his attention to the sea when he could not expect to extend his kingdom any further on land[7]. According to him, Shivaji launched his naval programme after his flight from the Mughal capital. But as usual Cosme da Guarda was inaccurate, for we read of the maritime activities of the Marathas in the letters of the English factors of Bombay and Surat as early as 1664. The Dutch spy saw at Goa a *Pataxo* of Dariya Sarang one of Shivaji's naval commanders in January 1667[8], and the Dutch factors of Surat mention in their account of the first sack of Surat a rumour "that Sivagy had about 40 frigates in the river, also intent on plunder[9]. A still earlier date is supplied by a Portuguese official letter. On the 16th August 1659 the Governors of Goa wrote to His Majesty the King of Portugal—" A son of Xagi, rebel captain of King Idalxa, has made himself master of the lands near Bassein and Chaul. He is powerful and obliges us to have great care as he has made some ships of war at Biundy, Galiana, and Panvel, ports in the district of Bassein. We have ordered the Captain not to allow them to put out in the sea and to impede their exit "[10].

5. Elliot and Dowson, *History of India*, Vol. VII, p. 271.
6. Sen, *Siva Chhatrapati*, pp. 93-95.
7. Cosme da Guarda, *Vida e Accoens do famoso e felicissimo Sevagy*, Chap. XVI, p. 139.
8. Transcripts of Dutch Records, English Translation, Vol. 28 DCC XXX VIII, Letter from the Dutch spy at Goa, January 13th, 1667.
9. Dutch Records, India Office, English Translation, Vol. 27, No. DCCXI.
10. Pissurlencar, *Portuguese e Maratas*, p. 4.

Maratha Gallivats attacking an English ship.

(By Courresy of the Calcutta University Press.)

This is the earliest reference to Shivaji's fleet as yet available to us. It is quite natural that his first ships should have been built at Kalyan and Panvel near Bassein, for Kalyan was in those days a ship-building centre of some importance, the neighbouring forests offered abundance of excellent timber, and expert shipwrights could be allured from the Portuguese port of Bassein and the English island of Bombay. But Shivaji must have achieved a certain importance on the sea before his ship-building activity caused so much anxiety to his Portuguese neighbours. The degree of their anxiety is hardly indicated in the few sentences, quoted above, which announced a new menace to their naval supremacy. We learn from a petition, submitted to the King's council on the first of April, 1662 by Joao de Salazar de Vasconcellos, that such was the fright caused by the construction of this fleet by Shivaji that the Captain of Bassein, Antonio de Mello e Castro was ordered to impede its exit to the sea at any cost and the Governor promised favour and pardon to all offenders who might help him in this difficult task[11]. In any case 1659 is an important date in the military and naval history of the Marathas, for it witnessed both the discomfiture of Afzal Khan's expedition and the beginnings of the Maratha navy.

Of the numerical strength of Shivaji's navy we have different estimates. Krishnaji Anant Sabhasad says that Shivaji's fleet was divided into two squadrons of two hundred ships of varying type and dimensions. The total numerical strength, according to him, was four hundred, a very big figure, even according to modern standards[12]. Malhar Ram Rao Chitnis also says that " Four to five hundred ships of these different types were built and five to ten lakhs of Rupees were spent for the purpose "[13]. If these figures

11. Petitions in the Archivo Ultramarino of Lisbon, Petition dated April 1, 1662.

12. Sen, *Siva Chhatrapati*, p. 94. The total number subsequently given by Krishnaji Anant Sabhasad is 700, though he mentions only two squadrons of 200 each.

13. Sen, *Siva Chhatrapati*, p. 192.

appear high, the one given by Cosme da Guarda is certainly low. He says that Shivaji's fleet consisted of twenty-five ships only, all purchased from his subjects and designed for the capture of the small coasting craft called *Parangues*[14] belonging to the country merchants. Fryer saw on his way to "Serapatan (Kharepatan), to the South of *Dan de Rajapore*, a Strong Castle of Seva Gi's defended a deep Bay, where rode his Navy, consisting of 30 Small Ships and Vessels, the Admiral wearing a White Flag aloft "[15]. But different squadrons of Shivaji's fleet were stationed at different ports like Rajapore, Jetapore[15a], Malwan and Suvarnadurg, and Fryer does not pretend to speak of the entire fleet. The most reliable figures are supplied by the English factory records. Oxinden wrote on the 26th June, 1664—" Wee are heere allarmed to expect him by sea; for which intent report speaks him to bee fitting up some and building of others, to the number of 60 saile of frigotts, to surprize all jouncks and vessayls belonging to this port "[16]. On the 26th November of the same year, the Surat council informed their masters at home that Shivaji had fitted up four score vessels and sent them down to Batticola[17]. The fleet that conveyed Shivaji and his army to Barcelore in 1665, consisted, according to a letter of Streynsham Master, of "85 frigotts and three great shipps "[18]. We read in a letter written in 1667 that Shivaji had "in readiness 50 or 60 small frigotts "[19]. In 1675 the Rajapore factors wrote to their colleagues at Bombay that Shivaji had ordered about forty small vessels to be got ready[20]. In October, 1670, Bombay was alarmed by the appearance of 60 or 70 vessels belonging

14. Cosme da Guarda, *Vida e Accoens do famoso e felicissimo Sevagy*, Chapter XVI, pp. 139-140.

15. Fryer, *A New Account of East India and Persia*, p. 145.

15a. Jaytapur, a small town in the Rajapore sub-division in Ratnagiri district.

16. Foster, *The English Factories in India*, 1661-1664, p. 345.

17. Foster, *The English Factories in India*, 1661-1664, p. 358.

18. Foster, *The English Factories in India*, 1665-1667, pp. 77-78.

19. Foster, *The English Factories in India*, 1665-1667, pp. 268-269.

20. Factory Records, Surat, Vol. 88, Pt. II, fol. 33.

to Shivaji near the mouth of the port[21] and in November of the same year he fitted out a grand fleet "of 160 sayle of vessels small and great"[22]. From these figures it appears that Sabhasad's estimate may not have been greatly exaggerated. We have conclusive evidence that Shivaji built new ships from time to time, and it will not be unreasonable to suppose that when he sent Dariya Sarang to an unknown destination at the head of 160 ships in the November of 1670, he had not completely denuded his naval bases of their protecting fleets and that the total numerical strength of his navy may be reasonably put at 200 ships, big and small. Krishnaji Anant Sabhasad and Malhar Ram Rao Chitnis were probably thinking of the mercantile fleet as well when they made their estimate, for, of the different types of vessels included in their lists, *Taru*[23], *Tarandi*, *Pagar*, *Dubare*, *Vabhor* and *Tirkati* were not used in naval engagements; while we read not only of Shivaji's salt boats but also of his regular "May fleet" plying between his ports and those of Arabia and Persia. Whether the trading or the fighting fleet came first into existence, we cannot as yet decide.

The Maratha navy contained five types of fighting ships. Of these the most important were the *Ghurab* and the *Gallivat*, but we also read of *Pals*, *Shibars* and *Manchuas* of war. There were probably few *Ghurabs* in Shivaji's fleet, the small frigates, mentioned in the English factory records, being rowing *Gallivats*. "The grabs," says Robert Orme, "have rarely more than two masts, although some have three; those of three are about 300 tons burthen; but the others are not more than 150: they are built to draw very little water, being very broad in proportion to their length, narrowing however from the middle to the end, where instead of bows they have a prow, projecting like that of a Mediterranean galley, and covered with a strong deck level with the main deck of the

21. Factory Records, Surat, Vol. 105, fol. 55.

22. Factory Records, Surat, Vol. 105, fol. 78, and Vol. 3, fol. 111. (consultation Swally Marine, 24th November, 1670).

23. Babu Jadunath Sarkar persists in writing *tarambes* (*Shivaji and His Times*, First edition, p. 336), not knowing that *tarven* is plural of *taru*.

vessel, from which, however, it is separated by a bulkhead which terminates the fore-castle: as this construction subjects the grab to pitch violently when sailing against a head sea, the deck of the prow is not enclosed with sides as the rest of the vessel is, but remains bare; that the water which dashes upon it may pass off without interruption. On the main deck under the forecastle are mounted two pieces of cannon of nine or twelve pounders, which point forwards through the port holes cut in the bulkhead, and fire over the prow; the cannon of the broadside are from six to nine pounders." A *Ghurab* never went into action unless it was accompanied by one or more *Gallivats* which, Orme says, "are large row-boats built like the grab, but of smaller dimensions, the largest rarely exceeding 70 tons: they have two masts of which the mizen is very slight; the main mast bears only one sail, which is triangular and very large, the peak of it when hoisted being much higher than the mast itself. In general the gallivats are covered with a spar deck, made for lightness of bamboos split, and these only carry petteraroes fixed on swivels in the gunnel of the vessel; but those of the largest size have a fixed deck on which they mount six or eight pieces of cannon, from two to four pounders: they have forty to fifty stout oars and may be rowed four miles an hour"[24]. Captain Anselm of the *Derby*, who had first hand knowledge of Sambhaji Angria's ships, says that "his Gallivats had thirty oars or upwards" and they had remarkable speed[25]. Some of Shivaji's frigates, as we learn from the English factory records, did not carry more than four guns. Of the other vessels the *Pal* has been likened by an eighteenth century Portuguese writer with the frigates of Europe[26]. Gemelli Careri, who travelled in a Portuguese *Manchua* in 1695, describes it as follows:—"These *Manchucas* had such a Main Sail as the *Lentis* of *Trapan* in the Kingdom of Sicily, 12 oars and four

24. Orme, *Military Transactions in Indostan*, Vol. I, pp. 401-402.

25. *A Faithful Narrative of the Capture of the ship Derby*, p. 101.

26. Jose Freire Monteroyo Mascarenhas, *Epanaphora Indica*, Pt. II, p. 8 and Pt. III, p. 27.

small guns."[27] Hamilton calls a *Shibar* a half galley[28]. These boats were all designed for shallow water, and from the few accounts of the naval actions that have come down to us it appears that they generally waited for the calm when they had to fight against a European ship as their oars placed them at an advantage over their antagonist, and, when discomfited, they readily retired to shallow waters where their heavier rival could not follow.

How these ships were manned and armed in Shivaji's days is not precisely known, but probably there was not much difference in the naval practice of Shivaji and that of the Angrias. The *Ghurabs* in the days of the Angrias carried 16 guns and 150 armed men, while the *Gallivats* had six guns and sixty fighters. The ship's crew were divided into two classes, viz., gunners and ordinary soldiers intended for boarding the enemy vessels[29].

These seldom had any fire arms but carried the ordinary weapons of offence like the sword, spear, bow and arrow. There was a scarcity of expert gunners, who were much in demand, and we may reasonably surmise that they were mere mercenaries and readily transferred their services from one master to another. Sidi Kasim seduced a number of gunners from Bombay by offering them higher pay, and when the English expostulated, he wrote to them: "You write me concerning a gunner and I would faine know what service you want by him, but if you have need of him and will content him, by paying him what is his due you may send for him. I have taken severall gunners from our enemys (i.e., Shivaji) and have many others, therefore by that reason I shall not be revenged and besides you have one of my gunners in your service, who if he be contented to come to me, you may give him leave and send him to me"[30].

Most of the captains of Shivaji's fleet were Muslims by faith. Krishnaji Anant Sabhasad says that the chief

27. Churchill's *Voyages*, Vol. IV, p. 212.
28. Hamilton, *A New Account of the East Indies*, Vol. I, p. 132.
29. *A Faithful Narrative of the Capture of the ship Derby*, p. 53.
30. Factory Records, Surat, Vol. 108, fols. 59-60.

commanders of Shivaji's fleet were Mai Naik, a Bhandari, and Dariya Sarang, a Musulman. Dariya Sarang commanded the fleet when it was sent on a mysterious and futile expedition in 1670 and Mai Naik led the Khanderi expedition in 1679. Both these officers are frequently mentioned by English and Dutch factors. A third officer, Ibrahim Khan, is mentioned by Sabhasad in his general list of infantry, cavalry and naval commanders[31], but he does not seem to have played a distinguished part, like Daulat Khan, who occupied as important a position in Shivaji's navy as Mai Naik or Dariya Sarang. Sidi Sambol and his relative Sidi Misri entered Shivaji's service after the former had been replaced in the command of the Janjira fleet by Sidi Kasim by the order of the Great Mughal. The bulk of the common crew probably consisted of Kolis and Bhandaris, hardy races of fishermen of the coast who were employed for their courage and endurance by the English of Bombay and the Sidi of Danda Rajpuri. The navy was clearly not a Maratha institution as the army was.

Did Shivaji employ European sailors in his navy? We have reason to believe that he did. Europeans had enjoyed the reputation of being good gunners and good sailors since the date of their first appearance in India, and Indian merchants were eager to secure the service of European captains and European sailors for their sea-going vessels. If they were welcomed by owners of merchantmen, it is but natural that they should have been welcomed by the leaders of the fighting fleet at an epoch when foreigners were not excluded from the military or naval services of the State. In a petition, already referred to, submitted by Joao de Salazar de Vasconcellos, we read that when the security of Bassein was threatened by Shivaji's fleet in 1659, and the Captain of that city had been ordered by the Governors of Goa to prevent the exit of that fleet at any cost, it was suggested that the danger could be evaded by causing the defection of three hundred soldiers in Shivaji's service. This was effected by

31. Sen, *Siva Chhatrapati*, p. 138.

the petitioner, Joao de Salazar de Vasconcellos, because he was a friend of the Captain, Ruy L. Viegas, who was obviously a Portuguese. The men under his command are described as " soldados " soldiers and " home's de guerra ", fighting men, and it is difficult to say whether they properly belonged to the navy. The petitioner, however, confidently asserts that their desertion effectively prevented the exit of the fleet and removed the anxiety of the Governor of Bassein[32].

Like the army the fleet had to spend the rainy season in enforced idleness. The little vessels could not face the fury of the Arabian Sea and had to retire to the ports when the monsoon broke. They were probably hauled ashore like the Sidi's boats at Bombay. On the return of the fair season they repaired and refitted; and if a large expedition was contemplated, all the carpenters of the locality were impressed for this service, which made it very difficult for the ordinary merchant to secure any artificers for his private work.

Of Shivaji's naval expeditions or enterprises, only three deserve mention here. In the beginning of February, 1665, he himself set out with his army in a fleet, consisting of 85 frigates and three great ships, for Barcelore. He was evidently on friendly terms with the Portuguese at the time, for when he passed Goa on his way to the south, the Viceroy did not deem it necessary to dispute his progress[33]. He disembarked at Barcelore and plundered it. The major part of the fleet was sent back with the exception of 12 frigates kept for transporting his forces across the rivers[34]. This was probably the only occasion when Shivaji himself embarked on

32. Petitions in the Archivo Ultramarino of Lisbon Petition dated, April 1, 1662.

33. Cosme da Guarda mentions one naval action between Shivaji's fleet and a Portuguese squadron in which the Marathas were defeated. It is evidently to this battle that Sebastiao Nunes Olares refers in his petition dated the 13th August, 1688 (Archivo Ultramarino of Lisbon). He says that he was employed in the fleet sent by the Viceroy Antonio de Mello e Castro against Shivaji's armada in 1665. The naval engagement mentioned by Guarda and Olares probably took place after the Barcelore expedition in February.

34. Foster, *The English Factories in India*, 1665-1667, p. 77-78.

a sea voyage, but a force of 3,000 soldiers was transported by sea in 1670 to an unknown destination.

This expedition was organised on a very elaborate scale, and caused much anxiety and speculation at Surat and Bombay, but it ended in nothing. In November, 1670, Shivaji assembled a vast fleet of 160 sail at Nagaon[34a] and mobilised a considerable army. The army and the fleet were supplied with provision for forty days and all the necessary instruments of mining, such as " pickaxes, shovells and crows of iron ". They were ready to depart at a moment's notice, but their destination was absolutely unknown. Bombay had been alarmed in the previous month by the appearance of a big Maratha fleet near the harbour, so the Deputy Governor and his council were naturally suspicious of the intention of their neighbour, particularly as their relations of late had been considerably strained by the Sidi's fleet " wintering " in the English island. The Bombay authorities wrote to their friends at Surat on the 17th, November :—"Where he aimes wee cannot tell or imagine, but tis good in such case to be jealous knowing who he is, for yesterday was in this place a Bramen of his (who came as wee since understand from him directly) and meeting some friends falls into discourse, and they enquiring what news he told them his master was bound upon some desperate designe nominated for 8 places which he thought his master must aime at, amongst Bombay one, but his business here as he said, was to get some pilots, he stayed not above 2 hours on the island, for had he made any longer stay, wee would assuredly have knowne more or secured his person "[35].

34a. Babu Jadunath Sarkar is wrong in calling the place Nandgaon (*Shivaji and his Times*, First Edition, p. 343). From another Bombay letter we learn that Shivaji's grand fleet assembled at "Nagaum a towne hard by Tull." The place, therefore, must be Nagaon in Kolaba district, which is only three miles from Alibag and only six miles from Thal. It is still a large and rich coast village, and in 1790 Ahilya Bai built a temple here (*Bombay Gazetteer*, Kolaba, p. 351). Nandgaon, which lies about four miles, and not ten miles, as Jadu Babu thinks, north of Janjira, cannot be by the widest stretch of imagination, described as a "towne hard by Tull." It is, moreover, too near Janjira to be the starting place of an important expedition.

35. Factory Records, Surat, Vol. 105, fol. 72.

The rest of the story may very well be told in the language of the Deputy Governor of Bombay. He wrote on the 21st of November, 1670:—"The General and the Admirall of the fleete which consists of 160 small vessels counted by my owne servant (who I sent as a spie) is one Ventgee Sarungee commonly called Durrea Sarungee with whom I having had a correspondence these 7 or 8 years, and always found him reall and oblidgeing, I was resolved to try if I could get out anything of his designe, soe wrote him a civill letter, wishing him good success in his voyage; and promising what assistance lay in my power; in lading three of his owne shipps, that are here to take in salt; desiring him if he could without prejudice to himselfe, advise me where he was bound to which he assured, that though his designe was carried very privately yett if I would send a trusty person, he would by word of mouth give me notice, soe I sent the Moodys son to him who arrived the next with orders from Sevagee (at the place of his rendevouzes) he tooke him aside and swore him his master was marching to Surat, with 10,000 horse and 20,000 foote and that he with 3000 souldiers and a great number of pioneers was to meet him then, the Bramanys have told him, that the 29th day of this month, Surat Castle should be delivered him; which if he carried, he would then to Broach, he likewise bid me keepe good watch and trust noebody and that I should doe well to lett noe vessel enter unsearched." In a postscript it is added: "The Saurngee likewise told him that if the Christians did not attempt to hinder his designe, his master would not meddle with them "[36]. The Bombay authorities, as they themselves write, did not trust the Admiral and were on their guard; the English President at Surat suggested that the three Christian powers should make a defensive and offensive compact to oppose Shivaji, but their fears and anxieties were soon laid at rest. The expedition came to naught. A week later another letter from Bombay informed them:—" Sevagees fleet was to the northward a Thursday morning from Nagaum a towne hard

36. Factory Records, Surat, Vol. 150, fol. 78.

by Tull and Friday past by here, and Saturday past by Mahim, soe wee concluded them bound according to the Generalls information (to the Deputy Governor) for Surat, but a Satturday morning at 8 o'clocke by Sevagees order, there was two frigatts well man'd with oars sent out after them, with 2 malldars[37], who have order to bringe the fleete back againe; Sevagee himselfe being returned back againe after he had gone three days march"[38]. On the 17th December the Bombay council wrote that they had certain intelligence of the return of the Maratha fleet to Dabhol. The expedition, whatever its destination was, had failed but the fleet had not returned unscathed. The Maratha fleet had met and captured a Portuguese ship near Daman and the Portuguese soon retaliated. They encountered twelve Maratha ships, captured them all and triumphantly carried them to Bassein[38a] and then went out to seek the rest of the grand armada. It was probably of this engagement that Father Naverette heard while he was at Surat in January, 1671[39].

But the enterprise, on which Shivaji had set his heart most, was the conquest of Janjira. The war with the Sidis had begun as early as 1648 and they had been steadily driven from their territories on the mainland. Then began a fierce struggle for the hill-girt island stronghold of Janjira. Shivaji tried his best to reduce it by storming it from the mainland. He tried to build a mole, he ineffectually attempted the expedient of a floating battery. Once he was almost on the brink of success and the Sidi commander, driven to his last resources, had agreed to sell the island to his enemy; but his colleagues foiled him and saved the little state from being absorbed in the growing Maratha kingdom by transferring their allegiance from the weak Sultan of Bijapur to the powerful Emperor of Delhi. Neither Shivaji nor his successors ever accomplished the conquest of Janjira.

37. Macebearer.

38. Factory Records, Surat, Vol. 105, fols. 86-87.

38a. Factory Records Surat, Vol. 105, fols. 96-97.

39. Navarette quoted in *Orme's Historical Fragments of the Mogul Empire*, p. 207.

The Island of Bombay played in this struggle an important and unhappy part. Every year the Sidi's fleet came to "winter"[40] at Bombay. There they were provisioned and refreshed. But the Sidi's sailors were an unruly lawless band. They not only committed acts of violence in the island of their unwilling hosts, but from his safe retreat the Sidi led plundering raids against the mainland opposite, which belonged to Shivaji. Shivaji protested and so did the English authorities, as they entirely depended on Shivaji's country for their fuel and food. The Maratha King quite rightly complained that the English were guilty of violation of neutrality when they allowed the Sidi to make use of their port. He also complained that the provisions obtained from his country were being diverted to the benefit of his enemies. The Bombay authorities complained to their superiors at Surat, but they were absolutely helpless. They dared not disoblige the Mughal Government, they had to think of their masters' interests in the Mughal's country and counselled patience. Every year they promised to persuade the Governor of Surat of the unreasonableness of the Sidi's conduct and every year they heard fresh complaints from their Bombay colleagues. Their position in truth was a difficult one. They dared not break with the Mughal, for they had so many factories in his empire; they dared not break with Shivaji, for Shivaji could stop their supplies of fuel and provisions. He would have been quite satisfied if the English had rendered him secret assistance in his attempts against Janjira by selling him artillery and ammunition; but they preferred the weaker Sidi as a neighbour to the stronger Maratha. They had definitely rejected Revington's suggestion of assisting Shivaji to conquer Janjira when it belonged to Bijapur, and in 1669 Henry Young seriously thought of purchasing the island, in order to save it from falling into Shivaji's hands[41]. They tried to induce the Sidi to refrain from hostilities against Shivaji's lands during his stay at Bombay but the Governor of Surat laughed

40. The season meant is the Indian rainy season from June to August.

41. Factory Records, Surat, Vol. 105, fol. 150. Letter dated 16th October 1669.

at their protest and the Sidi paid no heed to their expostulations. These conditions continued even after Shivaji's death and on the 28th December 1680, the Surat Council wrote to Bombay:—" We are sorry to finde you to be soe involved in troubles betwixt Sombajee Rajah and the Siddy and which wee here seriously considered how to advise you best to direct yourselves in soe knotty an affaire, tis true the countenance, assistance and harbour given to the Siddy to the prejudice of the Rajah being both our friends will heardly pass with the Law of Nations which wee should not be the least deviate from if necessity forced not, as wee feare in our case it will, our present condition being such that wee must be forced to disoblige one or the other, the choice of which is very disputable "[42].

Shivaji was greatly exasperated with the English for their failure (though for no fault of theirs) to keep their promise. The Sidi's fleet alone stood between him and Janjira, for on the high seas his light vessels were no match for the heavier craft of the Sidi. And however friendly he might appear in his ordinary correspondence with the English, he could not forgive them for admitting the Abyssinian Admiral to their harbour. On the other hand, it would have been impolitic to drive them definitely over to his enemy's side by any hostile action directed solely against them. In 1678 the Sidi " had much provoked him by making slaves of the people and Braminys he tooke in his incurssions into his terrytorys", and Shivaji could wait no longer. He ordered Daulat Khan and Dariya Sarang to cross over to Bombay at the head of 4,000 soldiers and burn the Sidi's fleet at Mazagon. These two

42. Factory Records, Surat, Vol. 90, Pt. II, fol. 5. It should be noted that the English sometimes tried to keep the balance between the two enemy powers by extending their protection to Shivaji's fleet, as they did in 1672. We read in a Bombay letter, dated the 2nd December, 1672 (Factory Records, Surat, Vol. 106, Pt. II, fol. 24) :—" Wee have thought good to advise you that there is laid up in this harbour, six small vessells, belonging to Sevagee with his concent, all new and lately built at Cullian Buindy, wee give out here that wee have seized on them on account of our demands made to him, and wee desire you likewise to give out at Suratt that the onely reason why they are seized on here is to prevent their attempting the Surrat armada.

officers accordingly proceeded to Panvel; but lack of boats prevented them from crossing, and the Portuguese Government, which was fully as apprehensive of the growing Maratha power by land and sea as the English, would not permit them to make use of its territories. So the two Admirals had to return without effecting any result. The English were on their guard; and the Sidi left Mazagon and took shelter with his fleet under the bastions of the fort of Bombay[43].

Shivaji was, however, resolved to prevent the Sidi's depredations; and in order to bring force to bear upon the English, he sent Mai Naik and Daulat Khan to occupy the small and hitherto uninhabited island of Kenery. The twin islands of Henery and Kenery commanded to a certain extent the harbour of Bombay, and once established there, it would not have been difficult to surprise the Janjira fleet. The English had by some means obtained notice of Shivaji's design. On the 4th September, 1679, the Surat council issued an order to the Bombay authorities "that they immediately erect an English flag on the highest part of the Island (and if it may be done without any danger from the Mallabars) that a file of souldiers be kept there to guard it; and the *Hunter* friggat be ordered to attend upon them, plying up and downe neere the said Island giving the Commander orders, in a friendly way to acquaint those that are appointed by Sevagee, for the management of that designe, when they offer to erect their fort, that the Island belongs to His Majesty of Great Brittaine, and that none can attempt anything upon the place, without an open breach of friendship"[44]. But the resolution came too late; the Marathas had acted more promptly than the English anticipated, and Mai Naik with 150 men was already in possession of the island and had raised a clumsy breast-work of dirt and stone, with guns behind it, before the English were prepared to step in. When requested to withdraw, he firmly replied that he had occupied the island at Shivaji's command

43. Factory Records, Surat, Vol. 107, fols. 112-113 (Bombay 23rd July 1678); fol. 116 (Bombay 29th July 1678); and Vol. 90, Pt. I, fol. 24 (Mazagon, 24th July, 1678).

44. Factory Records, Surat, Vol. 4, Pt. II, fols. 63-64.

and would not retire without his order. The Surat council resolved on the 15th September to " repell them with force as an open enemy." This was followed by a rash assault on the island, in which Ensign (?) Thorpe lost his vessel and his life. This disaster was followed by a naval action between the English squadron and Daulat Khan's fleet (" consisting of upwards sixty vessells small and great "). At the first onslaught of the Maratha armada most of the English ships were struck by panic and the *Dove*[45] surrendered without firing a shot. Captains Keigwin and Minchin in the frigate *Revenge*, left alone to face the enemy, coolly awaited the Marathas. Better artillery and science prevailed in the end over number, and Daulat Khan's fleet was put to flight. The defeat of the Maratha fleet, however, did not lead to the abandonment of Kenery. The Sidi shortly appeared on the scene and began to batter the hastily built ramparts of the island but after a few days the English ceased to co-operate with him. His occupation of the sister island of Henery was not calculated to conciliate the English and although Bombay advocated a vigorous policy of hostilities, Surat counselled a more moderate policy. Their man power was limited; they had been enjoined by their masters to effect economy, and the military experts, they had consulted, were of opinion that their resources were scarcely sufficient for the defence of Bombay. They counselled a diplomatic course of shifting the burden of war to the Sidi or the Portuguese[46] Government and retiring from the arena. Peace proposals from Shivaji offered an easy and honourable solution of their difficulty. Kenery was but a small island and its ownership was disputed by the Portuguese. So the Deputy Governor was instructed to send a friendly and conciliatory reply. The island was held by Shivaji's men in spite of the repeated attacks of the Sidi, and early in 1680 a treaty was concluded between Shivaji and the English[47].

45. Miscalled *Dover* by Jadunath Sarkar (*Shivaji and his Times*, p. 357).

46. Factory Records, Surat, Vol. 4, Pt. II, fols. 69-70, 82-84, 86-88 and 107-108; Vol. 108, fols. 2-3, 30, 34-35, 39-42.

47. Factory Records, Surat, Vol. 108, fols. 44-48.

The occupation of Kenery and the capture of the *Dove* were the last achievements of the Maratha navy before Shivaji's death. His maritime aims were not accomplished. The Sidi's fleet remained unbeaten and the island of Janjira, a mere dot in the sea, still defied the most strenuous efforts of the Maratha. Though Shivaji's captains had often captured Portuguese ships, he had failed to extort from them freedom of navigation for merchantmen belonging to his own ports. The only concession that he managed to obtain was included in a treaty of 1670, whereby small boats carrying provisions and foodstuffs were permitted to ply between Karanja and Goa without a Portuguese pass[48]. This concession was persistently refused to the *Gallivats* and big coasting vessels. Shivaji's fleet was numerically superior to the fleets of European nations in Indian waters; but in artillery and in the art of navigation it was vastly inferior. Shivaji himself cannot be blamed, for these deficiencies. In twenty years he could hardly expect to create a navy and bring it to perfection. He had made a beginning and a good beginning; it was for his successors to build upon the foundation he had laid. In Sambhaji and Rajaram's days the Maratha fleet continued to compel alien traders to buy its permits and its power was felt at sea even after the Mughals had conquered practically the whole of Maharashtra. But nothing more was done. In its organisation, in the type of its men of war, in its policy of selling *carṭaz* and making prize of merchantmen that did not possess it, and in the art and science of maritime warfare the Maratha navy remained where Shivaji had left it, until in the beginning of the next century its control definitely passed from the Chhatrapati to a family of hereditary naval chiefs.

---

48. Biker, *Tratados da India*, Vol. IV, pp. 174-175.

CHAPTER XI.

The Maratha Navy under the Angrias.

After Shivaji's death the Marathas passed through a great crisis. During the stormy days of Sambhaji and Rajaram most of their older leaders passed away. At one time it appeared that the nascent Maratha power might be crushed out of existence by the sheer weight of the Mughal empire, but the unusual crisis brought a number of young men of exceptional energy and ability to the forefront, and the new leaders not only saved the newly founded kingdom from imminent extinction but added to its power and prestige both by land and sea. And while Balaji Vishwanath, the founder of the Peshwa family, was gaining Shahu's confidence, the chief command of the Maratha fleet had already passed to Kanhoji Angria, the founder of a family which made itself feared and respected by all the sea powers of the coast, Indian and European.

The principal commander of Shivaji's fleet, as has been stated, were mostly Musulmans; but apparently the prospects of the sea-service had quickly attracted ambitious Maratha youths, and early in Sambhaji's reign Santaji Pavla, Govindaji Jadhav and Govind Kanho had earned some reputation as naval officers[1], though Mai Naik, Daulat Khan and Sidi Misri still directed the destinies of the Maratha fleet. But before Sambhaji's downfall a Maratha Admiral, competent to assume the responsibilities of the Commander-in-Chief, had already been found in Bhim Rao, otherwise known as Sidoji Gujar. Kanhoji Angria was one of his lieutenants.

Kanhoji's origin was obscure, and he certainly did not belong to the nobility of the land. Of his early career little or nothing is known. A Portuguese Viceroy states that he started life as a humble servant of other Hindus in the island

1. Malhar Ram Rao Chitnis, *Sambhaji Maharaj ani Thorle Rajaram Yanchin Charitren*, ed. K. N. Sane, pp. 14-15.

of Versova[2]. The rapid growth of his power, however, soon attracted the wondering notice of his contemporaries, and all sorts of probable and improbable stories about his birth and early career obtained currency among the credulous seamen who frequented the ports of western India. These stories were widely disseminated through the literary efforts of an English sailor, Clement Downing[3], and the account of Angria's Arabian origin was so commonly accepted that an unknown writer, who claimed to narrate an "authentic history and fighting adventures" of Kanhoji's son, Tulaji, had no hesitation in calling him "the Arabian pirate"[4]. Among modern writers, Mr. Enthoven believes in the Abyssinian origin of the Angrias, but he adduces no evidence for his belief[5]. According to the official history of his family, Kanhoji was a Maratha Kshatriya by birth and the original surname of his ancestors was Sankpal. The new name of Angria was supplied by the village of Angarvadi, where the family had long resided[6]. Tukoji, father of Kanhoji, had served under Shivaji[7]; and the son had naturally followed in the footsteps of the father. Malhar Ram Rao Chitnis says that when Rajaram sought refuge in Jinji he was accompanied by the Commander-in-Chief of the navy Sidoji Gujar, and Kanhoji was left in charge of Suvarnadurg. Here he distinguished himself against the Sidis of Janjira who had reconquered their lost possessions on the mainland and was appointed Subhedar of the Armada with the title of Sarkhel by Rajaram. When exactly this happened we do not know, but by 1703 he had attained so much importance that Caetano de Mello e Castro,

2. Biker Manuscripts (Archivo Ultramarino of Lisbon, Fundo geral 8548) p. 149; Instruccam que deixou o Conde de Ericeira Dom Luiz de Menezes V. Rey e Capitao Geral da India a Francisco Jose de Sampayo que lhe foy succeder no dito emprego no anno 1721. (Bibliotheca Publica of Evora cod. CV/1-1) fols. 201-203.

3. Clement Downing, *A History of the Indian Wars*, pp. 7-9.

4. *The Arabian Pirate; or Authentic History and Fighting Adventures of Tulagee Angria.*

5. Enthoven, *Castes and Tribes of Bombay*; Vol. I, p. XIII.

6. Mawjee and Parasnis, *Kaifiyats Yadis*, p. 1.

7. Malhar Ram Rao Chitnis, *Thorle Shahu Maharaj Hyanchen Charitra*, ed. Sane, p. 38.

Viceroy of Goa, addressed a friendly letter to him, sent him some presents and permitted the merchants of Chaul to purchase a vessel which Kanhoji had probably captured as a prize and was anxious to dispose of[8]. In 1710 he captured a Dutch sloop[9]. In 1712 he was simultaneously at war with the Portuguese, the Sidi and his own countrymen of Shahu's party, while his relations with the English were at the breaking point, but his power on sea was so well recognised that a Portuguese writer did not hesitate to compare him with the famous Barbarossa two years later[10].

Kanhoji had not the genius or imagination of Shivaji. But the Maratha navy had been an active unit for nearly forty years when he succeeded to the chief command. Its aims and objects were well known and clearly defined. The Maratha merchantmen were to be protected from the pirates who infested the Malabar coast, Maratha subjects were to be protected against the depredations of the Sidi and the sovereignty of the sea was to be secured for the Maratha State. It was, however, no easy task and Kanhoji had to contend against no less than five rivals, the Sidi of Janjira, the Savants of Wari, the English of Bombay, the Dutch at Vingurla and last but not least the Portuguese of Goa. The Sidis demanded his attention first. They had taken the fullest advantage of the Mughal occupation of Maharashtra and had re-established their dominion on the mainland. It was Kanhoji's duty to drive them back to their island retreat and recover the lost possessions of his master. The Sidis were no longer so formidable at sea, as they once had been, but the Maratha fleet consisted of no more than eight or ten small vessels, as we learn from Conde de Ericeira, when Kanhoji was called upon to assume its command[11]. Money was,

8. Sen, *A Preliminary Report on the Historical Records at Goa*, p. 59.

9. *Press List of Ancient Dutch Records* from 1657 to 1825 (*Madras Records Department*), pp. 7-8.

10. *Relacam dos Progressos das armas Portuguezas no Estado da India no anno* 1713, Pt. I, p. 19.

11. *Instruccam que deixou o Conde de Ericeira* (Bibliotheca Publica of Evora, Cod. CV/1-1) fol. 201.

therefore, needed for additional ships and for the enlistment of more men for the army; and money could be obtained in one way only namely by exercising the sovereignty of the sea as Shivaji and his sons had done and compelling alien traders to purchase Kanhoji's *cartaz*. This at once brought him into conflict with the Portuguese.

When exactly Kanhoji first challenged the Portuguese supremacy on sea we do not know, but his first victim was not a merchantman. It was a Portuguese *Pal* of war, richly laden and carrying on board the retired Governor of Chaul, who ultimately died from the rigours of his imprisonment[12]. Kanhoji next fought two *Manchuas* of war belonging to the Portuguese fleet of the North. He burnt one and captured another with 27 Portuguese prisoners. They were all put to the sword, according to a Portuguese official account, except one captain who purchased his life and liberty by paying a ransom of 12,000 Xerafins[13]. Many merchantmen sailing under Portuguese colours shared the same fate and contributed to Kanhoji's coffers; but the richest spoil that he obtained at the cost of his Portuguese neighbours was in 1712 during the Viceroyalty of Rodrigo da Costa, when he boldly attacked the merchant fleet sailing for the ports of the North. The fleet was convoyed by two frigates under the command of Luiz da Costa. Kanhoji fell upon the frigates with his *Pals*, dismantled the Portuguese flagship, and captured no less than forty *Parangues*. This was a great blow to Goa, for a large number of its citizens lost all the capital they had invested in this mercantile enterprise[14]. The next year the merchant fleet was better convoyed, but Kanhoji did not hesitate to attack two *Pals* that were lagging behind. The engagement lasted for two days and nights and Angria's fleet had at last to retire with much loss[14a].

12. Biker Manuscripts, p. 150.

13. Biker Manuscripts, p. 150.

14. Instruccam que deixou o Conde de Ericeira, fol. 161, Biker, *Tratados da India*, Vol. V, pp. 292-293.

14a. Biker, *Tratados da India*, Vol. V, p. 293.

The Portuguese, however, found themselves in a very sorry plight. Their possessions on the Bombay coast had been isolated and Angria was in a position to cut off their communication by land and sea. Success had augmented his self-confidence and he exacted a fee not only from Portuguese subjects fishing in the sea and the estuaries, but also levied a contribution on their villages. In 1713 he gave the Portuguese authorities further offence by attacking a frigate of 34 guns that had just landed a Portuguese force at Chaul. In this combat also the Angria's fleet, though numerically superior, was discomfited; whereupon the Viceroy resolved to take the offensive and sent Antonio Cardim Froes with a fairly numerous flotilla to reduce Kolaba. Having sailed with six *Pals* and some *Gallivats* he blockaded the port. The Angria, who was not inclined to hazard a naval action, responded by hauling his fleet ashore out of range of the Portuguese guns and leaving Froes to continue his ineffectual blockade[15]. Three months later the Portuguese Captain was forced to depart by the receipt of news of the arrival of the Arab fleet at Surat. In consequence, possibly of the Viceroy's complaints against the Sidi [16] for lukewarmness, the latter in December, 1713 also sent an expedition against Kolaba[17]; but as Angria obtained his provisions by land, the Abyssinian was no more successful than his European ally.

The Portuguese and the Sidi were not the only enemies that Kanhoji had to reckon with. In 1712 he had captured the Governor of Bombay's armed yacht with another English vessel, the *Anne* of Carwar. As a partisan of Tara Bai, he had waged a successful war against Shahu and extended his dominions on the mainland by the reduction of the strong fortresses of Lohagad, Tung and Tikona. Shahu's Peshwa, Bahiro Pant Pingle, had been taken a prisoner by his forces.

15. Biker, *Tratados da India*, Vol. V. pp. 304-305.

16. J. A. Ismael Gracias, *Uma Dona Portugueza na Côrte do Grao Mogol*, p. 139.

17. Relacao do Successo que houve no Estado da India no anno de 1714 sendo Viceroy e Capitao geral do mesmo estado Vasco Fernandes Ceaser de Menezes (a contemporary letter in Archivo Ultramarino of Lisbon Fundo, geral 465), pp. 91-92.

But these successes did not turn Kanhoji's head. As a practical man he realised the limits of his resources and decided to conclude peace with Shahu and the English so that he might be free to defend his territories against the joint efforts of the Sidi and the Portuguese. A treaty with the English involved little difficulty, but peace with Shahu was not so simple an affair. Consequently, he decided to come to terms with the English at once, and sent a messenger to Bombay in February, 1713 with proposals for peace, offering to deliver the captured vessels, if an Englishman of credit was sent to Kolaba. The Governor and Council proposed the following terms :—

1stly—" That he deliver up all that he has taken that belonged to the Company and our people."

2ndly—" That upon no pretence whatever he meddle with any English ships or with the ships belonging to the merchants who live under the protection of the English as Madrass, Bengall or any other factorys or colonys belonging to the English whatsoever."

3rdly—" That whatever ships or vessels belong to any nation whatsoever that are coming into our harbour and in sight thereof he is not (to) meddle with them that is between Mahim stakes and Cundry and at their going out the same rule is to be observed."

4thly—" That he grants our merchants the free liberty of his ports they paying usuall customs being conformable to the rules thereof. If any vessells belonging to Sevagee Rana (Raza) or Sow Razah shall take or molest any vessells belonging to Bombay they having his convoy which he is obliged to give he shall be answerable for the damage."

5thly—" Wee on our parts promise that wee will permit no ships or vessells whatever to wear English colours, but what belong to the subjects of the

English nation, which shall be incerted in all their ships."

6thly—" Wee grant him free liberty of our port of Bombay to buy sell and merchandise he paying the usuall custome and observing the rules of our port, which if he complys with that wee send the *Blenheim Ann* and *Manchua* to fetch the Companys effects which he has taken and our people "[18].

These terms were accepted by Kanhoji, as they imposed little or no sacrifice on him. If his ports were to be thrown open to the Bombay traders, he at any rate obtained similar concessions from the English; and this no doubt was to the mutual advantage of both parties. The English, it is true, refused to supply him with " powder and shott " and did not consent to give him a place for manufacturing powder, while to a proposal of mutual military assistance in times of need they gave only an evasive answer. But as regards " mariners and inhabitants of Bombay that of their own free will will serve him " the English promised " not to hinder them "; and they also consented to another request of his " that his Groabs and Galevatts have free liberty to come and return to and from this port (of Bombay) without impediment." Kanhoji was henceforth to desist from interfering with all ships coming to or going from Bombay; but complete immunity was granted only to vessels belonging to the Company and their subjects, while foreign vessels that came to or sailed from Bombay would be safe only within a certain specified distance. He obtained a further undertaking from the English that they would convoy foreign vessels only " out of sight " of Bombay, after which, as the tenor of the correspondence indicates, Kanhoji would be free to deal with them as he pleased. The most important clause of the treaty was the fifth which obliged the English not to permit foreign ships or vessels to wear their

18. Bombay Public Consultations, Range, CCCXLI, No. 4, (Consultation, 12th February, 1712-13).

colour [19]. It was the interpretation of this last term which led to hostilities a few years later between Kanhoji and the English.

In his treaty, or more accurately his agreement, with Shahu, Kanhoji showed wisdom and moderation. Recognising that his strength lay mainly in the sea, he relinquished his recent conquests on the mainland. The possession of the coast, on the other hand, was essential not only for the maintenance of uninterrupted commuication between different ports, but also its revenue on which the navy, as in Shivaji's days, ordinarily depended. He, therefore, received from Shahu Rajmachi and other places and the important island of Kenery [20]. In acknowledging Shahu's supremacy, he recognised the right of the stronger of the two claimants to the headship of the Maratha Government; and although he thereby incurred the displeasure of Sambhaji of Kolhapur, he practically secured himself from any invasion from the mainland by the promise of the Peshwa to help him whenever occasion should arise. This treaty was concluded in the latter part of 1713 or in the earlier months of 1714. As an immediate result of it the Sidi after further territorial losses came to terms with the Angria and withdrew altogether from the struggle, leaving the Portuguese to carry on the war alone. This explains the bitter complaints made by the Viceroy in 1715 against the Chief of Janjira. In 1716 the Portuguese sought a new ally in the Raja of Kolhapur with whom they concluded an offensive and defensive alliance against Kanhoji [21]; but Sambhaji of Kolhapur possessed neither energy nor ability and the net result of these diplomatic efforts was nil. The Angria's fleet rode the sea boldly, seizing merchantmen of all nationalities which had omitted to purchase his passports, and the Portuguese found themselves powerless to circumscribe his activities. Of all their possessions on the coast, Chaul

19. Bombay Public Consultations, Range, CCCXLI, No. 4, (Consultation, 14th February, 1712-13).

20. Malhar Ram Rao Chitnis, *Thorle Shahu Maharaj Hyanchen Charitra*, pp. 39-40; Mawjee and Parasnis, *Treaties Agreements and Sanads*, pp. 197-199.

21. Biker, *Tratados da India*, Vol. VI, pp. 2-4.

suffered most; for the main source of its income was the volume of dutiable commerce which suffered heavily from Angria's interference. His fleet, which originally consisted of eight or ten small *Gallivats*, now comprised far more than forty vessels of varying type; and adventurers of all nationalities, European and Asiatic, flocked to his service. It was, indeed, reported that Kanhoji boasted that he could capture Chaul whenever he liked. But luckily for the Portuguese they soon found an ally more formidable than the weak Sidi or the incapable Sambhaji. In 1721, only eight years after the conclusion of their treaty with Kanhoji, the English formed an offensive and defensive alliance with the Portuguese against him, though their actual breach with the Maratha admiral had taken place much earlier.

The amicable arrangement between Kanhoji and the English was short lived. Though he had promptly restored the two captured English vessels after the conclusion of the treaty, their cargo he had omitted to return. This was, however, not the only source of dissatisfaction. In 1715 Kanhoji complained to Governor Boone " of ill usage in return for the good offices he had done," while in March 1716 Boone wrote to his masters at home that he was not pressing the outstanding claims against Angria " as they were not in a good posture to oppose him "[22]. He was temporising in expectation of a suitable opportunity of vindicating English claims. The matter was eventually brought to a head by Kanhoji's capture of three ships in succession and his forcible appropriation of some timber from one of the Company's vessels.

The first ship that Angria captured was the *Success*. The English contended that it belonged to their broker Govardhan Das and was therefore an English ship. As the Bombay authorities were still unable and unwilling to break with Kanhoji the President permitted the broker to try private negotiation; and it was ultimately settled that the ship should be returned in exchange for some presents. But owing to

22. Foster, Downing's *History of the Indian Wars*, p. XIII.

mutual distrust and suspicion the arrangement fell through, and another ship, the *Robert*, was captured by Angria's officers. On the 3rd January, 1717-18 the Bombay Council met to discuss yet another act of aggression by Kanhoji, " Cannojee Angria" we read in the Bombay Public Consultations, " two or three days since having carried the Rt. Hon'ble Companys Surat boat into Collaby one of his ports and taken out some pieces of timber, brought in a debate in what manner we should resent this insult, on consideration that wee are not in a very good condition, being so bare of ammunition, soldiers and seamen to perform anything with our arms. Tis agreed that the President expostulate the affair with him by letter, and endeavour by that means to bring him to reason and prevent if possible such insults for the future "[23]. For identical reasons the Council decided on the 22nd January, to send a Prabhu to Captain Henry Cornwall who was then in one of Kanhoji's ports in connection with the negotiation about the *Success* with instructions to expostulate with Angria about the *Robert*[24].

Kanhoji positively refused "to deliver up the ship *Robert* or free the Englishmen belonging to her, on pretence of her belonging to the Moors "[25]. The English were still unable to retaliate. " Our condition at present obliging us to dissemble these insults and the President embarquing to-morrow for Surat directed that Mr. Parker during his absence endeavour by Rama Comatee to get the Europeans taken in said ship set at liberty, but that wee do not appear in it ourselves till a more favourable opportunity should offer "[26]. Kanhoji having captured another ship, the *Otter*, the Council decided on April 5th " to serve him in the same kind " and authorised the Governor to issue private instructions to the English frigates to take and destroy Kanhoji's " grabbs should they fall their way." But war had not yet been declared. Open hostilities

23. Bombay Public Consultations, Range, CCCXLI, No. 4, p. 2.
24. Bombay Public Consultations, Range, CCCXLI, No. 4, p. 11.
25. Bombay Public Consultations. Range, CCCXLI, No. 4, (Consultation, 6th February, 1717-18), pp. 31-33.
26. Ibid.

were hastened by the detention at Mahim of a *Shibar* belonging to Angria's port Alibag, which evoked a wrathful letter to Boone from Kanhoji. "Our friendship is over," said he, "and from this day forward what God gives I shall take." Angry correspondence followed, which was not calculated to improve the impaired relations between the two powers and Boone and Kanhoji freely and in no ambiguous language cast reflections upon each other's good faith[27]. At last, on the 17th June, 1718 war was openly declared against Kanhoji Angria by a proclamation published at Bombay [28].

The nationality of the three captured ships was a highly controversial question. The owners of the ships were not English, but the cargo belonged to English subjects, and Kanhoji contended that they were not entitled to exemption from the ordinary rules of passports. He wrote to Captain Cornwall "that the ships belonging to Bombay, Bengall or Madras shall not be molested by him but that if the English will freight on countrey shipping they must expect that he will make prise of them"[29]. This he reiterated in his letter to Boone. "The English," he wrote, "freight the ships of foreign merchants and lade them with their goods, and receive no molestation they having English colours. This is gain to the owners of the ship; yet how can they carry on their trade without a pass. To-day you freight the ship *Sacry*; to-morrow Your Excellency will say that you have a mind to freight fifty or a hundred ships of the Surat merchants. If so what occasion have they to take a pass they always took of mee, and if Your Excellency intends to carry on the trade alone under your colours, why did the Bombay merchant who hired the ship of the Duan of Chaul write to mee and take my pass for her?" To this Boone retorted—"Let the bottom be whose it will, the money lent on it is worth more than the ship, and

27. For these letters see Bombay Public Consultations, Range, CCCXLI, No. 4, pp. 58-61 (Consultation 13th April 1718) and pp. 77-83, (Consultation, 7th May, 1718).

28. Bombay Public Consultations, Range CCCXLI, No. 4, p. 96.

29. Bombay Public Consultations, Range CCCXLI, No. 4, pp. 31-32. (Consultation 5th February, 1717-18).

the goods are English you well know, or else you would not have attempted so barbarously to beat the Captain and other Englishmen into a confession of what made for your purpose."

Modern practice will not uphold Boone's contention that a ship loses its original nationality when it carries foreign cargo of superior value; but Kanhoji's excuse for taking the East India Company's timber was palpably unsound. He pleaded necessity—"I had wrote Your Excellency before the necessity I was in for timber, and then I had timber coming from Bombay of foreign merchants, which was chosen by my people, which I gave you notice of, and had your licence for a carpenter to come from thence, which you repealed and hindred the timber to be brought. In this manner things go on, demonstrating that tis not Your Excellency alone that governs. Your Excellency has no intention to do anything contrary to our friendship, but you find it necessary to act according to what is told you by bad men who live with you. As I had a great necessity for timber, when the boat came from Surat, I brought her in, in a friendly manner, believing that you observed the friendship without scruples, and what's a little timber? Had I wrote to you, you would have given it mee, but as it might have hapned that somebody or another would have stopt it, as they did before, and my work thereby be put to a stand, I took the timber here and wrote Your Excellency to let mee know the price thereof, and had for answer you wanted timber, which I took well, expecting when mine would come to repay you. In this there is no cause of difference."

Kanhoji's excuse for retaining the cargo of the *Anne* and the Company's yacht was equally ingenuous, but neither the cargo nor the timber mentioned above would have proved an insuperable obstacle to peace. The real ground of contention was that the English had to load foreign boats with their goods and demanded for these boats the same immunity to which ships of undoubted English nationality were entitled. Kanhoji was unwilling to grant this demand, which would have meant financial loss to him. Five years earlier he might have been more compliant, but his treaty with Shahu had strengthened his position on the mainland, and his victory over the Sidi and the Portuguese had added to his confidence, while the English had suffered a loss of prestige after the ill success of the Carwar expedition in 1717. But while unwilling to make concessions to the English, Kanhoji was prudent enough not to offer any additional offence to the Portuguese. Conde de Ericeira tells us that Kanhoji did not give Portuguese subjects any trouble during the term of his Viceroyalty[30]. One enemy at a time was enough for him.

The English commenced the war with resolution and vigour and sent a number of minor expeditions against Kanhoji's coast. The following extracts from Bombay Public Consultations will give some idea of their scope and frequency[31].

"Sunday 25th May:—Sailed our Galevats in order to make further depredation in the territories of Angria.

Monday June 2nd:—Last night sailed two Galevats with about thirty sepoys to make a descent in another part of Angria's country.

Wednesday 4th June 1718:—This morning returned the two Gallevats from Angria's country having pillaged one town and brought sixteen prisoners".

Similar expeditions were sent out in July, September and October, but they were not always successful. The failure was attributed in some cases to adverse weather and in others to the unwillingness of the men to land. Boone did not rely solely on these punitive expeditions; he realised that he could not bring Kanhoji to terms unless some of his principal strongholds were reduced. Before embarking, however, on any serious enterprise, he tried to exploit the difference between Angria and his quondam sovereign, the Raja of Kolhapur. On the same day that the war was proclaimed at Bombay, "The President wrote a short letter to Mr. George Taylor Chief of Carwar acquainting him of our breach with Angria

30. Instruccam que deixou o Conde de Ericeira (Bibliotheca Publica of Evora, Cod C V /1-1) fol. 201.

31. Bombay Public Consultations, Range CCCXLI, No. 4, pp. 87-90.

and directing him to lay before Sambajee Rajah, the many injuries done to us by him and to acquaint said Rajah if he will chastise him, as soon as the fortresses in his possession are delivered up to him wee shall lay down our arms, or else endeavour to exterpate said pyrate ourselves tho' far from any design against His Highness or any of his loyal subjects"[32]. The English negotiation with Sambhaji in 1718 seems to have had no better result than the Portuguese treaty of 1716. A defensive and offensive alliance with the Portuguese against the common enemy was discussed in October, 1718, but how far it progressed we do not know. Conde de Ericeira however, writes of a sound scheme which he had planned for capturing or burning the Angria's *Pals* at Gheria, which, he complains, was frustrated by carelessness on the part of the English[33]. We read of a futile attempt by the English to burn the *Ghurabs* at Vissundroog[33a] in November, 1719, and apparently therefore, the alliance, if ever seriously concluded, must have ended after this event. Conde de Ericeira, moreover, was highly suspicious of the English and did not think much of their military resources, which were at that moment undoubtedly limited and insufficient.

The first serious expedition was led by Boone in person and was made against the island stronghold of Kenery, first fortified by Mai Naik in 1679 and now held by Angria's men. After a severe cannonade a landing was effected but no more than 40 persons could be induced to volunteer for an assault. The assault made by such a small party naturally failed, though the failure was attributed to the treachery of Ramji Kamathi, a Hindu inhabitant of Bombay. He was accused of carrying on a treasonable correspondence with Angria and was condemned, though without sufficient evidence, to life-long imprisonment, while his property was confiscated.

From Kenery the fleet sailed to Kolaba and bombarded the place at intervals, without however effecting any

32. Bombay Public Consultations, Range CCCXLI, No. 4, p. 98.

33. Instruccam que deixou o Conde de Ericeira (Bibliotheca Publica of Evora, Cod. C V/1-1) pp. 202-203.

33a. Vijaidurg.

appreciable loss, and they then left for Gheria. All that they effected was to capture from one of Kanhoji's squadrons four of their prizes, the *Ghurabs* escaped as there was very little wind[34].

While the English fleet was sailing to the south, some of Kanhoji's *Ghurabs* appeared near Bombay. They were sighted by Captain Eustace Peacock of the *Morrice*, who hastily returned with other vessels to Bombay for safety and did not resume his voyage until the enemy had been put to flight by the frigates *Victoria*, *Revenge*, *Defyance* and the galleys *Hunter* and *Hawk* in the third week of January, 1719 About this time peace proposals were made by Shahu and hostilities were for the time being suspended[35].

On the 30th January, 1719, the President informed the Council that Shahu Raja had sent an envoy to him to conclude a peace with the English nation, " in which Cannojee Angria his servant should be included and the Angria had also requested his permission to send his servants." Certain preliminary Articles proposed by the President were agreed to by the Maratha envoy but the gist of these is unknown. Captain John Milles was sent with the President's letter to Kolaba to bring the English prisoners. He returned on the 12th February without his compatriots, who were at Gheria. Kanhoji promised to send the English prisoners quickly with one of his own officers but informed Boone that he had certain objections to the Articles sent to him. What his objections were we do not know. Some Articles alone were discussed, but the treaty was not ratified by Kanhoji[36], and the English, after another futile expedition against Kolaba and the capture of the ship *Charlotte* by Angria in 1720, concluded

34. Foster, Downing's *History of the Indian Wars*, p. XVI.

35. Bombay Public Consultations, Range CCCXLI, No. 4, (Consultation 30th January, 1719.)

36. Robert Cowan in his letter to Baji Rao says :—(3rd January 1721-22) " Two years since His Excellency the Shaw Rajah sent his envoy Sevajee Vissanat who with Damajee Pillaji in behalf of Angria agreed with the President and Governor sundry articles of peace and signed them but Angria has never complyed with these articles." Bombay Public Consultations, Range CCCXLI, No. 5.

an alliance with the Portuguese which resulted in their joint expedition against Kolaba in December, 1721.

An alliance between the two European neighbours against their common Indian enemy was perhaps the most obvious course to pursue in existing conditions, but mutual suspicion had so long stood in its way. The Portuguese had very reluctantly parted with Bombay, and the steady growth of English influence on the Malabar coast was certainly not to their liking. They often suspected the English of piratical practices, and the Conde de Ericeira seriously believed that Angria got his artillery and ammunition from Bombay. He also feared that the English would quietly withdraw from the war when they saw the Portuguese involved in it. Moreover, the man power at the disposal of the Bombay Government was not calculated to create confidence. He informed his successor that Bombay had no more than 80 Englishmen, all of whom were merchants and clerks. The Count, therefore, strongly urged the new Viceroy not to conclude any alliance with the English, the only power whom he could recommend as reliable being the Sidi of Janjira[37]. But when Robert Cowan, the English agent, reached Goa in March, 1721, they had been at war with Angria for three long years, and the loss they had suffered probably provided sufficient evidence of their resolution. Moreover, a squadron of four ships under Commodore Thomas Mathews had left England for the East in February of that year, and the news must have reached the European settlements in India sometime before the conclusion of the treaty, which was signed on the 20th of August, 1721, only a week before the arrival of the English fleet at Bombay. The treaty consisted of fourteen Articles and provided for equal division of the spoils of the war and the conquered territories. Of the naval strongholds of the Angria, Kolaba was to be awarded to the Portuguese, while Gheria was to fall to the English. Evidently, the allied powers were planning the complete conquest of the Angria's possession and the total destruction of his power. It was therefore decided that no

37. Instruccam que deixou o Conde de Ericeira, pp. 201-203.

peace proposal was to be entertained by either of the allies; all such questions were to be jointly decided[38].

The success of the scheme depended upon its secrecy. But the Portuguese began to enlist Pathan mercenaries at Bassein, and before long Kanhoji became aware of the new menace that threatened him. He promptly tried to avert the danger by diplomacy and sent peace proposals to the Portuguese authorities[39]. The Viceroy, however, curtly rejected Kanhoji's offer and continued his warlike preparations. The Angria not only strengthened his position by enlisting fresh forces but applied for help and reinforcement from his liege-lord, the Chhatrapati of Satara.

We need not go into the details of this expedition; suffice it to say, that it totally failed. Angria, forewarned of the coming danger, was well prepared to face it. The morale of the Bombay men, "habituated to defeat in their attacks on Angrian strongholds," was naturally not very high. Mathews was a brave officer but did not possess tact and other qualities of leadership. The first serious reverse so infuriated him that he insulted his Portuguese colleague, and the breach between the allied armies was so great that Col. Biddulph thinks that "a little more enterprise on the part of the Mahrattas would have destroyed the whole force".

Kanhoji Angria was a diplomat of uncommon ability. We have already seen how he had tried to prevent the conclusion of the Anglo-Portuguese alliance. In his letter he had made a pointed reference to the English failure in 1719 against Kolaba and Kenery, and although he had refrained from mentioning it, the Viceroy was well aware of the results of the Portuguese expedition against Angria's headquarters under Antonio Cardim Froes in the following year. Better success

38. Biker, *Tratados da India*, Vol. III, pp. 242-244; Sen, *A Preliminary Report on the Historical Records at Goa*, pp. 63-66.

39. Angria's letter to the Captain of the Province of the North was according to a manuscript chronicle in Archivo Ultramarino of Lisbon (Noticias da India desde o fim do governo do Vice Rey Vasco Fernandes Ceaser (de Menezes) athe o fim do anno 1738 em que governava o Viceroy Conde de Sandomil, fundo geral 465) was addressed a fortnight before the Anglo-Portuguese agreement was signed.

was expected from the reinforcement Mathews had brought; but enthusiasm and confidence aroused at Goa by the arrival of the English fleet had now been rudely shaken. The Maratha Admiral did not fail to exploit the mutual recrimination and suspicion which now recurred and again made peace proposals to the Portuguese. In spite of the best efforts of the allies Angria's fleet still kept the sea and the Viceroy learnt that Angria's captains had captured a Portuguese boat near Diu[40]. Kolaba itself was well provisioned and strongly garrisoned with one thousand infantry and seven hundred cavalry. Fresh reinforcements from Poona and Satara were daily hurrying to the field of war. First Pilaji Jadhav and then Baji Rao had appeared in the neighbourhood with an enormous Maratha horde that now numbered twenty-five thousand cavalry. Whatever chance of success there had been at the earlier stage of the campaign now completely vanished. The Portuguese Viceroy, therefore, deemed it wise to accept peace proposals and return to Goa. But his English ally would not agree to such a course, and, according to the lately concluded treaty, he was unable to come to terms with Kanhoji without the concurrence of the English. A way out of this difficulty was soon discovered. Peace was negotiated not by Kanhoji but by Baji Rao, and the Portuguese came to terms not with the Angria but with his master, Shahu. This point was emphasised not only by the Viceroy but also by the Bishop of Nanking, then at Goa, and by Joseph Ferreira de Horta in their letters to Conde de Unhao[41]. The treaty was thus observed in the letter, though it was violated in the spirit. The Viceroy had, it is true, invited the English agent, Robert Cowan, to take part in the peace conference, but he naturally complained that the Portuguese had sacrificed English interests and the English took no part in the negotiations. On the 9th January, 1722, a treaty was formally concluded between the Peshwa and the Viceroy at the camp of Alibag.

40. Biker Manuscripts, p. 277.

41. Varias Cartas da Asia ao Conde de Unhao. (Bibliotheca Publica of Evora, Cod. CXX/2-1).

The Portuguese undertook not to convoy ships belonging to the enemies of the Marathas but to help the Marathas against their enemies, who were not at peace with the Portuguese. The ports of the two nations were thrown open to the merchants of either party, and the Portuguese promised to furnish the Peshwa with ammunition at a just price, while the Marathas on their side undertook to restore the Portuguese ships captured by the Kolaba fleet[42]. A copy of this treaty was delivered to Robert Cowan and the English were called upon to accept similar terms within eight days[43]. Thus ended the short-lived Anglo-Portuguese alliance. The English were left alone to fight the Angria as best they could.

The ill-success of the Anglo-Portuguese expedition undoubtedly contributed to Kanhoji's prestige, and he was soon free to seek his enemies at sea. On the 14th of March, 1722, Goa received the news of a naval victory obtained by him. His fleet, consisting of four *Pals* and twenty *Gallivats*, had attacked two English *Pals* between Chaul and Rajapore. One of the two English vessels was burnt and the other was put to flight[44]. About the same time Angria captured a big English ship richly laden with coins and valuable goods. But his success was by no means uniform; for one of his ships surrendered to the English near Henery sometime between March and October. In October, 1722, Kanhoji sailed in person with five thousand men from Kolaba, leaving his eldest son in charge of the government. The Portuguese say that he openly declared that he would not return so long as the name of the English was heard on that coast[45]. It does not appear that he achieved anything. He tried his best to conclude an offensive alliance with the Portuguese against his

42. Biker, *Tratados da India*, Vol. VI, pp. 10-12.

43. Bombay Public Consultations, Range CCCXLI, No. 5, The Portuguese Viceroy's letter to Robert Cowan, dated 15th January, 1722.

44. Noticias da India desde o fim do governo do Vice Rey Vasco Fernandes Ceaser (de Menezes) athe o fim do anno 1738 (Archivo Ultramarino of Lisbon, fundo geral 465) fol. 111. The battle was fought on the 27th February, see Bombay Public Consultations No. 4. Consultation 22nd March 1721-22.

45. Noticias da India desde o fim do governo do Vice Rey Vasco Fernandes Ceaser (de Menezes) athe o fim do anno 1738; fols. 118-119.

enemies of Bombay. The Portuguese Government were notoriously short of funds and would not embark on a policy of aggression, although their relations with their former allies were far from friendly, but Kanhoji offered the Viceroy whatever financial assistance he might require and was ready "to swear perpetual friendship on the head of his sons". Jealous as the Portuguese were of their prosperous European neighbour, they were nevertheless more suspicious of the rising power of the Maratha Admiral; and they promptly composed their differences with the English[46].

In 1724 Kanhoji addressed a letter to William Phipps, who had succeeded Charles Boone as Governor of Bombay in January, 1722[47], proposing a treaty of peace. Phipps replied in a haughty tone, commenting on the character of Kanhoji's government, but Kanhoji renewed his proposal of exchanging prisoners, adding retorts to Phipps' criticism, which were full of sarcasm. He was impelled to make this proposal, as we are informed by a Portuguese writer, by the desire of securing the liberty of Shivaji Naik, one of his captains, who had been taken prisoner when a *Pal* of Angria's fleet surrendered to the English near Cape Rama. Eventually, an exchange of prisoners was effected in 1725, though the main differences between the two combatants still remained unadjusted[48].

But Kanhoji had stronger grounds than the Portuguese suspected for soliciting a cessation of arms. In 1723 he came to blows with the Savant of Kudal with whom he had hitherto maintained friendship and amity. The quarrel arose, as Captain Alexander Hamilton informs us, out "of a dispute about a Prize which Connajee Angarie laid claim to"[49]. The Chief of Kolaba was by far the stronger of the two, and he

46. The Portuguese Government referred the points of difference to their masters in Europe.

47. Forrest, *Selections from the letters Despatches and other State Papers*, Home series, Vol. II, pp. 37-38.

48. Noticias da India desde o fim do governo de Vice Rey Vasco Fernandes Ceaser (de Menezes) athe o fim do anno 1738, fols. 122-123. The exchange of prisoners was effected in the Portuguese island of Karanja on the 26th July 1725, see Bombay Public Consultations, Range CCCXLI, No. 6.

49. Hamilton, *A New Account of the East Indies*, Vol. I, p. 245.

captured and burnt the Savant's fleet and then effected a landing near Vingurla and burnt and destroyed the villages near that port. The Savant was hardly a match for him; but Kanhoji was aware of the danger of his allying himself with his European rivals, and about this time rumours reached his ears of the machinations of his enemies at Shahu's court [50]. The Savant in his distress had already applied to the Portuguese for help, and Kanhoji considered it wise not to give them any fresh cause of offence. Prudence also induced him to volunteer proposals of peace to the English. About this time fresh dissensions had taken place between himself and the Sidi of Janjira, who appeared in 1725 before Kolaba with a large fleet of twelve *Pals*, two frigates and one hundred *Gallivats*[51]. It is quite impossible that Kanhoji should have been ignorant of the intended invasion, and this offered an additional ground for his pacific attitude. For reasons unknown to us, the Maratha Admiral considered it unsafe to face the Sidi on the sea, and, as was usual in that age, silver served to avert a danger when steel offered little or no remedy.

The last three or four years of Kanhoji's life were probably quiet and uneventful. His rivals at sea caused him no anxiety, and in 1725 he considered conditions sufficiently peaceful to justify his leaving his headquarters and journeying to Satara to pay his respects to his sovereign and liege-lord. He was received there with great honour and respect and after a short absence returned to Kolaba, where he died on the 20th June, 1729[52].

50. The suspicion of intrigue at Satara was not without basis. See Bombay Public Consultation, Range CCCXLI, No. 4, 23rd January 1722.

51. Noticias da India desde o fim do governo do Vice Rey Vasco Fernandes Ceaser (de Menezes) athe o fim do anno 1738, fol. 123. The ineffectual Dutch invasion of Kolaba in 1724 must have also added to Kanhoji's anxiety; it explains, in part, his moderation and caution.

52. This date is given by Noticias da India desde o fim do governo do Vice Rey Vasco Fernandes Ceaser (de Menezes) athe o fim do anno 1738, fol. 142. Grant Duff and Nairne think that Kanhoji died in 1728 (Bombay Gazetteer, Vol. I, Pt. II, p. 87) while Grose and Low were of opinion that he died in 1731. The writer of the Kolaba volume observes in a foot-note: (Bombay Gazetteer, Vol. XI, p. 149). "The fact that Kanhoji's name is mentioned in the treaty between the English and the Savantvadi Chief in 1730, supports Grose's date." The treaty was concluded on the 12th

Kanhoji Angria may be regarded as the second founder of the Maratha navy, just as Baji Rao I. has been styled the second founder of the Maratha empire. He was inspired, as he wrote in his letter to Governor Phipps, by Shivaji's example, and whatever may be said of his naval practices, he undoubtedly re-established Maratha prestige at sea. Even when he was at open war with the Portuguese, their subjects acknowledged his naval supremacy by purchasing his passports for their trading vessels. He defied the joint efforts of the English, the Portuguese and the Sidi, and in his wars by land and sea he had given evidence not only of good seamanship but also of wise diplomacy. In his foreign relations he could hardly be accused of treachery or faithlessness. Regarding the interpretation of the 5th Article of the treaty of 1713, which provided the immediate cause of his war with the English in 1718, there was room for an honest difference of opinion. He never violated the treaty which his master, on his behalf and on behalf of the Maratha State in general, had concluded with the Portuguese State in India in January 1722. In October of that year his fleet met some Portuguese boats on the high sea but permitted them to proceed on their journey as soon as their nationality was known [53]. In 1723 he permitted Portuguese vessels to take provisions at the port of Gheria[54], and, according to Portuguese accounts, the Angrias never interfered with their merchantmen or fighting fleet until they were at war with the Peshwa's Government. On the other hand, one eminent Portuguese writer, who was intimately acquainted with the inner policy of the Goa Government, cynically informs us that they secretly helped the Sardesai of Kudal in his war against Kanhoji Angria, because they preferred to have the weaker of the two combatants as their next door neighbour[55].

January 1729-30, and the text is to be found in Bombay Public Consultations, CCCXLI, No. 7, pp. 49-50. Article 5 mentions "The sons of Conajee Angria" and we can safely assume that he was not alive when this treaty was concluded.

53. Noticias da India desde o fim do governo do Viċe Rey Vasco Fernandes Ceaser (de Menezes) athe o fim do anno 1738, fols. 118-119.

54. Ibid, fol. 117.

55. Ibid, fols. 118-119.

As to his methods of enlistment and payment we know very little. But he made no improvement in naval strategy and armaments, which remained in the days of his sons as crude and as primitive as when Shivaji launched his fleet on the Arabian Sea. But he left an extensive province and a strong and respectable fleet to his heirs, who, had they possessed his prudence and moderation, might have added immensely to the prestige and power they had inherited from their famous father.

Kanhoji left many children by his wives and concubines. Of these six are known to history, Sekhoji, Sambhaji, Manaji, Tulaji, Yesaji and Dhondji [56]. Sekhoji was probably the eldest; for his succession to his father's office was uncontested and his authority was acknowledged and respected by his brothers without reluctance. It was during his regime in 1731 that Portuguese vessels at sea were again attacked. The Marathas had made inroads into Portuguese territories to demand and enforce the payment of *sardeshmukhi*; and the Portuguese had retaliated by sending a punitive expedition against Kalyan. The Viceroy despatched a fleet to assist his countrymen in the province of the North. This fleet was driven by inclement weather to take shelter near Angria's stronghold of Gheria and was attacked by him [57]. The Portuguese accused Sekhoji of treachery, but it should be remembered that the treaty of 1722 had been concluded between the Peshwa as the representative of Shahu on one side and the Portuguese State on the other. Sekhoji's father was included in the treaty as a servant of Shahu; he was not a principal. Consequently, Sekhoji could not be held responsible for the breach of peace, which was due to the aggressions committed by the Peshwa's officers. As the hereditary Admiral of the Maratha navy he could not permit Portuguese vessels carrying reinforcements against his master's territories to make free use of his ports or to proceed to their

56. J. F. M. Mascarenhas in his *Epanaphora Indica*, pt. V, pp. 28-33, gives an interesting but inaccurate account of Kanhoji and his sons. He mentions another son, Appaji.

57. Noticia da India desde o fim do governo do Vice Rey Vasco Fernandes Ceaser (de Menezes) athe o fim do anno 1738, fols. 151-152.

destination unimpeded. When once peace was terminated Sekhoji did not hesitate to harass Portuguese trading vessels. In 1731 he captured two merchant *Pals* and one *Gallivat*[58], and in 1733 eleven of his *Gallivats* appeared near the bar of Goa and prevented free navigation until they were driven off.

Sekhoji made an attempt to compose his differences with the English [59]. Their alliance with the Savant of Wari in 1730, though fruitless and ineffective, was a warning which he did not ignore. In 1731 the Portuguese fleet had again agreed to co-operate with the English against their common enemy at sea. Sekhoji, therefore, in June 1733 sent two envoys with proposals of peace to Bombay, but events over which he had no control prevented their acceptance. In that very year Peshwa Baji Rao had commenced a war against the Sidi of Janjira. The English and the Portuguese could not remain indifferent witnesses of the extermination of the only country power which offered any check to the naval supremacy of the Marathas. The Viceroy of Goa sent Antonio Cardim Froes with two ships to Janjira, ostensibly to mediate between the two combatants, but really to help the Sidi openly, should such assistance be absolutely necessary. The English openly sided with the Chief of Janjira, and this involved them in open hostility with Sekhoji, who was co-operating with the Peshwa. His brother, Manaji, had inflicted a defeat on the Sidi's fleet and but for English intervention the island of Henery would certainly have changed masters. The English occupied the little island and hoisted their own flag there, to which Angria responded by an ineffectual bombardment from the neighbouring stronghold of Kenery. Shortly afterwards, the career of Sekhoji was cut short by his death, which occurred in September 1733. With his demise the most successful period of the Maratha naval history came to a close.

Sekhoji was succeeded by his brother Sambhaji, an intrepid but short-tempered seaman, who did not possess the

58. Ibid, fol. 152.

59. Sekhoji's moderation is all the more remarkable as he had gained an important victory over the English fleet in November, 1730. See Bombay Public Consultations, CCCXLI, No. 7, pp. 184-185.

wisdom and diplomatic qualities of his father and elder brother. He permitted himself to be involved in simultaneous hostilities with the English and the Portuguese. His relations with the Peshwa were most unfriendly and he could not even depend upon the loyal allegiance of his father's army and navy, his authority being successfully contested by a half brother Manaji. This domestic dissension ultimately led to the ruin of the Angria's power.

This fraternal strife commenced in 1734 within twelve months of Sekhoji's death. Apparently, Sambhaji was quite willing to assign subordinate commands to his brothers as Sekhoji had done, and the precise reason of Manaji's defection cannot be definitely stated. Anyhow, while his brother was fighting the common enemy, he took possession of Kolaba with the help of the Portuguese and put out the eyes of Yesaji who had been left in charge of that fort. That done, Manaji made overtures to all the old enemies of the Angria family, the Portuguese, the English, and the Sidi, for help and support against his brother. He, however, relied mainly on the patronage of the Peshwa, who did not look with satisfaction upon the growing power of the Angrias and had decided that they must at all costs be rendered innocuous. The Portuguese and the English both befriended the weaker Manaji. To the latter, who had for nearly twenty years tried in vain to destroy the Angrias, this family feud offered an excellent opportunity of securing their object. They decided to assist Manaji with money and military stores and to take every opportunity of inciting him to nurse his resentment against his brother [60]. It was the duty of the Peshwa as the virtual head of the empire to mediate between the two brothers and bring about a reconciliation. He actually did so in 1735, but his decision served merely to aggravate the quarrel. Kanhoji Angria's fleet and territories were divided between the two brothers, Manaji being given the new title of *Vazaratmav*, with Kolaba for his head-quarters, while the command of the other half of the fleet fell to Sambhaji, who retained the paternal title of *Sarkhel*, with his head-quarters at Suvarnadurg. As the

60. Bombay Public Consultations, CCCXLI, No. 7b, pp. 406-407.

arrangement did not please him, he appealed to Shahu on several occasions but without effect. His failure merely caused him to nurse his grievance and watch for a suitable chance to recover his position.

In the meantime war broke out between the Peshwa and the Portuguese, and the two Angria brothers served their suzerain's cause to the best of their ability. Sambhaji and Manaji, it is needless to say, followed no concerted plan, each acting on his own account. They might have helped the Peshwa's forces operating against Bassein and other Portuguese places in two ways. First, they could have blockaded these ports and cut off communication with Goa, but this was neither effected nor even attempted. Not only did the Portuguese safely send reinforcements to Bassein, as occasion demanded, but the besieged themselves on certain occasions despatched expeditions to other places on the coast. The Angrias with their fleet were certainly cruising in the sea, but they never thought of attempting a regular blockade. There was yet another way of striking their enemies at a vital point. Goa depended absolutely for its food supply on the regular import of rice from the ports of Canara. If this supply was cut off, not only Goa but the besieged city of Bassein also, which mainly relied on Goa for its provisions, would be reduced to grave straits. Concerted action by the two brothers, or even resolute operation by Sambhaji alone, might have starved the Portuguese into submission. But no systematic effort was ever made by either of the two Angrias to intercept the Portuguese merchant flotilla. This can be explained by the fact that whereas the Peshwa was fighting against the Portuguese alone, the Angria brothers were fighting also against the English; and they were prone to be diverted from their main objective by the sight of vessels belonging to other nations. They had forgotten their father's policy of fighting one enemy at a time and so narrowing the field of operations.

For our information about the maritime operations of the two Angria brothers during the Maratha-Portuguese wars we are mainly indebted to contemporary Portuguese letters and narratives. In 1735 the Portuguese fleet encountered two *Pals* of Sambhaji Angria and put them to flight after half-an-hour's fighting [61]. In 1738 however his arms were more successful, for a Portuguese *Pal* belonging to Diu surrendered to Sambhaji's captains near Dahanu without much resistance [62]. In the same year a squadron of Sambhaji's fleet consisting of five *Pals* and eleven *Gallivats* captured the Portuguese *Pataxo* [62a] of war, *Sao Miguel*, near Gheria, and Antonio Fernandes informed Conde de Unhao that this *Pataxo* carried on board a cargo of ivory worth 100,000 Xerafins and other merchandise of great value belonging to the traders of Goa [63]. He had also captured, as we learn from the same source, three *Parangues*, one of which had on board forty thousand Rupees in cash alone. These successes naturally emboldened Sambhaji's men, and the Portuguese captains, convoying the grain boats from the south, were alarmed at the news that Angria's fleet was waiting for them. Their relief may be imagined when they shortly afterwards learnt that Sambhaji had sighted two Dutch vessels, captured them and carried them to Gheria, leaving his principal opponents to bring their much needed provisions safely to port [64]. Had he waited a little longer, Sambhaji might have intercepted the whole fleet. This would have involved the earlier capitulation of Bassein, but Sambhaji cared more for his own immediate profit than for the rapid success of the Peshwa's arms.

The capture of the two Dutch ships was a tactical blunder. For, the next year witnessed the appearance of a Dutch fleet of eight men-of-war and some light vessels near the bar of Agoada intent upon making a demonstration

61. Relacao dos successos acontesidos no Estado da India (Archivo Ultramarino of Lisbon, fundo geral, No. 929) fol. 4.

62. Relaçao dos successos acontesidos no Estado da India (Archivo Ultramarino of Lisbon, fundo geral, No. 929,) fol. 15.

62a. A pinnace.

63. Varias Cartas da Asia ao Conde de Unhao (Bibliotheca Publica of Evora, Cod. CCX/2-1) letter dated 30th December, 1738. Also see Relacao da guerra que o Inimigo Marata fes no Estado da India (Archivo Ultramarino, fundo geral, No. 1605), fol. 25.

64. Relaçao da guerra que o Inimigo Marata fes no Estado da India (Archivo Ultramarino, fundo geral, No. 1605), fols. 28-29.

against Gheria, one of Sambhaji's naval strongholds. The Portuguese Viceroy, anxious to exploit every opportunity, at once proposed an alliance with the Dutch not only against the Angria, against whom they had a legitimate grievance, but also against the Marathas. The principle he advocated was that all European nations should act in concert against their Asiatic enemies. Nothing, however, came out of these negotiations, and the Dutch fleet soon left the Malabar coast without effecting any thing[65].

What he had omitted to do in 1738 Sambhaji tried to accomplish in 1739. The Portuguese frigate, *Nossa Senhora da Victoria*, had convoyed 47 *Parangues* laden with salt to the ports of the south. As usual, on their return journey they were laden with rice for Goa and found Sambhaji's fleet of seven *Gallivats* and ten *Pals* ready to contest their advance near Mangalore. The Portuguese frigate carried thirty-two pieces of artillery and was commanded by Antonio de Brito Freire, an officer of long experience and great reputation. On the 5th of March he left the *Parangues* in the harbour and boldly sallied out to fight, whereupon the Maratha fleet at once divided into two squadrons and attacked the frigate. The battle raged for a whole day, but the superior artillery of the Portuguese enabled them to inflict some damage on two of the Angria's *Pals*. These injuries were repaired under cover of night, and the battle was renewed the following morning without, however, any better results. The Angria's fleet eventually retired before the guns of their enemies, and Antonio de Brito Freire conducted the *Parangues* safely to Goa [66].

Manaji Angria, however, was more fortunate in his naval operations than his brother. A few days after Sambhaji's

65. Relaçao dos successos acontesidos no Estado da India (Archivo Ultramarino, fundo geral. No. 929), fol. 25. *Press List of Ancient Dutch Records, from 1657 to 1825*. (Madras Records Department), p. 26.

66. Relaçao dos successos acontesidos no Estado da India (Archivo Ultramarino, fundo geral, No. 929), fol. 29; Relacao da batalha naval que a nau Nossa Senhora da Victoria teve na costa do sul (Archivo Ultramarino, caixa 26, X, 5, 15 No. 2) Diogo da Costa, *Relacam das guerras da India desde o anno de 1736 ate o de 1740*, p. 149.

defeat near Mangalore, Manaji proceeded against the island of Karanja with forty *Gallivats* and 2,000 men. He safely effected a landing and the garrison capitulated on the 21st March after a seige of only five days. Manaji then proceeded to lay seige to the Portuguese port of Chaul [67].

On the 23rd May, 1739, the Marathas took possession of Bassein, but the capitulation did not bring immediate peace. In 1740 the two Angria brothers inflicted more loss on the Portuguese than they had ever suffered within living memory, and such prestige as had attended their declining fortunes owing to the naval victory of Mangalore was entirely obliterated. Sambhaji's fleet first met the Portuguese frigate, *Oliviera*. near Gheria but after a few hours fighting left it alone and proceeded southwards along the coast. It entered Onore to obtain some masts and there got news of certain Portuguese grain boats sailing under a strong convoy from the south. Some stray Portuguese ships, which had been warned of the movements of the Maratha fleet, effected their escape by hard rowing [68]; but the main flotilla, unaware of the near approach of the enemy, advanced without suspicion. The convoy consisted of two *Pals*, two galleys and a *Charrua*. The Maratha victory was swift and complete. After little or no resistance the Portuguese Admiral surrendered, and practically the whole of the grain fleet fell into Sambhaji's hands. So confident was Angria of his naval power that on his way to Gheria, he passed with his valuable prize within sight of Anjidiv and at a little distance of Agoada; but the Portuguese attempted no rescue. To the credit of the Maratha Chief it must be remarked that his prisoners were not ill-treated. He set them at liberty, treated them courteously and sent them back to Goa. The Portuguese chronicler, who bitterly laments this disaster, was not willing, however, to give Sambhaji Angria his due. His generous treatment of the captives was attributed to his parsimony, coupled with an

67. Relaçao dos successos acontesidos no Estado da India (Archivo Ultramarino, fundo geral, No. 929), fols. 36 and 41.

68. Diario das Viagens de Piloto Francisco Pessoa de Magalhaes (Bibliotheca Publica of Evora Cod. CXVI/2-10).

insinuation that he restored the Portuguese Admiral and his colleagues to libeity to save their boarding expenses [69].

This was not the only disaster that befell the Portuguese in this unlucky year. Manaji captured a *Pataxo* of war belonging to the Diu fleet. By a clever stratagem the vessel had been lured on by a single ship, and it discovered too late that behind the harmless bait waited four *Pals* of Manaji[70] Both the brothers were able seamen and but for their mutual dissension they might have easily accomplished their father's ambition—the conquest of the whole coast from Bombay to Goa. But unluckily they could not compose their differences, and the same year that witnessed their success against the Portuguese also found them fighting bitterly against one another.

Sambhaji was the aggressor on this occasion. Unreconciled to the loss of Kolaba, he was only waiting for a suitable opportunity to recover it from his brother. Early in April he suddenly landed at Alibag, captured Hirakot and Sagargad, and then laid siege to Kolaba. Manaji in his distress appealed to the Peshwa and the English for help. He had not been always friendly to the English, and only a year previously the Bombay Government had found it necessary to chastise him. But though they disliked Manaji, they feared Sambhaji more, and neither the Peshwa nor the English could afford to be indifferent witnesses of Manaji's ruin, which would mean a further increase of Sambhaji's power. A Maratha force under Balaji Baji Rao and an English naval squadron almost simultaneously appeared before Kolaba, and Sambhaji had to beat a hasty and ignominious retreat[71].

This discomfiture must have convinced Sambhaji of the necessity of some alliances even if he had been totally

69. Relaçao dos successos acontesidos no Estado da India (Archivo Ultramarino, fundo geral, No. 929), fol. 49.

70. Ibid, fol. 50.

71. Manaji let his brother escape when he found that the Peshwa was exploiting his adversity; otherwise Sambhaji's fleet would have been completely destroyed, as he was caught between the Peshwa's land force and the English fleet.

ignorant of a clause aimed against him in the treaty which the Portuguese concluded later with the new Peshwa. His relations with the English and the Portuguese were equally bad, but these were the only two powers whose alliance was worth securing. Though he had captured the *Derby* in 1735, he had a taste of the English naval power when his fleet fled before Commodore Bagwell's squadron in 1738, and in 1739 he made overtures to the English Government for peace. His father in a similar situation would not have been very arrogant about the terms; but Sambhaji was not endowed with his father's diplomatic moderation. "He demanded that the English should provide all their trading vessels with his passes, and pay him 200,000 Rupees annually for the free navigation of the seas." These terms were at once rejected as "absurdly extravagant"[72]. The next year his unsuccessful encounter with the *Harrington* did not improve his relations with Bombay; and, convinced of the futility of his attempt to win the friendship of the English, he turned his attention southwards. He was not at peace with the Portuguese, and in November 1741 his fleet again fought, though without success, a Portuguese vessel. But alliance and hostilities in those days were always uncertain and lasted just as long as they suited the interests and the convenience of the parties concerned, and Sambhaji shared at least a common hatred with the Portuguese. Neither party had any reason to love the Peshwa. Even during the fateful years that preceded the fall of Bassein, while openly fighting against the owners of Goa, the two Angria brothers are proved by some letters in the eighth volume of the Livros dos Reis Visinhos to have been secretly coquetting with them. His approaches, therefore, could not be characterised as abrupt. What terms he actually offered we do not know, for his letter has not been preserved; but the answer that the Marquis of Louriçal addressed to him on the 2nd December[73] made a

72. Sambhaji had made several attempts to come to terms with the English, but the English were unwilling to allow him to recapture Kolaba, which was Sambhaji's sole object in seeking English friendship.

73. Livros dos Reis Visinhos, (Goa), Vol. IX, fol. 148.

complimentary reference to his father "the great Canogi Angria" and the "firmness of his word". Sambhaji was invited to depute a reliable person to Goa with a view to concluding a treaty against their common enemies. But this letter probably did not reach Sambhaji, who died ten days later on the 12th of December, 1741.

Of the numerical strength of Kanhoji Angria's fleet, the conditions of his service and the naval strategy of his age, we have no very clear knowledge; but, fortunately, an obscure pamphlet published in 1738 by a friend of Captain Anselm of the *Derby* in defence of the Captain's character, throws some light on Sambhaji's tactics, and on the numerical strength of his fleet in 1736, when Captain Anselm was his prisoner. Sambhaji was a hard-working man, as we learn from the Captain, and personally supervised everything. His men, including the gunners among whom there were some Europeans, were very poorly and irregularly paid and had no share in the prizes they seized. A very small fraction of their salary was paid in cash, the highest officers receiving only "one month and a half's pay out of twelve in money", "the rest one month's pay", "and some but half a month in twelve". When the *Derby* was captured, the men were in arrears for eighteen months. To meet their daily needs, they received food and clothing from their master. It was he who planned every expedition, and on their return the men were thoroughly searched. None could leave Suvarnadurg without Sambhaji's knowledge and permission, and everyone was expected to pay his respects to the Chief in the morning so that he could easily discover who was absent[74].

"Sambhaji", says Captain Anselm, "got seven of his Grabbs afloat, which was all he intended to launch, not having men for his other two. He has in all thirty fighting Gallivats, rowing with thirty oars and upwards; 14 of which are very large carrying six Guns"[75]. Nearly twenty years later, in 1754,

74. *A Faithful Narrative of the Capture of the Ship Derby*, pp 110-111, also see pp. 107-108.

75. *A Faithful Narrative of the Capture of the Ship Derby*, p. 101.

Edward Ives found the band of the Angria's fleet to consist of "a plain brass tube, shaped like a trumpet at both ends, and about ten feet in length; and a kind of drum called *Tom tom*, being a skin stretched out on a large shallow brass-pan, on which they struck with two large sticks "[76]. Probably these instruments constituted the military band in Sambhaji's time also.

About the up-keep of Sambhaji's men-of-war Captain Anselm writes:—" He keeps his Grabbs in very good order; every cruise they are hauled ashore, cleaned and breem'd, and their bottoms well oil'd[77]. They mount 16 guns, but their prow-guns do the most execution. If a ship has anything of an appearance, they send a Gallivat to see what she is. They will not come near unless it is a calm; and to a ship that does not feel her helm, they will slide a knot or two. They row with eight oars on their prow, and by the help of the Gallivats (as each Grabb has one to attend to it). I have seen them go at the rate of three knots. They will be under the stern of a ship and can never miss hitting with their guns "[77a]. Sambhaji did not issue any written instructions to his officers but gave his orders publicly, and when they had sailed, some of their relatives were sent into the fort probably as hostages. The Angria fleet generally kept close to the coast, though not invariably, as Captain Anselm learnt to his cost.

Of their method of fighting, Benjamin Hall, Purser of the *Derby*, has left the following account:—" Their manner of fighting a ship is as follows. Their Grabbs and Gallivats, be there never so many of them in number, always keep astern of our ships, or any other they may engage, and so close, that there is no danger of their missing you when they fire their prow-guns, which were six-pounders. They tack and give you a Broad-side, and so shear off and load again. But in the mean time another Grabb comes up, and fire on us in

76. Ives, *A Voyage from England to India in the Year MDCCLIV*, p. 43.

77. Stavorinus says that the use of this oil served to make the planks last longer. See *Voyage to the East Indies*, Vol. III, p. 22, Foot-Note.

77a. *A Faithful Narrative of the Capture of the Ship Derby*, pp. 52-53.

the same manner, and so goes off, that the next may come up. This is the method they take, till they have all fired round, when the first comes up again. As to their Gallivats. they run in between the Grabbs, and keep constantly firing at you. Their Grabbs are the oddest built vessels you ever saw; they have a very long prow, which is almost even with the surface of the Water, and very high-sterned. They carry 16 Guns each, and 150 men, all in arms proper for boarding any vessels. But in time of engagement, they are all, excepting the Gunners who manage their Guns, under Deck, where there is little danger of killing them with our Guns. These vessels are built purposely for fighting and they manage them with so much dexterity, that they can tack on you any way in a moment, and always keep their Grabbs astern, so that we shall not be able to bring a Broadside to bear on them. As to their Gallivats, they carry six guns each, and sixty armed men, and are always ready to supply their Grabbs with ammunition and men, in case of any accident "[78].

These accounts show that the Maratha navy had not yet emerged from the primitive galley stage. The seamen had, indeed, learnt to make a skilful use of their sails, but as both the English and the Portuguese agree that they always preferred a calm sea for a naval engagement, it is clear that their strategy depended rather upon oar than upon canvas. Their Gunners were often foreigners; and Muslim Captains were still welcomed in the Angria's service. Inferior as it was to the fighting fleets of contemporary Europe, Sambhaji Angria's navy enjoyed a great reputation on the Malabar coast and was considered an excellent school for naval training. Both Ismail Khan, whom the Portuguese writers delighted to style as 'valoroso' or valiant, and Apaji Gopal, the Commander-in-Chief of Gaikwad's fleet, who had earned the encomiums of his Portuguese opponents by his intrepedity and skill, began their naval career in Sambhaji's service [79]. But the Maratha navy was like a child of arrested growth. It

78. *A Faithful Narrative of the Capture of the Ship Derby*, pp. 52-53.
79. F. R. de Moraes Pereira, *Annal Indico Lusitano*, p. 79.

progressed satisfactorily up to a certain stage and then ceased to progress.

Sambhaji's death failed to restore unity in the Angria family. Tulaji succeeded his brother in the principality of Suvarnadurg, while Manaji continued to rule at Kolaba, and the breach between the two brothers was as wide as in Sambhaji's time. Manaji had been very shabbily treated by the Peshwa, some of his forts were taken by Sadashiv Rao, and he bitterly complained to Shahu of the ungracious treatment meted out to him, but even the common antagonism to the Peshwa could not induce the two brothers to forget their family feud and offer united opposition to deliberate aggression from Poona. On the other hand, Manaji was openly jealous of his younger brother and claimed that, as the elder of the two, he should be honoured with his father's title of *Sarkhel.* Shahu seems to have hinted that this honour could only be earned by some distinguished deed of valour, and Tulaji proceeded to prove his superior ability by capturing Anjanvel. Manaji, however, did not despair, and resolved to win the higher title of *Sawai Sarkhel* by some noteworthy achievement. On the 8th November, 1774, he attacked the Portuguese merchant fleet with nine *Pals* and eight *Gallivats*[80]. The combat lasted for six days and five nights, during which, as we are informed by Jose Freire M. Mascarenhas, the Portuguese had only a brief respite of two hours in the evening, while the Hindu sailors of Angria's fleet laid down their arms and performed their daily worship. The Portuguese convoy consisted of two frigates only, *Nossa Senhora da Oliveira* and *Penha da Franca*; but they fought valiantly against the superior squadron of Manaji, who at length withdrew without accomplishing his purpose. After this he seems to have attempted to cultivate the friendship of the Portuguese. The Marquis of Alorna writes that Manaji had always solicited his friendship and, since his arrival in India,

80. Varias Cartas da Asia ao Conde de Unhao (Bibliotheca Publica of Evora, Cod 2-1/CXX) Letter of Pedro Vicenti Vidal, dated Bombay, the 24th November, 1744.

he had received repeated offers of co-operation from Manaji against Balaji Baji Rao [81].

Tulaji also was aware of the designs that the Peshwa had against him, but, like his brother Sambhaji, he was no diplomat. Although tentative proposals for peace were made by him from time to time, no systematic or serious effort was made to compose his differences with the Portuguese until 1755, when he found himself on the brink of ruin. In 1748 and 1749, Tulaji was at peace with the Governor of Goa; in the previous year he had even sent one Rudraji Dhulap to Goa to negotiate an alliance [82]; but the resources at the disposal of the Viceroy were so very inadequate that he was forced to return a non-committal reply. In 1749, a naval action had actually commenced between Tulaji's fleet and a Portuguese frigate, when Captain Antonio de Britto Sancho received information from the Maratha Admiral that he had commenced the attack without knowing the nationality of the frigate, but, as he was on friendly terms with the Portuguese, he would no longer interfere with its journey [83]. In 1751, however, Tulaji captured two boats belonging to Portuguese subjects; in the following year he renewed his proposals for an alliance against the Sardesai of Kudal, but did not hesitate at the same time to attack the frigate *Mizericordia* off Calicut in December. In the five hours' fighting that followed, the Angria's fleet suffered severely from the Portuguese fire [84] and had to retire. These occasional defeats, however, made little impression on his power, for in 1753, a Portuguese writer compared him with the Hydra [85] which was furnished with a fresh head from every wound it received. The Marchioness of Tavora rightly wrote

81. *Instruccao do Ex mo Vice-Rei Marquez de Alorna*, p. 25.

82. *Epanaphora Indica*, Pt. VI, pp. 61-62.

83. *Epanaphora Indica*, Pt. VI, p. 18.

84. Balthazar Manoel de Chaves, *Annal Indico Historico do governo do illustrissimo e excellentissimo Senhor Marquez de Tavora*, Pt. III, pp. 80-84.

85. *Relacam Verdadeira dos felices successos da India, e victorias que alcansaram as armas portuguezas naquelle Estado, em o anno de* 1752, pt. I, p. 1.

that his policy was uncertain and regulated by the needs of the moment [86].

The Portuguese were not the only European nation to suffer from Tulaji's fleet. The French and the Dutch had also suffered similar losses; but the English suffered most, probably because their mercantile interests were far superior to those of any other nation. On different occasions the Angria had seized and carried away the following vessels belonging to the East India Company or their subjects:—"The *Charlotte*, belonging to Madras, the *William* belonging to Bombay, the *Severn*, a Bengal freight ship, the *Derby*, the Grab *Restoration*, the Sloop *Pilot*, and the *Augusta*, the *Dadaboy* from Surat, the *Rose* from Mangalore, the Grab *Anne* from Gombroon, *Benjimolly* from the Malabar coast and the *Futte Dowlat* from Muscat." It is needless to remark that the heavy financial loss caused by the Angria brothers greatly exasperated the English, but their fleet and several strongholds were still considered invincible and all attempts against them had for nearly half a century proved futile. Mutually antagonistic and disunited as they were, the Angria brothers could still defy any single maritime power of the coast. Unfortunately for Tulaji he had to contend against a simultaneous invasion by the strongest sea power and the most formidable land force that India knew at that time. When Kolaba was attacked by the joint Anglo-Portuguese army in 1721, his father obtained strong reinforcements from Poona led by Peshwa Baji Rao in person; but when the English bombarded Suvarnadurg in 1755, the Peshwa's army co-operated with the invaders and Tulaji had no ally to befriend him.

Various conjectures have been made as to the cause of the Peshwa's attitude towards Tulaji. It has been suggested that Tulaji had failed to send the annual tribute and had further insulted the Peshwa by mutilating his messenger. It

86. Carta da Marqueza de Tavora que de Goa escreveo a' seus filhos, (Bibliotheca Publica of Evora) No. 25 of 2-11/CXVI. The letter is undated, but seems to have been written shortly after the assumption of the Government by her husband.

has also been hinted that Tulaji was a cruel persecutor of the Chitpavan Brahmans and that Balaji Baji Rao was consequently actuated by feelings of revenge. But the apologists of Balaji Baji Rao conveniently forget that fifteen years before the joint Anglo-Maratha assault on Suvarnadurg the Peshwa had provided for a Portuguese alliance against Angria in his treaty with that nation concluded at Poona in 1740. It should also be remembered that the docility of Manaji did not save him from unfair and unjust treatment. The Peshwa regarded the Angrias as possible rivals whose maritime power placed them in a position of special advantage. He could enforce his will on the Dabhades, on the Gaikwads and the Bhonslas but the Angrias were beyond his reach. That was the sole reason of his alliance with the English. The English of course welcomed this opportunity of removing the only power who could challenge their supremacy by sea; but the Peshwa gained practically nothing and only set a bad example to the other Maratha chiefs by co-operating with a foreign nation against one who claimed to be a subject of the Satara Raja. The story of Tulaji's fall need not detain us long. Negotiations for an alliance between the Peshwa and the Governor of Bombay had been opened early in 1755, and a treaty was concluded on the 29th March. But both allies had been busy with their military preparations and within three days of the conclusion of the pact Commodore James left Bombay with his fleet. Their first objective was Suvarnadurg and a joint attack was promptly made. After very little resistance the fort capitulated on the 3rd of April, but the Angria's fleet had already effected its escape. The Peshwa was eager to finish the war that year; but his fleet, though numerically considerable, was no match for that of Tulaji and he had to rely absolutely on the co-operation of the English squadron for the reduction of the Angria's naval stronghold. The English Commodore and his official superiors at Bombay were unwilling to expose their vessels to the fury of the monsoon and Gheria, the principal head-quarter of Tulaji, was, therefore, left unconquered when the campaign of the year came to a close.

The respite thus given to Tulaji enabled him to seek an ally. He applied for help to the Portuguese, who demanded a very heavy subsidy. Tulaji had no time to haggle and promptly paid a portion of the stipulated sum. On the 5th November 1755, a treaty was concluded, by which the Viceroy undertook to send a reinforcement of five hundred men to Gheria [87]. A Portuguese detachment had already been despatched to the Angria's head-quarters when an angry protest from the Peshwa reached Goa [88]. The palmy days of Portuguese authority in India had passed away and the Viceroy did not dare to offend the powerful leader of the Maratha State. The reinforcement was, therefore, quickly recalled on a hollow excuse that deceived nobody, and Tulaji was left to his doom. He could not count even on his own servants, for we learn from a Maratha chronicle that Ramaji Mahadev had bribed most of them. This statement is corroborated by the little resistance that the garrison of Suvarnadurg offered. Clive and Watson found the capture of Gheria as easy as James had found the reduction of Suvarnadurg. Despairing of success, Tulaji left the fort, and the garrison, in the absence of their master, did not exert themselves to defend it. Edward Ives, an eye witness, observes :—" the fort was so strong both by art and nature at the time we attacked it, that it might have held out a long time against all our efforts, had it been defended with any tolerable degree of skill and resolution "[88a]. The victors found in the fort 250 pieces of cannon, six mortars, an immense quantity of stores and ammunition. One hundred thousand pounds sterling in silver rupees and about thirty thousand more in valuable effects; but the great fleet which for sixty years had terrorised merchant vessels in the Arabian Sea was reduced to ashes either by the fire of Watson's fleet, as the English reports state, or by its despairing master, as the Portuguese account suggests, before the garrison capitulated. The last days of Tulaji were spent as a prisoner of the Peshwa. After his death his sons managed to reach Bombay, but all trace of them from that date is lost.

87. Biker, *Tratados da India;* Vol. VII, pp. 36-38.
88. Biker, *Tratados da India,* Vol. VII, pp. 42-46.
88a. Ives, *A Voyage from England to India,* p. 88.

The Portuguese papers mention a Raghunath Angria, who was a Captain in Hyder Ali's fleet, but there is no evidence forthcoming of his relation to Tulaji.

After the fall of Gheria the Angria tradition was maintained, though feebly, by the Kolaba branch of the family. Manaji's vessels had taken part in the expedition against Janjira in 1758, and after his death in that year his son assumed the command of the fleet. Raghuji took part in the conquest of Henery in 1760, and in 1778 captured a Portuguese sloop of war belonging to Diu, after which he concluded a treaty with the Government of Goa on terms of equality [89]. As certain changes in these terms were suggested from Lisbon this treaty was not ratified; but it shows that Raghuji, like his father and grand-father, deemed himself competent to conclude treaties and alliances with foreign powers without any reference to the Peshwa. John Mc Cluer, who surveyed the Malabar coast in 1787 and 1788, met Raghuji at his capital. He describes him as "an arrant pirate who will make free with any vessel he can manage." But he remarks that Raghuji "behaves very civil to any English vessel that goes nigh Kenery" which was in his possession [90].

As Raghuji may be rightly regarded as the last of the Angrias, we may here quote Mc Cluer's account of his interview with the Chief of Kolaba. "When we landed there was a numerous train to receive us, many of them Purvoes who spoke good English, and no doubt carry on a regular correspondence with their friends at Bombay. We were shewn to an open booth, near the gate of the fort, and there seated on a carpet till the great man came out. Some time before he made his appearance, his approach was noticed by the clashing of cymbals, and rattling of tomtoms. He came out in great state, attended with fifty or sixty armed men, whose arms were all covered with red clothes. At first I took them for flags that they carried. He received us very kindly, seemed very happy to see his friends, as he called us, and

89. Biker, *Tratados da India*, Vol. VIII, pp. 47-49.
90. Mc Cluer, *Description of the Coast of India*, p. 12 and also p. 11.

asked a number of questions which I knew wanted no answers, as he seemed well informed of everything transacted in Bombay. After a discourse of about half an hour upon various subjects, we took our leaves of him, and at parting we were almost suffocated with perfumes, and drowned with rose water. Nor did his civility end here, for he ordered a boat to attend us to the vessel, with a trey of sweetmeats, which part of the ceremony I could have gladly dispensed with, as it entirely prevented my sounding between the shore and the vessel "[91].

Though Raghuji could still indulge in the pomp and splendour associated with his house, its power for ever vanished with Tulaji. His fleet no doubt still rode the sea and harassed merchantmen, but no power except the Portuguese now feared the Angria's fleet. After Raghuji's death there was endless confusion in the small principality owing to the minority of his son and the ambition of his unscrupulous relatives. The remnant of the once powerful Kolaba fleet was burnt by a fire which broke out in the harbour. Its disappearance was of little moment, as the rising power of the English had long rendered it an anachronism. After the annexation of the Peshwa's territories, the Angria of Kolaba became a feudatory of the English and the small principality was annexed when its last representative died without an heir of his body in 1840 [92].

---

91. Mc Cluer, *Description of the Coast of India*, p. 14. Another Englishman who had a personal interview with Raghuji Angria was Forbes; see his *Oriental Memoirs*, Vol. I, pp. 133-136.

92. *Bombay Gazetteer*, Vol. XI, p. 157.

CHAPTER XII.

THE MARATHA FLEET UNDER THE PESHWAS

It is uncertain at what date the Peshwa first cast their eyes towards the sea and decided to extend their authority in that direction. The treaty of 1713 left the best ports and harbours in the possession of Kanhoji Angria, and no mention is made of the Peshwa's fleet either in the treaty concluded in January 1722 between Baji Rao and Francisco Jose de Sampaio e Castro or in the treaty of 1732 (1731-32 $\frac{\text{30 January}}{\text{10 February}}$) between Krishna Rao Mahadev, Governor of Kalyan, and Martinho de Silveira de Menezes, Captain General of the fortresses and lands of the North. But Baji Rao must have organised a navy sometime between this date and 1739, for reference is made to the Peshwa's fleet in Baji Rao's treaty with the English in 1739[1], as well as in the treaty of 1740-41 concluded between the Governments of Poona and Goa[2]. By 1750 the Peshwa's fleet had also begun to exercise authority by sea like the older navy of the Angrias; for on the 14th January 1751 Padre Angelo dos Serafins wrote from Goa to a friend in Portugal that in spite of the amity established between the two States by the treaty of Poona the Marathas did not desist from harassing Portuguese trading vessels at sea [3]. In 1755 Edward Ives saw the Peshwa's fleet near the harbour of Bombay [4]. He writes :—" During my stay at *Bombay* two fleets of country vessels came into the bay : One of them belong to the *Nanna* or prince of the *Maharattas*, the other to *Monagee Angria*, the brother of *Angria* the pirate. These vessels were not unlike the *Tartans* of the *Mediterranean*, only a great deal lower; they carried two

1. Forrest, *Selection from State Papers*, Appendix A. pp. 699-704.
2. Biker, *Tratados da India*, Vol. VI, p. 207.
3. Fr. Angelo dos Serafins, *Relacao da viagem que o illustrissimo Marquez de Tavora Vice-Rey do Estado da India fez do porto desta cidade de Lisboa ate o da cidade de Goa*, p. 8.
4. Ives, *A Voyage from England to India*, p. 43.

guns in the bow, and a vast number of men. *** Each fleet consisted of about 30 sail." But this was not the total strength of the Peshwa's fleet in the middle of the eighteenth century. It consisted of more than fifty vessels when it was sent to co-operate in the same year with Commodore James. As Commodore James complained of the cowardice of the Peshwa's fleet, stating that it rendered him no assistance but only caused loss of time, we may assume that the Peshwa had not yet been able to enlist experienced seamen. His Admiral was Naro Pant who, according to Captain Low, had earned some distinction as a soldier on land, but had had no experience of the sea [5].

Naro Pant still held the chief command of the Peshwa's fleet when Balaji Baji Rao attempted to conquer Janjira after the reduction of Gheria. Gheria, however, had been reduced by the prowess of Watson and the intrigues of Ramaji Mahadev and not by the valour of Naro Pant who preferred to lie behind whenever a bombardment was imminent. The Peshwa solicited English assistance in his attempts against Janjira, but here his interests were not identical with those of his late allies and they refused to fight against the Sidi. Henery was reduced by the joint efforts of the Kolaba fleet and the Peshwa's navy, though the exact share of the latter in this achievement is not specifically recorded. It soon became evident that the Peshwa's naval strength was very inadequate for the reduction of the Sidi's island and he applied for help to the Portuguese [6]. The Portuguese welcomed the suggestion and were sanguine about their success. But when they appeared near the island, they found the English flag flying there. The Portuguese were annoyed, but were not prepared for a war with the English. Henery was, therefore, occupied by the Peshwa's troops and a small squadron was stationed there, while the other island remained in possession of Raghuji Angria. The proximity of the two islands led, as Mc Cluer informs us, to constant bickerings between the two chiefs about the division of the spoils.

5. Low, *History of the Indian Navy*, Vol. I, p. 131.
6. Biker, *Tratados da India*, Vol. VII, pp. 175-179.

Foiled in their attempt against Janjira, the Peshwa's fleet employed itself for the next fifteen years in their ordinary work of issuing passports and seizing ships that did not possess them. These duties could not always be effected without fighting. In 1763, for example, the Peshwa's captains seized a Dutch ship off Anjidiv[7]; they also took a Danish vessel, which was rescued later by a Portuguese squadron[8]. The Portuguese themselves lost several boats, as Conde de Ega informed the home authorities in 1764[9]. The Maratha fleet, he wrote, infested the sea and respected no nation except the English. They had in the previous year captured a Portuguese ship of Macao, a *Pal* belonging to Mozambique and some small vessels belonging to the traders of Portuguese India. Their loss might have been much heavier had the Maratha Admiral been better versed in the art of navigation, for both the north and the south going Portuguese merchant fleets had been attacked by numerically superior Maratha squadrons[10]. In 1767, the Maratha fleet of 6 *Pals* and 54 *Gallivats* attacked Portuguese squadron of one *Pal* and four *Manchuas* convoying a big merchant flotilla near Gheria but after two hours' obstinate fighting the Peshwa's fleet had to retire[11]. Gheria still continued to be a point of danger for merchant fleets, though its prestige had evidently much declined since the days of Sambhaji and Tulaji Angria.

During the first Maratha war, the Peshwa's fleet caused some anxiety to the Bombay Government, who wrote thus to the Governor-General and Council :—" As a considerable part of our marine force is employed at Bassora and in the Persian Gulf, we have at present not a sufficient marine force for the protection of our trade on the Coast of Malabar from the Maratha fleet, which, it is most probable, will attempt

7. Officios dos Governadores, (Archivo Ultramarino, of Lisbon) Maco 2, Letter No. 4, 20th January, 1764.

8. Ibid.

9. Officios dos Governadores (Archivo Ultramarino of Lisbon) Maco 2, Letter No. 15, dated 20th January, 1764.

10. Officios dos Governadores (Archivo Ultramarino of Lisbon) Maco 2, Letter No. 4, 20th January, 1764.

11. Officios dos Governadores, Maco 12, No. 21.

making some depredations on it "[12]. But actually little damage was done, and the Maratha fleet proved vastly inferior to that of its English opponents. Only two naval actions were fought during this war. The first took place in 1755 near Gheria. The frigate *Revenge* and the Ghurab *Bombay* encountered the Maratha fleet near that port. The latter tried to flee, but one of their largest ships, the *Shamsher Jang*, was overtaken. After three hours' fighting the Maratha man-of-war blew up and the Captain perished with most of his crew[13]. The second action, which was fought after the conclusion of peace, was lost by the English. The *Ranger*, a small brig of twelve guns, was conveying from Bombay to Calicut a number of high military officials, when it encountered the Maratha fleet under Anand Rao Dhulap, the best known, if not the ablest of the Peshwa's naval officers. The Maratha Admiral was ignorant of the termination of war, and the English Captain chose not to enlighten him. After a most stubborn fight the *Ranger* was captured and carried to Gheria, but not before the great majority of the men on board had been either killed or wounded. The *Ranger* was restored to the English Government as soon as Anand Rao Dhulap learnt of the conclusion of peace [14].

In 1787 the Maratha Government proposed an alliance with the Portuguese, soliciting their co-operation in naval engagements against Tipu's fleet. This clearly shows that the fleet [15] had not yet earned the full confidence of the Poona Government, and, six years later when they planned for the last time the conquest of Janjira, they again deemed it necessary to purchase the co-operation of their Portuguese neighbours[16].

The last achievement of the Peshwa's fleet was the capture of Ximpi [17] in 1791. The Portuguese Government had

12. Forrest, *Selections from State Papers*, Maratha Series, p. 208.
13. Low, *History of the Indian Navy*, Vol. I, pp. 156-157.
14. Low, *History of the Indian Navy*, Vol. I, pp. 157-159.
15. Officios dos Governadores, Maco 20, Letter No. 95, 12th March, 1787; Biker, *Tratados da India*, Vol. VII, pp. 221-222.
16. Officios dos Governadores, Maco 29, Letter No. 37, 12th March, 1793.
17. Officios dos Governadores, Maco 26, Letter No. 33, 18th April, 1791.

planned to forestall the Marathas and occupy the stronghold of Piro on their own account, but in the name of their protege the Raja of Sunda, Babu Rao Saloc [17a], the Maratha Admiral, took possession of the neighbouring island of Ximpi with two big *Pals* of 3 masts, 2 *Ghurabs* and 4 *Gallivats*. As Ximpi was fortified both by nature and by art and was deemed almost impregnable, the Portuguese were greatly surprised at its speedy reduction by the Maratha fleet. After this the Maratha fleet proceeded to Onore, where it divided into two squadrons. One of these started for the north, while the other waited at the port with the intention of capturing a ship belonging to their enemy, Tipu Sultan[17b]. On the whole, it may be safely asserted that the record of the Peshwa's fleet was neither great nor glorious, and, while the Maratha horseman has left a reputation behind him, the existence of the Maratha sailor will hardly be suspected by the average student of Indian History to-day.

We have more precise knowledge about the internal administration of the navy under the Peshwas than in the previous periods. The military head of the navy was the Subhedar or Admiral. The first Admiral of the fleet, of whom we know nothing but the name, was Baji Rao Bekse. He was succeeded in his office by his son Trimbak Rao in 1749-50. The Admiral then enjoyed a salary of 1,000 Rupees a year besides allowances in cash and kind which amounted to 186 Rupees in cash and 16½ maunds of grain [18]. Thirteen years later, however, we find that the revenue of some *Mahals* was granted to Anand Rao Dhulap for meeting the expenses of the fleet in which his own salary and allowances were undoubtedly included [19].

The civil administration of the fleet was at first vested in certain hereditary officers commonly styled *Darakhdars.*

17a. This is the Portuguese spelling of Babu Rao's surname, the more accurate transliteration would be Salokhe.

17b. Officios dos Governadores, Maco 27, Letter No. 30, 19th April, 1791.

18. *Peshwas' Diaries*, Vol. III, p. 185.

19. *Peshwas' Diaries*, Vol. IX, p. 339.

They were clerks by profession, and although the muster rolls and the accounts of the navy demanded little technical knowledge, the purchase of provisions for the navy and the repair of old and damaged ships in particular could not be satisfactorily performed by civil servants, who had no knowledge of the needs of the fleet. In 1765-66, therefore, a *Karbhari* and an *Amin* were appointed to supervise the civil administration of the fleet and the Admiral was also associated with them in this work [19a]. The *Amin* was generally responsible for the accounts, muster rolls, purchase of provision, etc. Even this arrangement did not prove entirely satisfactory, and in 1781-82 the *Darakhdars* were recalled and Anand Rao Dhulap became the undisputed civil and military head of the Peshwa's fleet. He was directed to fit out a fleet of three *Pals*, three *Ghurabs* and thirteen *Gallivats*, and to meet the expenses of the fleet from the revenue of the *Mahals* granted for the purpose as well as from the income derived from prizes taken at sea for not possessing Maratha passports. The Admiral was further empowered to impress the service of carpenters, black smiths and cobblers living in the districts granted to him [20].

The salaries of the ordinary sailors and petty officers of the navy were as follows during the regime of Balaji Baji Rao [21].

Sar Tandel	... Rs.	10-0 per month.
Tandel	... ,,	7-8 ,, ,,
Sailor	... ,,	4-8 to 5 per month.

Besides this they received a food allowance in kind which varied with the rank of the men. In 1782-83 the salary of a soldier serving in the navy including all allowances was 65 Rupees per year; that of a sailor 61 Rupees 8 annas, while a gunner drew a slightly higher salary, viz., 67 Rupees 8 annas[22].

The officers and sailors of the navy were suitably rewarded by the Peshwas for good service in war. Madhav Rao I distributed Rs. 4,250 among officers and sailors of the navy for

19a. *Peshwas' Diaries*, Vol. IX, pp. 340-343.
20. *Peshwas' Diaries*, Vol. VI, pp. 195-196.
21. *Peshwas' Diaries*, Vol. III, pp. 186-187.
22. *Peshwas' Diaries*, Vol. VI, pp. 196-198.

their services against Hyder Ali. Three officers, Damaji Naik Kuveskar, Shivaji Rao Surve and Vithoji Naik Bamkar were given Rs. 300, Rs. 250 and Rs. 200 respectively. Balaji Hari Fadnis received Rs. 500 and to *Serangs* and sailors were allotted Rs. 3,000 in all [23].

From our brief survey of the naval history of the Marathas it will be apparent that during the 150 years of its existence the Maratha navy made no progress either in the art of navigation or in the method of warfare. Mc Cluer visited the principal ports of the coast in 1787 and 1788 and left a brief account of the Maratha ships and their method of attack:— " They send," he tells us, " 2 large ketches, with a number of gallivats to cruize; each gallivat carrying 80 or 90 men armed with lances, musquets, and stones. One large carriage-gun is lashed down in their prows to the beams with strong ropes, so I suppose when the gun fires the vessel recoils with it "[24]. Compare with this the accounts of Angria's ships and the method of attack left by Captain Anselm and Benjamin Hall fifty-three years previously, and they will be seen to tally in every detail. The ships were similarly manned, similarly armed and similarly manœuvred for a century and half while immense improvement was being effected in naval engineering and naval strategy in the west. The Marathas knew and acknowledged the superiority of the European's at sea; they considered the naval superiority of the western nations as a possible source of danger; but they made no effort to learn, to improve or to invent. In 1679 Daulat Khan's fleet of sixty sails fled before a single English man-of-war; in 1739 a single Portuguese frigate defeated Sambhaji Angria's squadron of seventeen vessels; in 1752, again, a single Portuguese ship beat back an Angrian fleet of twenty-one; while in 1767 an unequal combat between 60 Maratha men-of-war and five Portuguese vessels ended in the discomfiture of the numerically superior fleet. While European sailors traversed the oceans and the seas of the world the Maratha preferred

23. *Peshwas' Diaries*, Vol. IX, p. 344.

24. Mc Cluer, *Description of the Coast of India*, p. 25.

to hug the coast; while the European captain was armed with the best artillery of the age, the Maratha still retained his lance and spear, bow and arrow, and even that pre-historic weapon, an unhewn stone. In war as well as in civilization there must be progress or decline; as the Maratha sailor did not or could not go forward, he was gradually relegated to the background. This fate was inevitable; for nature planned the survival of the fittest, and in war the strongest is the fittest, and the strongest must survive. In primitive times mere physical strength sufficed for battle; but in the eighteenth century war had already become scientific and a constant intellectual effort was required to maintain military and naval efficiency. The Maratha soldier and the Maratha sailor were both temperamentally conservative. They clung steadfastly to the ways of their forefathers, and in consequence sank into hopeless decrepitude.

CHAPTER XIII.

PIRACY OR SOVEREIGNTY OF THE SEA.

The downfall of the Maratha naval power was due to its inefficiency, but prejudice has handed down the names of the Maratha captains as pirates. Naval practices both in Asia and Europe have undergone revolutionary changes since the days of Kanhoji Angria and Anand Rao Dhulap, and the freedom of the sea in times of peace, if not in times of war, is to-day accepted as an axiom of international relations. Their interference, therefore, with free navigation and appropriation of alien vessels wrecked on the coast at once condemn the Maratha admirals as guilty of piracy in the eyes of a generation that does not know how universal these practices were one hundred and fifty years ago on the Malabar coast, if not elsewhere. And it is generally ignored that the Marathas were not the only nation guilty of such practices. They were simply following the precedents of their European neighbours.

The first European nation to reach the Indian waters in modern times were the Portuguese. Their powerful navy gave them an overwhelming advantage over the Indian princes and they were resolved to make the fullest use of it. They claimed the sovereignity of the sea and compelled all powers, friendly or otherwise, to respect their claim. None were allowed to navigate the Arabian Sea or the Indian Ocean without their express permission, and such permission had to be purchased by every trading vessel. Even Indian sovereigns were not exempted from this acknowledgement of Portuguese naval supremacy. In 1534 Bahadur Shah of Gujarat concluded a treaty with Nuno da Cunha, and one of the clauses clearly laid down that all ships sailing from Bahadur Shah's ports would have to come to Bassein to take *cartaz* from the officers of the King of Portugal, whatever might be their destination, exception being made only in favour of ships going to Mecca [1].

1. Biker, *Tratados da India*, Vol. I, p. 63.

16

In 1547 Joao de Castro conceded to King Nizamshah free *cartazes* for five ships only, on condition that they should not give passage to any Turk [2]. In 1548 similar favours were granted to the Sultan of Bijapur by a treaty[3], but in another treaty concluded with that prince in 1574 it was stipulated that if any vessel sailing without Portuguese *cartazes* was seized in a port of Adilshah by his subjects, half of the prize should belong to the Portuguese and the other half to King Adilshah even if the captured boat happened to be the property of one of his subjects [4]. But it was not the Muhammadan princes alone who were subjected to these humiliating terms. In 1631 Virappa Naik, King of Canara, and the Zamorin of Calicut undertook not to allow any vessel to enter or leave their ports unless it had been furnished with Portuguese *cartaz* [5]. Only small rowing vessels were allowed free ingress and egress.

When other European nations came to India by the maritime route, the Portuguese attempted to shut them out of the Indian trade by exercising the sovereignty of the sea, which they claimed and which their Indian neighbours had to respect. In 1608 the ships of William Hawkins with their crew and cargo were seized and taken away by the Portuguese Captain-mor, and when he expostulated with a Portuguese officer, he was quietly told that " these seas belonged unto the King of Portugal, and none ought to come here without his license ". The angry Captain swore, fulminated and challenged his adversary, but to no effect[6]. Three years later, Sir Henry Middleton met with similar opposition from a Portuguese Admiral. He writes :—" The nine and twentieth, there came a small Portugall frigat from the Admirall of the Armada (as they terme them) wherein was one Portugall and his boy who brought me answer of my letter sent the day before from the Captaine Major, wherein hee used some complements certifying me that he was glad to heare I

2. Biker, *Tratados da India,* Vol. I, pp. 120-122.
3. Biker, *Tratados da India,* Vol. I, pp. 122-127.
4. Biker, *Tratados da India,* Vol. I, pp. 160-167.
5. Biker, *Tratados da India,* Vol. I, pp. 270-275; and 281-293.
6. *Purchas, His Pilgrimes,* Vol. III, pp. 4-5.

belonged to a King a friend, and that he and his would be readie to doe mee service in anything he might, provided I brought a letter or order from the King of Spaine or the Vice-Roy, for my trading in these parts, which if I could shew him, he would willingly obey; if otherwise, he must guard the port he had in charge, where the King his Master had his factorie "[7].

The Portuguese power in the east gradually declined, but they did not give up this claim. Towards the close of the seventeenth century, the Italian traveller, Gemelli Careri, still found them exercising this right. He writes :—" So that being become formidable to all the Princes of *Asia*, they had made all the Country about Tributary; and being Sovereigns of the vast Ocean by means of their mighty fleets, no ship of any Nation whatsoever could sail those Seas without their Leave and Pass; seizing the Ships and Goods, and Imprisoning the Men for presuming to Sail without their Protection. This authority the Portugueses, tho weak, still exercise over all Ships of Moors and Gentils; for the *Europeans* are got above it "[8].

In the next century also the Portuguese " still exercised this authority over all ships of Moors and Gentils "[9]. Among the instructions issued by the Viceroy, Conde de Sandomil, on the 12th September, 1735, occurs the following:— " Whenever the captain takes or sees a ship he will immediately send for its *cartaz* and if it does not possess one or possesses only an old *cartaz* or if it is discovered that the ship has made a voyage to a forbidden port or carries forbidden cargo, he shall formally cause it to be taken and have the date and the latitude where the capture took place and whether there was any fighting or not, recorded through his scribe "[10]. In 1736 Antonio de Britto Freire was expressly ordered to give chase to all ships he might meet on his way, if he could do so without any prejudice to his voyage or to

7. *Purchas, His Pilgrimes,* Vol. II, pp. 172-173.
8. Chuichill's *Voyages,* Vol. IV, p. 220.
9. Ibid.
10. Toma que hao' de guardar as Capitaens de mar e guerra ou quaesquer outros das embarcacoens de Estado no tomar das prezas (Bibliotheca publica of Evora. Cod CXV/1-5) fol. 3.

the safety of the *cafilla* he was convoying [11]. The same instructions were repeated on the 13th September, 1737, and the 5th September, 1738, when the same officer was entrusted with the responsibility of convoying Portuguese merchant fleets [12].

It is needless to say that if such orders were issued to Portuguese naval officers in the middle of the eighteenth century when the Portuguese naval power was undoubtedly on the wane, they had sent out their fleet in earlier times with the sole purpose of taking prizes. The Dutch Governor-General and the Council of India wrote to the Directors of the Dutch East India Company in 1668:—"The Portuguese vessels are now mostly engaged in piracy, they principally attack ships belonging to Canara several of which had been brought to the port of Goa"[13]. In the previous year the Portuguese Government had actually suggested to the Dutch that they should join their naval forces and make prize of Moorish ships in the Indian waters, as such an enterprise would be immensely profitable [14]. In 1682 Captain Smith of the *Returne*, while sailing from Bombay, obtained among others the following instruction:—"Whereas the Portuguese have beene lately very insolent and were so bold as to fire at the *Eagle*; if you should meete with any of them offer noe affront or violence to them; but if they fire at you and assault you defend yourselfe the best you can"[15].

But the Portuguese were not the only nation who made use of their maritime power against weaker states and denied to them the right of free navigation. On the 11th February, 1664, the Dutch East India Company concluded a treaty with "Adersia, Ruler and Chief of the Moors, in the countries

11. Regimento com que sahy commandando a Armada da costa do Norte em 11 de dezembro 1736 (Bibliotheca publica of Evora; Cod. CXV/1-35, fol. 3).

12. Bibliotheca Publica of Evora Cod CXV/1-35 fol. 34.

13. Dutch Records, India Office transcripts, English translation, Vol. 29, p. 13, No. DCCXL.

14. Dutch Records, India office transcripts, English translation, Vol. 29, Letter No. DCCXXXVII, dated 20th March, 1667.

15. Factory Records, Surat, Vol. 4, fols. 122-123.

under the King Kalatry ", by which they not only secured a monopoly of the spice trade of the country but also restricted the right of free navigation of Adersia's people as the following significant Articles show :—

" 18. The Company shall have the right to submit all the coming and departing vessels to inspection.

19. No vessel shall be allowed to leave any port under the government of Adersia without a pass from the Director of the Company at Cannanore.

20. The passes will only be delivered on the recommendation of Adersia to prevent any pirates from obtaining them " [16].

How the Dutch enforced their rights against other nations in the 17th century we do not precisely know, but it appears from an entry in the Bombay Public Consultations that in the second decade of the next century they had also started the profitable business of capturing and confiscating alien ships. They had seized some English vessels apparently without any just reason, and the Bombay Council sent a strong protest to the Council of Cochin against their action[17].

The English East India Company's officers also issued passports and insisted on the trading vessels of the country to buy them. Khafi Khan thought that the English behaved much worse than the Portuguese on sea[18], and the account left by Sir Thomas Herbert, who visited the East in the earlier part of the 17th century (his book was published in 1634), substantially corroborates the Muslim historian[19]. But in the second half of the century their practice seems to have much improved. In 1672 Peter Johnson, Captain of the frigate, *Revenge*, brought a Calicut merchant ship as a prize

16. Dutch Records, India Office transcripts English translation, Vol. 27, No. DCCXII.

17. Bombay Public Consultations, Range CCCXLI, No. 4, p. 13, Consultation 23rd January, 1717-18.

18. Elliot and Dowson, *History of India*, Vol. VII, pp. 344-345.

19. *Relation of some Yeares Travaile, Begunne Anno 1626 into Afrique and the greater Asia especially the territories of the Persia Monarch and some part of the Orientall Indies*, pp. 184-185.

to Surat, as it had no English pass[20], and in 1675 the English factors of Broach warned the *Nakhodas* of some Malabar vessels that unless they provided themselves with English pass, their ships would be regarded as good prize if any English ship met them on the sea[21]. But in the same year the Carwar factors had to remonstrate with their superiors at Surat for the leniency shown to those delinquents who refrained from procuring their pass. " The owners of ships at Batticola and at other ports hard by make their braggs that the taking of their vessells chances soe seldome and when Your Honour doth take them without a passe Your Honour doth only hinder them in their voyage by carrying them to Bombay and afterwards lett them goe. But Your Honour doth use them soe civilly there that they thinke their time very ill spent to desire a passe of us, and wee know that if Your Honour &'s vessells should but look out with a vigilent eye they would find a great many Batticola and other vessells that belongs to the adjacent places without any passe, how beneficiall this would be to the keeping up our Honourable Masters credit here in these parts, which hath bin much impaired now a late dayes as to this perticular wee leave the negotiation to Your Honour etc.'s serious consideration "[22].

This remonstrance shows that English opinion in India was not in those days adverse to the seizure of unlicensed ships but held it as a lawful exercise of sovereignty of the sea. Three years later, on the 27th February, 1668-69, Captain William Norgrave was given the following instructions:—" Wee have appointed you upon the *Hunter* to transport Mr. George Bowcher to Callicut; to whom wee have given instructions to direct you to examine all vessells for English passes, you shall meet with in your going downe; and such as shall be found to have none, belonging to any port of the Mallabarr coast, to be secured and brought up to Bombay

20. Factory Records, Surat, Vol. 3, fol. 22, Consultation Surat, July 19th, 1672.

21. Factory Records, Surat, Vol. 107, fol. 120, (Broach to Surat 20th August, 1675).

22. Factory Records, Surat, Vol. 88, fol. 216, (Carwar to Surat, 3rd February, 1674-75).

especially such as may belong to Allee Rajah or the Moores of Burgora, Cotta, Durmapatam or Billiapatam, or the natives of Porcat, taking great care in your acts of seizure, you govern yourselfe and men with that moderation, discretion and conduct as to discharge yourselfe with courage and reputation and with that uprightness and faithfulness as to forbeare yourselfe and prevent your men from purloyning or embezzling any of their goods etc., a full return of all things being intended backe to the owners when wee shall receive satisfaction for the severall wrongs done us from those places "[23]. In this case the English authorities did not intend anything but what they considered just retaliation. The instructions of Sir John Gayer was generally lenient but did not repudiate the principle on which the Portuguese and the Dutch were acting. On the 28th May, 1695, he told Captain Leonard Edgecombe :—" If in your passage out or home you meet with any country ships demand to see their passes and if they have none threaten them hard what you will do to them if you meet them without again but let them by no means be abused by you or any of your ships company but if you find any English on board them that have not our orders for being there take them (away) "[24]. But Governor Boone upheld the prevailing practice when he detained the *Shibar Khanderao* belonging to a subject of Kanhoji Angria. In defence of his action he wrote to Angria :—"Concerning the Shybar Canderow belonging to Trimbuckjee Meggee, you write that his goods and those of the Surat merchants are stopt; as Trimbuckjee is an inhabitant of this place and has his warehouses here, and allways takes my pass for said Shybar, and this year without said pass pretended to go to sea, how could it be permitted? In the same manner all the merchants of Surat take my pass to carry on their trade, and if their goods were laded in this Shybar, why was not I acquainted therewith? The vessells and their cargos that sail without a pass, both the Portuguese and you make prizes of, as you well know; and when this vessell was taken without my pass, it was on the same penalty, but I am not yet

23. Factory Records, Surat, Vol. 4, Pt. II, fol. 21.
24. Factory Records, Bombay, Vol. 10a, Instruction dated 28th May, 1695.

determined to do so "[25]. Thus it is clear that the practice of controlling the navigation of the Arabian Sea by the maritime powers of Western India had been by common consent recognised as a lawful act, and although the greed and cupidity of naval officers had frequently led to misuse of the custom, there is no doubt that it originally arose from a much-felt need. The coast was in those days infested by numerous pirates. They could and did frequent the ports in the guise of inoffensive traders and assume their true character on the high sea when a suitable opportunity occurred[26]. Such practice could to a certain extent be stopped, by the issue of passes to genuine merchants, and the price demanded for these safeguards does not seem to have been very high. From the Portuguese *cartazes* granted to Maratha merchants it appears that the Goa Government demanded 20 Xerafins for each hundred *Khandis*[27] of the cargo carried by the vessel. The price of an English pass varied according to the distance of the destination; " the fee for a pass from Broach to Surat was 4, from Goa 2 and from Cambay 3 or 4 Rupees per 500 Candy "[28]. It was demanded in return for the service rendered by the government concerned to traders in general by policing the sea, and the payment was made without much demur, as Henry Grose tells us :—" Towards defraying the charges of this marine, the company required of all the vessels trading in those seas, those of the other European nations excepted, to take the passes of the Bombay Government, for which they paid a small consideration, at which I never heard the least murmuring, the merchants being duly sensible not only of the benefit their trade received from the English protection, but that this contribution was far short of the cost of it "[29]. How much Angria or the Peshwa's officers usually demanded for

25. Bombay Public Consultatoins, Range CCCXLI, No. 4, pp. 58-51.

26. Factory Records, Surat, Vol. 106, fol. 74, (Bombay 26th March, 1672).

27. 1 *Khandi*=20 maunds. This rate of duty is given in some *cartazes* published by Biker and quoted in Sen, *A Preliminary Report on the Historical Records at Goa*, pp. 49-51.

28. Factory Records, Surat, Vol. 107, fol. 120.

29. Grose, *Voyage to the East Indies*, pp. 68-69.

their passes we do not know[30], but there is no reason to suppose that the price was excessive for no complaint of that nature has come down to us. From the meagre references made by Portuguese and English writers to the naval practices of the times it appears that the Maratha fleet generally gave convoy to merchantmen sailing from their ports. Evidently, the purchasers of the Angria's pass also received a good return for their money.

The Maratha captains did not in general act differently from their brethren in the Portuguese, English and Dutch navy. They seized trading ships only when they had failed to purchase their passes, and in those days such an omission, as the Carwar letter already quoted shows, could be very well construed as a deliberate defiance. The merchantmen were generally well-armed, the few passengers that they took also provided themselves with muskets and blunderbusses and not infrequently put up a fight before the ship surrendered to a man-of-war. The capture of such armed ships could hardly be regarded as an act of cowardice as the torpedoing of an unarmed trading vessel by a submarine to-day. In any case the merchant ship was fully aware of the risk she was running, and the contest was not very unequal.

Both the Marathas and the Portuguese stoutly denied the charge of piracy, and their protest was couched in almost identical words. In 1700 the Portuguese detained a vessel belonging to the Sidi of Janjira or one of his subjects. When the Sidi remonstrated with the Government of Goa, they replied that the ship had been captured on legitimate grounds, viz., failure to buy their *cartaz*. The ship was eventually restored to its owner in consideration of the friendship then subsisting between the Portuguese and the Mughal. The letter concluded with a significant sentence that reminded the Sidi that "the Portuguese were the sovereigns of the sea and not pirates"[31].

30. I have not been able to trace more than one pass issued by Angria. It appears that Sambhaji Angria used to charge one Rupee per Khandi for his pass. Bombay Public Consultations, CCCXLI No. 8, 1736, p 348, Consultation 1st October, 1736.

31. Livros dos Reis Visinhos, (Goa) Vol. IV. fol. 28.

The Angria retorted to his English accusers that he was not a pirate but the Admiral of the Maratha empire. To the expostulations of the Bombay Government, Henry Grose informs us, the Angria " made no further a satisfactory answer, than that disclaiming the title of Pirate, he assumes that of Admiral to the Mar-rajah, to whom he insisted that the sovereignty of the seas belonged, and that he was determined to maintain it, against all such as should refuse to acknowledge, or not take his passes "[32]. It should be remembered that neither the *Success* nor the *Robert* nor the *Otter* had Kanhoji's pass, and he argued that, as their owners were not English subjects, they were not protected by the treaty of 1713. In 1791 the Portuguese Secretary of State wrote to Bahiro Pant Mehendale :—" The vessels of the *Sarkar* (*i.e.* Poona Government) took in the port of Angediva, a merchantman belonging to that place laden with cargo and at Chapora they robbed the canoes of the fishermen without leaving even their small sails, besides other incidents to which I do not refer, for it seems that some of these and other hostilities which I do not mention here, might have been committed by the Bhonsla, Melondim, and the Angria of Kolaba who use the banner of the Most Felicitious (i.e., Peshwa)". In answer to this complaint, Gangadhar Pant, Subhedar of Gheria, wrote to the Governor of Goa :—" The said vessel was in the sea and it got no *cartaz*, nor had it a passport, nor the banner of Your Excellency "[33]. It was, therefore, justly captured. It is remarkable how similar are the arguments put forward by Governor Boone in his letter to Kanhoji Angria, by the Government of Goa in their correspondence with the Sidi of Janjira, by Kanhoji Angria in his letter to Captain Cornwall, and by Gangadhar Pant in his reply to the Portuguese Governor in defence of similar actions at different times. The Maratha Government, however, did not always uphold the actions of their servants. In 1763 Madhav Rao I. promised to make an enquiry about the circumstances under which some

32. Grose, *Voyage to the East Indies*, pp. 150-151.
33. Biker, *Tratados da India*, Vol. IX, pp. 185-187.

Portuguese ships had been captured by his fleet and to restore them if they had been seized without sufficient reason[34].

On the 7th of June 1781, Naraen Sinay, the Portuguese envoy, complained to Anand Rao Dhulap that five Maratha *Gallivats* of his fleet had robbed some *Parangues* belonging to Portuguese subjects and the total loss sustained by them on that occasion amounted to Rs. 11,780,000, and in two month's time a *Shibar* captured on that occasion was restored to its rightful owners with some money compensation for other losses [35]. Sometimes the Portuguese Government actually solicited the protection of the Maratha navy for their ships in Maratha waters and such protection was not usually refused.

It is true that such interference with free navigation, though admittedly based on a common custom, doubtless caused great hardships to merchants of all nationalities. Shivaji himself had at different times to solicit passports for his own ships from the Portuguese and the English[36]. In 1670 he had tried to secure his ships from Portuguese interference by a treaty. The Portuguese, however, positively refused to allow any vessel but small rowing crafts and grain boats to ply without their *cartaz*. In 1782 Raghuji Angria of Kolaba suggested that Portuguese merchantmen of Goa, Daman and Diu should take his *cartaz*, while vessels belonging to his subjects should similarly purchase Portuguese passports. But the Governor of Goa answered :—" I am unable to accept this Article and it is impracticable, for the Crown of Portugal has the sovereignty and the dominion of the sea of Asia by first occupation and conquest, by possession and immemorial custom, and we cannot compel the subjects of the Majestic State to take the *cartazes* of any other potentate ", but as the Portuguese Government were no longer able to maintain the supremacy they once enjoyed in the Indian waters, he added :—" I desire

34. Officios dos Governadores (Archivo Ultramarino of Lisbon) Maco 2, No. 15, 20th January, 1764.

35. Livros dos Reis Visinhos, Vol. II.

36. Pissurlencar, *Portugueses e Maratas*, p. 26; Foster, *The English Factories in India*, 1665-1667, p. 275.

to preserve amity with the Magnificent friend on terms that will not be very onerous to etiher party. I shall not do anything to your merchants even if they do not possess my *cartaz*. In the same manner the fleet and the ships of the Magnificent ally should not interfere with the merchants of the Majestic State even if they do not possess the *cartaz* of the Magnificent ally "[37]. Three years earlier, the Portuguese had renounced by treaty their right of enforcing *cartazes* on the Peshwa's ships. Thus, by peaceful negotiation the antiquated and clumsy custom of interfering with free navigation by the maritime states of the Malabar coast was being gradually abolished.

The English had by similar means procured freedom of navigation for their own vessels and those belonging to their servants and subjects. In 1713 Kanhoji Angria had undertaken not to molest English ships, but a controversy about the status of foreign vessels laden with English goods had led to a breach between the two powers. The subject was, therefore, more clearly dealt with in 1739, when a treaty was concluded between Baji Rao I. and the Government of Bombay. Article I. of that treaty runs as follows:—" The English shall only issue passes to the Company's vessels, the merchants or servants, dependents, belonging to the island of Bombay, or other places where the English have settlement, and the English shall not interfere with Baji Rav's fleet, nor give convoy to foreign vessels; save that if two or three vessels should accidentally fall in company with the English, in such case Baji Rav's fleet shall not molest them". And Article II. provided that " the English, nor their subjects or dependents, shall not freight or put their effects on board any vessels not provided with passes from Baji Rav, but if any unavoidable necessity obliges them to the contrary of this, in case of such effects being seized by Baji Rav's fleet they shall be restored to the owners, they proving their property therein ". But all restrictions were finally removed by the treaty of Salbye, Article XI. of which laid down that "The Hon'ble East

37. Livros dos Reis Visinhos, Vol. II; Sen, *A Preliminary Report on the Historical Records at Goa*, p. 54.

India Company and the Peshwa mutually agree that the vessels of each shall afford no disturbance to the vessels of the other and the vessels of each shall be allowed access to the ports of the other, where they shall meet with no molestation and the fullest protection shall be reciprocally afforded ".

It is, however, curious that though the Angria has always been styled a pirate by his European opponents, such an epithet has never been publicly applied to the Peshwa's admirals, though their naval practices were not at all different. The reason is not far to seek. The peculiar constitution of the feudal empire of the Marathas with " its states within the state " led to a misconception of the political status of the Angria family particularly when they were on unfriendly terms with the Peshwa. The inconsistencies resulting from the inalienable hereditary rights claimed and exercised by each feudal family caused great confusion, and foreigners not familiar with such practices in their own country were naturally bewildered when they found that Angria did not respect the Peshwa's passports and the Peshwa's officers similarly took no notice of any safeguard granted by Angria. This led them to believe that Angria was nothing but a rebel against his sovereign, and the depredations which he committed on the sea were, therefore, regarded by them as acts of piracy. It is worth noticing that long after the fall of Gheria Raghuji Angria still claimed the right of capturing foreign boats furnished with the Peshwa's passport[38].

But however crude and fanciful the practices of the Marathas may seem, we have seen that they had the sanction of a well recognised custom behind them and had formed the subject matter of solemn treaties; their legitimacy cannot, therefore, be questioned. At least one English writer, Captain Alexander Hamilton, seems to have frankly acknowledged this, when, writing about the sovereignty of the sea claimed by the Chief of Burgara, he observes :— " Our own King was invested with the like sovereignty not only on his own coasts, but on those of France, Holland and

38. *Itihas Sangraha, Peshave Daftarantil Sanadapatrantil Mahiti*, pp. 154-155.

Denmark, and could have no greater right than he had, only he was in a better condition to oblige the transgressors of his laws to obedience than he was "[39]. In the first half of the eighteenth century might still constituted the best right in international affairs all the world over.

Another Maratha naval practice that led to much negotiation and controversy, was that relating to wrecks. By the immemorial custom of the coast a wreck was appropriated by the prince to whose shore it was driven, for they argued that it had been sent by God to his doors. Henry Oxinden was the first English envoy to negotiate about the English ships wrecked on Shivaji's coast, but that prince was at first reluctant to make any concession on this point. Oxinden wrote to his official superiors at Bombay that his request about the restoration of English wrecks was opposed by Shivaji's officers. "They say that should they grant us our wracks the French, Dutch and other merchants would demand the same which they cannot graunt being positively against the lawes and constitutions of their country now and formerly the Nisamshay Kingdome by which they are still governed "[40]. Ultimately Shivaji was prevailed upon to make this concession, but it appears that during the stormy days following his death the Marathas had again reverted to the original custom, for wrecks formed the subject of an Article of the treaty of 1739. Article IX. of that treaty laid down that—"Any vessel belonging to the English or Bajirav that shall be driven by stress of weather, or other accidents, for shelter on the coast of either jurisdiction, all possible assistance shall be given for the refittal; but if stranded or wrecked on either shore, half of the cargo and vessel shall belong to the Government, and the other half be reserved to the owner "[41].

But clear and simple as this arrangement may seem, it did not lead to an immediate end of troubles. Where

39. Hamilton, *A New Account of the East Indies*, Vol. I, p. 300.

40. Factory Records, Surat, Vol. 88, fols. 145-147, Oxinden's letter from Rairi, 30th May, 1674.

41. Forrest, *Selections from State Papers, Maratha Series*, Appendix A, p 703.

financial interests are involved, a point may be easily stretched and the slightest injury to a ship may convert it in the eyes of interested parties into a wreck. So a wreck had to be defined officially, and this was done by Article II. of the treaty, concluded between the Bombay Government and Peshwa Madhav Rao I. on the 14th September 1761. This provided that "all assistance be afforded in future to any vessel or vessels in distress, having English colours or passes, without subjecting the owners or proprietors thereof to any impediments under the pretence of their being wrecks from the splitting of a sail, the breaking of their masts or yards and such trifling misfortunes; whereas no vessels are to be deemed wrecks but such as are driven ashore, and there break to pieces by stress of weather when the Maharatta officer and the people of the vessels are to join in saving all that is possible, which must be lodged in secure warehouses, and then one-half of what is so saved shall belong to Madarao and the other half to the owners"[42].

The Bombay Government secured still better terms for the owners when Raghoba solicited their help against his countrymen of the ministerial party and the Maratha Government gave up all claims to wrecks by Article XIV. of the treaty of Purandar. They undertook to restore everything to the owners after all reasonable expenses had been defrayed by them.

The appropriation of a wreck no doubt caused a great hardship to the poor owners, but the custom was shared by the English and the Portuguese with the Marathas and probably originated from prudential considerations to prevent fraud by unscrupulous shipowners. In 1678 a ship was wrecked very near the harbour of Bombay and part of the cargo was saved. The Bombay authorities took compassion on the poor merchants and solicited the permission of their superiors at Surat to restore to them what little of their property had been saved. The reply of the Surat Council not only explains the prevalent custom but places before us its justification. The

42. Aitchison, *Treaties Engagements and Sanads* (1909 edition) Vol. VI, p. 18.

Surat authorities permitted the suggested restoration after deducting the expenses incurred by the Company in saving the property from the wreck. But they observed that restoration of such property was "contrary to the custome of most nations in such cases and which not withstanding may appeare severe and somewhat inhumane to add to those (that were too miserable before) a greater weight of unhappiness, yet this law was founded upon very high and prudent reasons, to prevent the severall abuses ill men employed upon shipping might otherwise undertake to act through some sinister ends of benefit acrewing to themselves by the willfull casting away of the ship"[43].

All customs, military, naval or administrative, are based on past experiences. In course of time they become antiquated and are then abandoned. But in the period of transition, before their anachronism is detected and before they are finally abolished, they cause hardship and inconvenience. But it will not be just to condemn as inhuman or heartless those who may administer such antiquated laws and pursue such out-of-date customs in a period of transition. The average man hardly perceives the absurdity of the institutions he inherits from his father. Such was also the case with the Maratha naval leaders. Judged by the standard of modern times, their actions will undoubtedly appear as high-handed, but they were simply observing in their daily official routine the same practices as their European contemporaries in Western India. The freedom of the sea was an idea yet unknown. Both on land and on sea might still constituted the best, if not the only right. We should not forget that this was the age of "Letters of Marque", and a King's Commission or letter patent formed the sole difference between piracy and privateering. Piracy was condemned, but privateering was held honourable. One was expected to respect the rights of his compatriots, but common usage allowed little consideration for the rights of the foreigner on the high seas, and the more remote a naval captain was from his home, the less was his disposition to be bound by inconvenient conventions. In Indian waters the

43. Factory Records, Surat, Vol. 89, fol. 134.

Portuguese had set up a precedent which was probably based on customs prevailing on the coast. The precedent was followed by other nations, European and Indian. They challenged the Portuguese claim to the sovereignty of the sea, but the principle of the sovereignty itself remained unchallenged. This led to the numerous controversies and inconsistencies that mark the naval history of the period. But, for these inconsistencies the Marathas alone were not responsible[44]. Had their naval power survived, they might have continued or abolished the antiquated claims they had once made. But as it is, they can hardly be condemned as pirates. Like the Portuguese naval commanders, Shivaji, Kanhoji Angria and Anand Rao Dhulap could also claim to be the sovereigns of the sea, but, saddled with a hereditary system of naval command and incapable of advancing with time, they failed to compete with their English rivals, and their naval efforts seem as ineffectual and ephemeral to-day as the short-lived reign of terror established by pirate chiefs of the west on the high seas.

---

44. "From the 15th century Denmark levied " Sound dues " on foreign vessels passing through the strait, the Hanse traders and certain others being exempt. In the 17th century quarrels arose on this matter between Denmark and the Neherlands and Sweden, while in modern times the powers found the dues irksome, and in 1843 and 1853 protests were made by the representatives of the United States of America, but Denmark based her right on immemorial custom, and adhered to it ". It was only from the 1st of April, 1857, that Denmark consented to waive this claim on receipt of a united compensation of 30,476,325 rix-dollars or about £ 4,000,000. *Encyclopædia Britannica* (13th edition), vol. 25, p. 460.

CHAPTER XIV.

CONCLUSION

The Maratha empire suffered from many maladies. The principal chiefs professed to serve the same master and the same State, but, divided by personal jealousy, they were seldom able to pursue resolutely a concerted plan or a coherent policy, and common interests were frequently sacrificed to private ends. The irregular cavalry was slow to mobilise and not generally available for prompt action or prolonged services in distant parts, and the personnel of the army, therefore, had to be largely changed; the non-Maratha recruits who replaced the Maratha horsemen were mercenaries of the worst type drawn by prospects of plunder and were not bound to their masters by racial or any other affinity. The policy of indiscriminate aggression for financial purposes initiated by Balaji Baji Rao led to incessant but incomplete and ineffective invasions, which naturally left bitter memories in the harassed principalities; the Marathas thus made many enemies, who were not without means and motives of retaliation and who waited for favourable circumstances, while they had very few firm friends to rely upon in any serious emergency. The proved superiority of trained sepoys commanded by European officers led to the employment of a large number of military adventurers of diverse nationality, unknown antecedents and doubtful character. The great majority of these officers were either English or French, and they naturally sacrificed their masters' interests to those of their own and of their respective nations. The craze for trained battalions of infantry led the Maratha chieftains to under-estimate the value of cavalry which had formed in the past the greatest source of their strength. Cavalry was, therefore, neglected and allowed to degenerate. The Marathas had long been familiar with artillery and firearms, but they neglected to learn the science and technique of these invaluable weapons and continued, till their final overthrow, to rely for their supplies on the European settlements at Bombay and Goa. Nor was this all, the last decade of the eighteenth century found the Marathas without any able military leader, and it was no wonder that the ill-led ill-organised, ill-equipped and ill-disciplined hordes with irreconcilable methods of fighting were easily discomfited and routed by Wellington and Lake.

The first step in the wrong direction was the revival of feudalism. Shivaji knew the defects of Maratha character better than any of his predecessors or successors, and he deliberately set himself to undo the evils of that disintegrating system. He found his countrymen divided by mutual jealousy and inherited rivalry and left them fairly united under a ruler of their own race with a national banner and a common object to strive for. But his success was by no means complete. Even in his life time one of his principal ministers, Niraji Raoji, served as an agent of the English East India Company at his court [1]. Though the rivalry of Moro Trimbak Pingle and Annaji Datto did not find expression in any overt act of hostility while their great master was alive, lesser officials did not hesitate to let private feelings colour their public acts. When the Subhedar of Chaul quarrelled with the English of Bombay, seized their ships and threatened to stop their supply of fuel and provisions from the mainland, his colleague, the Subhedar of Kalyan, encouraged the English by every means in his power and assured them of his friendship and support [2]. It was, therefore, obviously necessary that the anti-feudal policy, so wisely initiated by Shivaji, should have been vigorously pursued by his successors, but unluckily it was abandoned by them. Feudalism was revived under unusual circumstances, first for the defence and later for the expansion of the Maratha kingdom, and it certainly served its immediate purpose. The Mughals were permanently expelled from Maharashtra, and the Marathas soon afterwards penetrated into Gujarat and Malwa. But in the very prosperity of the

1. Sen, *The English Procurator at Shivaji's Court*, *Calcutta Review*, May, 1926.

2. Factory Records, Surat, Vol. 107, fols. 171-174.

Maratha empire lay the germs of its degeneration, decline and decay. While engaged against a powerful external enemy, the Maratha generals could be expected to forget for the time being their private differences, but hardly was that crisis over when they recklessly prosecuted their quarrels, oblivious of everything else. The Mughal hordes of Aurangzib found them resolutely united, but the triumph of the Maratha cause was before long marred by the ugly spectacle of Shantaji and Dhanaji engaged in a war of extermination. The crisis that culminated at Panipat rallied the Maratha chiefs to the Peshwa's banner, but the forces of disunion did not take long to assert themselves, and Bhonsla and Gopal Rao Patwardhan openly ranged themselves with the Nizam, the hereditary enemy of the Maratha empire. The inexcusable insult offered to the Peshwa and Nana Fadnavis again helped to bring together the principal chiefs at Kurdla, but soon afterwards followed a suicidal civil war which offered the English an effective opportunity of firmly establishing their suzerainty in India.

It is needless to say that their enemies always attempted to exploit the dissension and disunion of the Maratha chiefs. That astute diplomat, Nizam-ul-Mulk, not only took advantage of the rivalry between Kolhapur and Satara but further encouraged Trimbak Rao Dabhade to measure swords with the Peshwa Baji Rao. Nizam Ali profited by the difference between Madhav Rao and Raghunath Rao, and Hyder Ali pretended to espouse Raghoba's cause, not because he wished him success, but because it served his own interests best. It may appear strange that in the light of their past experience the Maratha chiefs did not improve their conduct. But feudalism is hardly conducive to unity, and it helped to accentuate that selfish individualism which was responsible for the political insignificance from which Shivaji had rescued them. As a matter of fact, they were often aware of the evil consequences of their selfish designs and yet they persisted in their policy of self aggrandisement, for national honour and welfare of the State were of little value to them. It is said that Malhar Rao Holkar had saved Najib Khan, an inveterate enemy of the Marathas in Northern India, from imminent ruin, because peace would necessarily reduce his own importance in the North. Raghoba feared that the English would make a puppet of him if he returned to Poona as their protege, for he had the significant example of Muhammad Ali before his eyes [3], yet he preferred to remain under their protection. To him, as to many of his contemporaries, his personal interests were of much greater importance than national honour and national independence, because the idea of nationality was yet unknown. It is on this account that high officials of the State did not hesitate to serve as agents of foreign powers and openly receive rewards for such services as they might render. Bahiro Pant Mehendale [4] served as an agent of the Portuguese Government at Poona, Naro Ram Mantri [5] and his adopted son, Ghanashyam Narayan, professed to be the friends of the Portuguese and Nana Fadnavis received a *jahgir* from the Nizam. It was quite in keeping with their own practice that Mahadaji Sindhia urged the Poona ministers to grant Anderson a *jahgir* worth 150,000 Rupees, while peace was being negotiated[6].

When self-interest prevailed so much over considerations of national welfare, it is no wonder that the Maratha chiefs should frequently fail to exploit the differences of their opponents by wise diplomacy and effective and timely aggression. We have already seen how Holkar was busy with some unimportant operations in Rajputana, while Abdali was destroying Sindhia's army in detail. During the first Maratha war the fighting was invariably carried on in the Maratha territories while those of the English were left undisturbed. An invasion of Bengal from Nagpur was often talked of but never carried into effect, because the Bhonsla judged it inexpedient to take any vigorous step when his personal interests were not at stake. When the English were involved in a war with Hyder Ali and eager to have peace on honourable terms, the Marathas failed to profit by their difficulties, because

3. Officios dos Governadores, (Archivo Ultramarino of Lisbon) Maco 5, No. 62.

4. Sen, *A Preliminary Report on the Historical Records at Goa*, p. 85

5. *Instruccao do Exmo Vice-Rei Marquez de Aloma*, p. 48.

6. Sane, *Patre Yadi Bagaire*, p. 232.

there was difference in their own ranks and Mahadaji Sindhia wanted early peace. The second Maratha war again found the great chiefs divided and disunited; the English secured the moral advantage and the prestige of the Peshwa's support, and while Sindhia and Bhonsla were beaten, Holkar still preferred to wait and watch, although the ultimate consequences of defeat were no longer obscure at that moment.

Shivaji had urged racial unity on a religious basis. He had attempted to suppress all separatist tendencies by doing away with the old feudal institutions. But new ideas require persistent propaganda before they are accepted and popularised. Such propaganda was ably carried on by Ramdas in Shivaji's time, but as Shivaji stands unique among his countrymen so does Ramdas. Neither of them found able successors to carry on their work, and the idea of nationality, which might have one day taken root in Maharashtra, died away in the uncongenial environments of feudalism. When the Maratha empire expanded across the Narbada, things became still worse. The first settlers in Central India had still some sentimental tie with the Deccan, the home of their childhood, but chiefs like Daulat Rao Sindhia and Jaswant Rao Holkar were Marathas by birth but not by breeding, and they could not be expected to have that sentimental respect for Poona or Satara which characterised Mahadaji Sindhia and Malhar Rao Holkar. The cleavage between the different parts of the empire therefore became still more accentuated.

When feudalism caused dissension between different principalities of the empire, it could not have a different result within the principalities themselves. When the head of a ruling family strove to improve his own fortunes at the expense of his lawful suzerain, it was futile to expect that his younger brothers and relatives should long remain contented with their subordinate position. Internal dissension weakened the empire and family dissension weakened the chiefs. During the first Maratha war the Nagpur and Baroda families were suffering from fratricidal wars, while the main war itself was the outcome of the inordinate and selfish ambition of a junior member of the Peshwa family. On the eve of the second Maratha war the widows of Mahadaji were in open war with Daulat Rao Sindhia, while Jaswant Rao and Kashi Rao Holkar were contending for the headship of the Holkar family and the person of the infant Khande Rao. At the same time the Southern Maratha country was being sadly harassed by a series of internecine wars, as Arthur Wellesley observes in one of his letters. He writes:—"In order, however, that the Commander-in-Chief may form a judgment respecting what has been done, it will be necessary to inform him, that since the year 1800, when I was in this country before, it has been one continued contest for power and plunder between the different chiefs who have armies under their command; between the Putwurdun's (Purseram Bhow's) family and Gocklah, in the countries bordering on the Toombuddra, Werdah, and Malpoorba; between the Putwurdun and the Rajah of Kolapoor in those bordering on the Gutpurba and the Kistna; between Bappojee Scindiah, the Killedar of Darwar, and the Rajah of Kittoor; between Gocklah and the Rajah of Kittoor, and Gocklah and Bappojee Scindiah; besides various others of inferior note, either immediately employed under these, or for themselves under their protection "[7]. A State, so divided and disunited, was doomed to destruction, and the Peshwas never made any serious effort to save it. Their own example of coalescing with a foreign power against Tulaji Angria was fraught with the worst consequences.

Dissension and disunion were not the only evils for which the Marathas were indebted to their love of feudalism. At the most critical period of its history the Maratha empire found itself without an able statesman who could put its undoubtedly great resources to the best use, as Sir Thomas Munro explained to the Governor-General: " It is not that they want resources, that they have not men and horses, but that there is no one amongst them possessed of those superior talents which are necessary to direct them to advantage "[8]. This lamentable dearth of talents must be ascribed to the feudal organisation of the empire, which confined the principal civil and military

7. Gurwood, *Dispatches of Wellington*, Vol. I, p. 124.
8. G. R. Gleig, *Life of Sir Thomas Munro*, Vol. I, p. 461.

offices of the State to a few families with inalienable hereditary claims. No family can produce great men for ever, and the direction of the Maratha empire inevitably passed to weak and inefficient hands in course of time. Shahu was the last person in the royal family who could claim to possess even average abilities. The Peshwa family was more fortunate; in the senior branch it produced four generations of able men; Sindhias were blessed with three generations of good soldiers in the eldest line; but Malhar Rao had no such good luck, and he did not stand alone in this misfortune. Baba Fadke could hardly be called the worthy son of a worthy father, and if the Bhanus had produced a Nana, they were responsible for a Moraba at the same time. In 1800 the Peshwa's *musnad* was occupied by a weak intriguer who has rightly been described as the "offspring of the weakness of Raghunath Rao and the wickedness of Anandi Bai"; the vast resources of the Sindhia's dominions were at the disposal of Daulat Rao, who was equally devoid of military ability and political foresight; Raghuji Bhonsla, who ruled at Nagpur, had inherited only the name of his grandfather, but he did not possess even the physical courage for which the Marathas were noted; Jaswant Rao Holkar was fully endowed with the warlike qualities of his family, but he was nothing better than a military adventurer, cruel, licentious and without any scruple. These were the men in whose hands rested the fate of the Maratha empire, because military and civil offices had been made hereditary in opposition to the principles and practice of Shivaji.

Once we recognise the lack of national unity and patriotism on the part of the Marathas, it is not difficult to understand why men of all nationalities were indiscriminately employed in the Maratha army. Maratha soldiers were generally averse to prolonged service in distant parts and the feudal force was slow to mobilise. Every chief of any importance therefore decided to maintain a standing army, and Sikhs, Arabs, Rohillas and Rajputs, who had no objection to serving throughout the year, were naturally preferred. If these men had been recruited directly by the State, punctually paid and placed under strict discipline, the mercenaries from other parts of India might have proved a source of strength instead of being a danger to the empire, but, as we have already seen, they were attached to the recruiting officers of their own race, and discipline was conspicuous by its absence among them. Had they been well-disciplined, remarks the Portuguese Viceroy, Marquis of Alorna, they would form the most invincible army in the world. They possessed courage and hardihood, but as they had no common interest with their employers and were very irregularly paid, they were easily accessible to corruption and bribe, and they had no scruple in changing masters as often as it was convenient to them or their recruiting officer.

The preponderance of the non-Marathas in the army naturally reacted on the warlike traditions of the Marathas, and the number of professional Maratha soldiers inevitably declined. In 1818 they formed only a small proportion of the entire population, as Sir Thomas Munro informed Mountstuaut Elphinstone from personal observation in the Southern Maratha country. "The number of horsemen", he wrote, "who depend for their livelihood solely on military service is very small; it probably does not exceed the proportion of one-tenth of the whole horsemen usually employed under the southern jagheerdars"[8a]. This explains why military traditions in Maharashtra died so quickly, for which Field Marshal Earl Roberts felt justified in classing the Marathas with the people of Bengal and Madras as a non-martial race.

The indiscriminate and unhesitating employment of English and French military adventurers were also quite in accordance with the traditions of India. Though they had been long familiar with the Europeans, even the ablest of the Maratha politicians felt no intellectual curiosity about Europe. The news of the War of American Independence and the French Revolution was brought to them by Europeans themselves. Of the traditional rivalry between France and England it was impossible to be ignorant, but they did not know anything about the constitution of those countries, about their social,

8a. G. R. Gleig, *Life of Sir Thomas Munro*, Vol. II, p. 270.

political and educational institutions, about their geographical situation, and moral and material progress. The hatmen (*topikar*), as the Europeans were called, were reputed to be good sailors, good soldiers and very obstinate (*hatti*); and obstinacy perhaps satisfactorily explained that sense of patriotism which the Marathas (like other Indians) did not at that time understand. Foreigners from all parts of Europe and Asia had been readily admitted to the services of the State by Muhammadan princes before the rise of the Maratha power, and adventurers from Persia and Central Asia not only supplied loyal servants but formed the principal support of the Mughal Government in India. The Portuguese soldiers, who were the first Europeans to seek service in the Indian states, seldom hesitated to fight against the State of their origin on behalf of their employers; some French deserters were found in the English service and instances of Englishmen in French employ, though rare, were not unknown. Maratha chiefs in the Nizam's service identified themselves, as much as possible, with their master's cause and took a prominent part in his wars against the Maratha empire. Sindhia, Holkar and other Maratha chiefs, therefore, argued that they could expect as much loyalty and devotion from French and English adventurers as from their Sikh, Rajput, Arab, Sindhi or Gossain soldiers. The European officers came in search of fortune and obtained from their Maratha employers good pay and rich *jahgirs*; some of them married in the country (both De Boigne and George Thomas had Indian wives), and their masters probably expected that like the Persian and Tartar immigrants of Mughal days these foreigners would also permanently settle in the country and spend the rest of their lives in the service of those who treated them so well and generously. In this expectation, if it was ever entertained, they were sadly disappointed; not only the English subjects in Sindhia's army but the great majority of French officers also accepted the Governor-General's offer and deserted Daulat Rao when their service was needed most, while Pohlman, a German, who was present at Assaye, behaved so despicably that Sir John Fortescue feels inclined to suspect disloyalty. The Marathas made a serious mistake in entrusting the defence of their empire to foreigners, and heavily did they pay for their mistake.

The employment of European officers involved a serious change in the Maratha army. Their method of fighting was fundamentally opposed to the Maratha military traditions. Whether those two opposite methods could be profitably combined remains a doubtful question, but it is unanimously agreed that the Maratha military leaders never made a serious effort to find a satisfactory solution, and both at Panipat and at Assaye their discomfiture was largely due to their attempt to reconcile their old tactics with those they had recently introduced in their army but had not assimilated. In the meantime their reliance on trained infantry had led them to neglect their cavalry, and two competent military critics like Sir Thomas Munro and Sir John Fortescue agree that the defeat of Assaye was due to the degeneration of Maratha cavalry. Sir Thomas Munro wrote to his brother [9] on the 12th February, 1804:—" I calculated, at the opening of the campaign, two years for the complete conquest of all the possessions of Scindia and the Berarman. I thought their cavalry would have shown a little more enterprise; but they ruined it and destroyed its spirit, by teaching the troopers that they did not depend upon cavalry, but upon infantry. By coming forward with regular infantry, they gave us every advantage we could desire. They opposed to us men that never could be made so good as our own, from the want of a national spirit among the officers, and of the support of European battalions; and they trusted the success of the war to the event of close engagements. More credit has been given to the firmness of their infantry than it deserved. They seem to have made but little opposition, except during the short time our army was forming, and to have relied more upon their artillery than their musketry, as is fully proved by our horse having suffered little loss, unless by round and grape-shot ". Sir John Fortescue's criticism is not so detailed, but he is equally positive about the mistakes made by the Marathas. " Had Pohlman done his duty ", he remarks, " he might at least have embarrassed

9. G. R. Gleig, *Life of Sir Thomas Munro*, Vol. I, pp. 354-355.

Wellesley greatly; and if the Mahratta cavalry had behaved with even a show of spirit, the issue would have been certainly doubtful, and most probably disastrous to the British arms "[10].

The degeneration of cavalry was also due to the departure from Shivaji's practice. Had the Peshwas continued to replace the *Silhedar* force by state-paid and state-equipped horse, the efficiency of their cavalry would certainly have been maintained. But the revival of feudalism naturally encouraged the employment of *Silhedars*, who were unwilling to risk their horse which formed their professional capital. At last even the *Jahgirdars* began to hire horse for their personal cavalry, as we learn from Sir Thomas Munro. " A great part of the horses employed in the Mahratta armies", he wrote, "are the property of men who do not belong to the military profession. Many of the wealthy inhabitants, most of the despandes, dessyes, and other hereditary civil officers of the potails and curnums of villages, and many even of the most substantial rayets, breed horses for the armies. They send them to the field mounted by their own domestics and labourers, and hire them to the jagheerdars or the Government. They are horse-dealers rather than soldiers "[11]. It is no wonder that untrained men mounted on hired steeds proved of little use in actual fighting.

If some defects of their military system were due to feudalism, others must be associated with the intellectual limitations of the Marathas. They readily adopted new arms but did not reject the old ones. While in Europe the cross-bow was replaced by the long-bow, the long-bow by hand-guns, the hand-guns by match-locks, and match-locks by fire-locks, in the Maratha army and the Maratha fleet muskets, bows and stones were simultaneously in use. During the hundred and fifty years under review the Marathas borrowed freely from their European neighbours but failed to make any contribution to military science either in strategy or in weapons. Yet they were not intellectually deficient; the failure, therefore, must be attributed to defects in education.

10. Fortescue, *History of British Army*, Vol. V, p. 32.
11. G. R. Gleig, *Life of Sir Thomas Munro*, Vol. II, pp. 269-270.

The Maratha Government did not recognise their responsibility for public instruction. Distinguished Brahman scholars and physicians of all castes and creeds were encouraged by liberal grants of rent-free lands and pensions, but private individuals were generally left to equip themselves as best they could for the professions of their choice. The great majority of the upper classes joined the army. They learnt to fight, but there was no systematic arrangement for any instruction in the science of war. Fighting was more or less a matter of experience, and the general education that was then available consisted wholly of cultural training in literature, grammar, politics, logic and philosophy. There was no treatise on the science of war, and if we except a single chronicle, that dealing with the campaign of Panipat, there was no record of the military experience of the Maratha generals. An officer never retired from service and had therefore no leisure for writing about the theories and practice of war. His experience was, therefore, lost to posterity and only his near relatives, who had the good fortune of serving with him, could profit by his teaching, and these could not always be expected to supply the best or the aptest pupils. The progress that Europe was making in the eighteenth century in theoretical science was absolutely unknown to the Indians of that age, and no Maratha chief ever attempted to master the superior military and nautical science of the west like Peter the Great. The Maratha officers began their military career too early, were too much tied to the time-honoured system to learn anything new and generally died early; if some of them had the good luck of attaining a ripe old age, they were too busy with their annual expeditions to leave a written account of their campaigns, and their limited education hardly qualified them for such a work.

At the same time the Maratha nobility had lost the simplicity of life that characterised their ancestors of Shivaji's time. What was condemned as an inexcusable vice by the founder of the Maratha kingdom was regarded as a necessity of life by his successors in the latter part of the eighteenth century. When the Peshwa's agent urged Tukoji Holkar to prohibit the sale of alcohol in his camp, he protested that alcohol was a necessity of life and soldiers could not be expected to dispense with it[12]. Shivaji never allowed "whores and dancing wenches" in his army. Govind Pant Bundele had to send handsome dancing wenches from Hindustan for the Peshwa Balaji Baji Rao[13]. The degeneration was thus all round. The State degenerated from a national monarchy to a feudal confederacy, the army degenerated from a well-disciplined national force to an ill-disciplined band of mercenaries, and the military leaders degenerated from simple hardy soldiers to ease-loving voluptuaries. There could be but one result of such a general and all-round degeneration.

A military empire cannot survive its military efficiency long, and unfortunately for the Marathas their rivals were endowed with those very qualities which they themselves lacked. The English were imbued with a strong sense of patriotism, they combined individual self-sacrifice with national ambition, their army was well-disciplined and scientifically trained, their generals were perfect masters of military science; and the badly led, badly armed and badly organised feudal army of the Maratha empire had to relinquish the unequal contest after a brief struggle. The Maratha chiefs were compelled to acknowledge their failure after two short wars, the Peshwa was pensioned off, the *Bargirs* converted their sword-blades into ploughshares, peace was restored throughout the length and breadth of India and the Maratha empire became a far-off memory.

---

12. *Itihas Sangraha, Holkar Darbarantli Hingnyanchi Vakili*, p. 19.

13. Rajwade, *Marathyanchya Itihasachin Sadhanen*, Vol. I, p. 319. Vol. III, p. 150.

ADDITIONAL NOTES.

Prohibition of women in Shivaji's Camp

Monsieur Germain, who was sent by Francis Martin to Shivaji's camp, found it " sans faste, sans femme, ni bagage; deux tentes seulement, mais de simple toile grosse et forte limitées, l'une pour lui, l'autre pour son premier ministre ". (Martin, *Memoire sur l'etablissement des colonies francaises dans l'Inde Orientale*, fol. 286 R°). This remark was repeated by Martin in fol. 287 R° of his Memoirs, where he says, "J'ay deia remarqué que son camp nestoit point embrassé de bagages ny de femmes."

Defenceless condition of Surat in 1670

Francis Martin, the future Governor of Pondichery, visited Surat in March, 1670, in company with Monsieur Carron, the Director General of the French East India Company. He found the city disturbed by a rumour of Shivaji's intended invasion and the Governor actually invited M. Carron to inspect the city walls and to advise him as to the best measures of defence. M. Carron gave him a number of suggestions, but the Frenchmen were surprised to find that no steps were taken, and they naturally suspected a secret understanding between Shivaji and the Governor of Surat. (Martin, *Memoire*, fol. 92 R°).

Chauth of Daman

Abbe Carré says that the Portuguese of Daman had stipulated to pay the neighbouring princes a certain sum per year for keeping their turbulent subjects in check and preventing them from committing any trouble in Portuguese territories. In 1673 Shivaji demanded that the stipulated money should be paid to him, and the Portuguese Government was not in a position to refuse payment. Carré was at Daman when Shivaji's envoy arrived there, but he does not say, probably because he did not know, whether the tribute demanded by Shivaji was called *chauth*. (Carré, *Voyage des Indes Orientales*, Vol. II, pp. 25-32). Professor Pissurlencar says that in 1684 the Portuguese had agreed not only to pay to Sambhaji the *chauth* of Daman but also *gaokhandi* of the district of Bassein, while Sambhaji undertook to defend the territories of the Portuguese. The extent and the precise nature of Sambhaji's obligations cannot be ascertained, as the original treaty has been lost and only a short summary given in a contemporary letter is now available. (P. Pissurlencar, *Prince Akbar and the Portuguese*, pp. 5-6).

Tulaji Angria and the French

In 1742 the Angrias took the *Jupiter*, one of the best vessels of Europe that La Bourdonnais had sent to Goa for provision. The next year they captured the *Neptune*, another French ship, near Calicut. But henceforth Tulaji completely changed his attitude and sought the friendship of the French. In 1747 he actually sent two envoys to Mahe with a proposal of an offensive alliance against their common enemy, the English of Bombay, but his offer was politely rejected by Dupleix. (Martineau, *Correspondence du conseil superieur de Pondichery et de la compagnie*, Vol. III, p. 392 and p. 407; Vol. IV, pp. 244-245. Also *Dupleix et l'Inde Francaise*, 1742-49, pp. 137-139).

BIBLIOGRAPHY.

MANUSCRIPS.

India Office, London.

Factory Records of Bombay and Surat, 1667-1682.

Original Correspondence, 1667-1680.

Dutch Records (transcripts and translation) 1660-1680.

Bombay Public Consultations, 1700-1756.

Goa Archives, Pangim.

Livros dos Reis Visinhos, Vols. 1-15

Archivo Ultramarino, Lisbon.

Officios dos Governadores, 1735-1800.

Stray documents consisting mainly of petitions.

Disposicoes da guerra do Angria, (Biker manuscripts) fundo geral, 8548.

Guerra dos Maratas, fundo geral, 465, 660, 1605, 4179.

Relaçao dos successos acontesidos no Estado da India, 1733-1740 fundo geral, 929 & 934.

Relaçao' da batalha naval que a nau Nossa Senhora da Victoria teve na costa do sul contra o pirate Sambagi Angria, caixa, 26, X-5-15; No. 2.

Conta que o general Marata Chimnagi Apa deu ao seu rei do conquista da praçca de Baçaim do Norte no anno 1746, fundo geral, 8106, Y-5-51.

Bibliotheca Publica of Evora.

Cartas de D. Manoel Mascarenhas.

Instrucçam que deixou o Conde de Ericeira a Francisco Jose de Sampayo e Castro.

Carta do Padre Belchoir de S. Payo.

Diario das viagens de piloto Francisco Pessoa de Megalhaes.

Carta escrita de Goa contendo novas da India dos annos de 1755 e 1756.

Carta da Marquesa de Tavora que de Goa escreveo á seus filhos.

Varias cartas da Asia ao Conde de Unhao.

Bibliothèque Nationale of Paris.

Mémoires sur la compagnie des Indes Orientales, 1642-1720, Fr. 6231.

Diverses relations sur les affaires des Indes, Fr. 12087.

Archive Coloniale of Paris.

Inde, C2—62.

Correspondance generale, Inde, 2e Serie.

Archive Marine of Paris.

Journaux des voyages de France á Suratte á la côte de Malabar, à celle de Coromandel Malaca Syam, etc., par le navire le Vautour de la compagnie des Indes, B.[4] 7.

Archive Nationale of Paris.

Mémoires sur l'établissement des colonies Françaises aux Indes.

Orientales, 1664-1694, T'1169.

PRINTED WORKS

MARATHI

ACWORTH and SHALIGRAM—Aitihasik Povade.

AMATYA, RAMCHANDRA PANDIT—Marathshahitil Rajniti.

APTE—Itihas Manjari.

Chandrachur Daftar.

ATRE—Malhar Rao Holkar.

BAPAT—Baji Rao I.

BHANU—Nana Ani Mahadaji.

Bharat Itihas Sanshodhak Mandal : Varshik Itivritta, Sammelan-Vritta.

Ahaval (13 volumes in all).

Bharat Itihas Sonshodhak Mandal Quarterly.

Shiva Charitra Pradip.

BHATE—Sajjangad wa Swami Samartha.

Bharatvarsha, The.

BHAVE—Marathi Daftar (Rumals I and II).

Dandekar and Nandurbarkar, ed. Shivadigvijaya.

Shri Shivaji Pratap.

Iniquities of the Inam Commission.

Itihas ani Aitihasik.

Kayastha Prabhunche Bakhar.

KELKAR—Maratha ani Ingraj.

KHARE—Aitihasik Lekha Sangraha, 12 Vols.

History of Ichalkaranji.

Adhikar Yoga.

Harivanshachi Bakhar.

Nana Fadnavis.

Kirtane, ed. Chitnis Bakhar.

LOKAHITAVADI—Aitihasik Goshti.

NATU—Mahadaji Sindhia.

PARASNIS—Itihas Sangraha, 7 vols.

Brahmendra Swami.

Maratha Armar.

POTDAR—Maratha ani Ingraj.

Prabhat, The.

RAJADHYAKSHA—Jivba Dada Bakshi.

RAJWADE—Marathyanchya Itihasachin Sadhanen, 22 vols.
Tanjavar yethil Shilalekha.
Sankirna Lekha Sangraha.

Raja Vyavahar Kosh.

Ramdas ani Ramdasi.

SANE—Patre Yadi Bagaire.
Sabhasad Bakhar.
Shrimant Sambhaji Maharaj wa Rajaram Maharaj Yanchin Charitren.
Thorle Shahu Maharaj Yanchen Charitra.
Peshavyanchi Bakhar.
Bhau Sahebanchi Bakhar.
Panipatchi Bakhar
Chitnis Bakhar.

SARDESAI—Marathi Riyasat, 5 vols

Saraswati Mandir.

Shahanav kalmi Bakhar.

VAD—Selections from Satara Rajas' and the Peshwas' Diaries, 9 vols. ed. Parasnis, Sane, Marathe and Joshi.
Selections from the Government Records in the Alienation Office, Poona.
(I) Kaifiyats Yadis, ed. Mawjee and Parasnis.
(II) Sanads and Letters, ed. Mawjee and Parasnis.
(III) Watan patras Nivad patras, ed. Mawjee and Parasnis.
(IV) Taha wa Kararmadar, ed. Mawjee and Parasnis.

Vividha Dnan Vistar.

PORTUGUESE.

BIKER, J. F. JUDICE—Collecçao de tratados e concertos de pazes que o Estado da India portugueza fez com os reis e senhores com quem teve relaçoes nas partes da Asia e Africa Oriental, 14 vols.

Breve noticia que se da ao publico para consolaçao dos portuguezes dos successos que acontecerao no Estado da nossa India desde o mez janeiro de 1759 até o de 1760.

CHAVES, DR. BALTHAZAR MANOEL DE,—Annal Indico historico do governo do illustrissimo e excellentissimo senhor Marquez de Tavora.

COSTA, DIOGO DA,—Relaçam das guerras da India.

CUNHA RIVARA,—O chronista de Tissuary.

DALGADO, S. R.—Glossario Luso-Asiatico, 2 vols.

FONSECA, F. F. DA,—Relaçao de hum grande combate e victoria, que contra o gentio e o arabio conseguio a armada que do porto de goa sahio de guarda costa em julho de 1753 commandada pelo valeroso Ismal Can.

GRACIAS, J. A. ISMAEL—Uma dona portugueza no côrte de Grao Mogol. Catalogo dos livros do assentamento da gente de guerra.

GUARDA, COSME DA,—Vida e acçoens do famoso e felicissimo Sevagy.

Instrucçao do Marquez de Alorna ao seu successor.

MACHADO, JOZE DA SILVA,—Relaçao dos successos da India.

MASCARENHAS, JOSE FREIRE,—Epanaphora Indica (in 6 parts).

PEREIRA, FRANCISCO RAYMUNDO DE MORAES,—Annal Indico Lusitano dos successos mais memoraveis e das acçoens mais particulares do premeiro anno do felicissimo governo do illustrissimo e excellentissimo senhor Francisco de Assis de Tavora.

PISSURLENCAR, PANDURANGA S. S.—Xivaji Maharaj com sangue Portugues?

Portugueses e Maratas.

Relaçam dos progressos das armas portuguezas no Estado da India no anno de 1713.

Relaçam verdadeira dos felices successos da India e victorias que alcansaram as armas portuguezas naquelle Estado em o anno de 1752.

Relaçam ou noticia certa do Estado da India, 1756.

Relaçao e verdedeiras noticias das ultimas acçoens militares ordenadas pelo illustrissimo e excellentissimo Marquez do Louriçal.

Relaçam das victorias alcançadas na India contra o inimigo Marata.

ROGER, J. Relaçao dos successos prosperos e infelices do illustrissimo e excellentissimo Conde de Alva.

SERAFINS, FR. ANGELO DOS—Relaçao da viagem que o illustrissimo e excellentissimo Marquez de Tavora fez de porto de Lisboa até o de Moçambique e depois ao da cidade da Goa.

FRENCH

BARBE, EMILE,—Le Nabab René Madec.

CARRE—Voyage des Indes Orientales mêlé de plusieurs histoires curieuses.

DE LA HAYE—Journal du voyage des grands Indes.

KAEPPELIN, PAUL,—La compagnie des Indes Orientales et François Martin.

Lettres et conventions des gouverneurs de Pondichery avec differentes princes Hindous, 1666 á 1793.

L. L. M.—Histoire de la derniére revolution des Indes Orientales.

MARTINEAU, ALFRED,—Correspondance du conseil superieur de Pondichery et de la compagnie. 4 vols.

Dupleix et l'Inde Française, 1742-49.

Memoire sur la carriere de M. le General Comte de Boigne.

SAINT-GENIS, VICTOR DE,—Une page inédite de l'histoire des Indes.

Voiage de Gautier Schouten aux Indes Orientales commencé l'an 1658 et fini l'an 1665.

HINDI

BHUSHAN—Poetical Works.

LALKAVI—Chhatra Prakash.

ENGLISH

ACWORTH—Ballads of the Marathas.

A Faithful Narrative of the Capture of the Ship Derby.

AITCHISON—Treaties Engagements and Sunnuds.

ANDERSON—The English in Western India (2nd edition).

Arabian Pirate, The. or Authentic History and Fighting Adventures of Tulagee Angria.

Asiatic Researches.

BIDDULPH—Malabar Pirates.

BLACKER—The British Army in India, 1817-19.

BROUGHTON—Letters written in a Mahratta Camp.

BRUCE—Annals of the East India Company. 3 vols.

BURWAY—Ahilya Bai.

Ranoji Rao Sindhia

Mahadaji Sindhia.

CAMPBELL—Bombay Presidency Gazetteer.

Churchill's Voyages.

COLEBROOKE—Life of Mountstuart Elphinstone. 2 vols.

COMPTON—A Particular Account of European Military Adventurers in India.

DA CUNHA—The Origins of Bombay.

Notes on the History and Antiquities of Chaul and Bassein.

DANVERS—The Portuguese in India. 2 vols.

DELLON—A Voyage to the East Indies.

DIROM—A Campaign in India in 1792.

DOWNING—A Compendious History of the Indian Wars.

DUFF, J. C. GRANT,—A History of the Mahrattas. 3 vols.

EGERTON OF TATTON—Indian and Oriental Armour.

ELLIOT AND DOWSON—History of India, 8 vols.

ELPHINSTONE—History of India.

A Report on the territories conquered from the Paishwa.

Encyclopœdia Britannica.

ENTHOVEN—The Folklore of Bombay.

Castes and Tribes of Bombay.

FITZCLARENCE—A Journey through India.

FORBES—Oriental Memoirs.

FORREST—Official Writings of Mountstuart Elphinstone.

Selections from the Letters Despatches and other State Papers preserved in the Bombay Secretariat, Home Series 2 vols.; and Maratha Series.

FOSTER—The English Factories in India.
FORTESCUE—A History of the British Army.
FRANCKLIN—Shah Allum.
Military Memoirs of George Thomas.
FRASER, BAILLIE—Military Memoirs of Col. Skinner.
FRYER—A New Account of the East India and Persia.
GLEIG—Life of Major General Sir Thomas Munro. 2 vols.
GROSE—A voyage to the East Indies.
GURWOOD—Dispatches of the Field Marshal the Duke of Wellington, 13 vols.
HEDGES, SIR W.—Diary during his Agency in Bengal, 3 vols.
HERBERT—Relation of some Yeares Travaile.
HAMILTON—A New Account of the East Indies, 2 vols.
HOPE—House of Scindea.
IRVINE—Later Moghuls, 2 vols.
The Army of the Indian Moghuls.
IVES—A Voyage from England to India in the year MDCCLIV.
JENKINS—A Report on the Territories of the Rajah of Nagpore.
JERVIS—Statistical Survey of the Konkun.
KARKARIA—Pratapgad.
KAYE—The Life and Correspondence of Sir John Malcolm, 2 vols.
KEENE—Hindustan under Free Lances.
Fall of the Moghul Empire.
Sindhia.
KINCAID AND PARASNIS—History of the Maratha People, 3 vols.
LOW—History of the Indian Navy 2 vols.
MAC CLUER, J.—Description of the Coast of India.
MACDONALD—Nana Furnuwees.
MACKINTOSH—An Account of the Origin and Present condition of the Tribe of Ramoossies.
MALCOLM—Central India, 2 vols.
Political History of India, 2 vols.
MALLESON—Final French Struggles in India.
Decisive Battles of India.
MANUCCI—Storia do Mogor, ed. and tr. W. Irvine, 4 vols.
MARTIN—The Despatches Minutes and Correspondence of the Marquis Wellesley during his Administration in India, 5 vols.
MILL AND WILSON—History of India, 9 vols.
MOLESWORTH—Marathi-English Dictionary.
MOOR—A Narrative of the Operations of Captain Little's Detachment.
Notes Relative to the late Transactions in the Mahratta Empire.

Origin of the Pindarries preceded by Historical Notices on the Rise of the different Mahratta States.

ORME—Hitsorical Fragments of the Moghul Empire.

War in Indostan, 2 vols.

OVINGTON—A Voyage to Surat in 1689.

OWEN—Fall of the Moghul Empire.

India on the Eve of the British Conquest.

Selections from Wellington's Despatches.

Selections from Wellesley's Despatches.

PARASNIS—Mahableshwar.

Poona in Bygone Days.

Panhala.

Satara.

Sangli State.

POGSON—A History of the Boondelas.

Press list of the ancient Dutch Records in the Madras Records Department.

PRINSEP, H. T.—History of the Political and Military Transactions, 2 vols.

Memoirs of the Puthan Soldier of Fortune.

Proceedings of the Indian Historical Records Commission.

Purchas His Pilgrimes, 20 vols.

RADDI—Shivaji.

RANADE—Rise of the Maratha Power.

Miscellaneous Writings.

SARKAR—Shivaji and his Times.

History of Aurangzib, 5 vols.

SCOTT, J.—History of the Deccan, 2 vols.

SCOTT WARING—History of the Marathas.

SEN, S. N.—Siva Chhatrapati.

Administrative System of the Marathas.

A Preliminary Report on the Historical Records at Goa.

SEWEL—A Forgotten Empire.

SLEEMAN—Rambles and Recollections, 2 vols.

SMITH, L. F.—A Sketch of the Rise, Progress and Termination of the Regular Corps formed and commanded by Europeans in the Service of the Native Princes of India.

SMITH, V. A.—Oxford History of India.

STAVORINUS, J. S.—Voyages to the East Indies, 3 vols.

SYKES—Special Report on the four Collectorates of Dukhan under the British Government.

TAKAKAV AND KELUSKAR—Life of Shivaji Maharaj.

THORN—Memoirs of the War in India.
TONE—Illustrations of some Institutions of the Mahratta People.
VALENTIA—Voyages and Travels, 4 vols.
WATTERS—On Youan Chwung, 2 vols.
WEST—A Memoir of the States of the Southern Marhatta Country.
WHITEWAY—Rise of the Portuguese Power in India.
WILKS—Historical Sketches of the South of India, 3 vols.
WILSON—Glossary of Indian Judicial and Revenue terms.
YULE AND BURNELL—Hobson Jobson.

JOURNALS AND PERIODICALS.

Calcutta Review.
Epigraphia Indica.
Indian Antiquary.
Journal of the Bombay Branch of the Royal Asiatic Society.
Journal of the Royal Asiatic Society.
Journal of the Asiatic Society of Bengal.
Journal of the Department of Letters, Calcutta University.

GLOSSARY

Aftabgir (or *Aftabgiri, Aftagir*)—" This sun screen (*aftab,* sun; *gir,* root of *giriftan,* to take), shaped like an open palm-leaf fan, was also called *suraj-mukhi* (Hindi, literally, sun-face). By the Moghul rules it could only be granted to royal princes (*Mirat-ul-Istilah,* fol. 3). In the eighteenth century, however, the Mahrattas adopted it as one of their commonest ensigns, and even the smallest group of their cavalry was in the habit of carrying one."—Irvine, *The Army of the Indian Moghuls,* p. 34.

Alvara—A charter or a prince's letters-patent,—Lacerda, *A New Dictionary of the Portuguese and English Languages,* p. 65.

Amin—" The word is Arabic *Amin,* meaning a 'trustworthy person'; and then an inspector, intendant, &c ".—*Hobson Jobson,* p. 17.

Arrack—" This word is the Arabic *arak* properly 'perspiration', and then first the exudation or sap drawn from the date palm ('arak al-tamar'); secondly, any strong drink, 'distilled spirit', 'essence'; etc. In India it is applied to a variety of common spirits; in S. India to those distilled from the fermented sap of sundry palms; in E. and N. India to the spirit distilled from cane-molasses, and also to that from rice ". Crooke-*Hobson Jobson,* p. 36.

Balparveshi—(A compound of *Bal,* child, and *Parwardan,* to rear or foster). " A pension or maintenance granted by a Government to the family of a soldier or servant who died in its service ". Molesworth, *A Dictionary Marathi and English,* p. 579.

Bania—A merchant, a man of the trading caste.

Bazar—A market.

Beldar Lugare—Beldar, a wandering caste of quarrymen. " They are strong and dark and the men wear the moustache and top-knot. They speak Marathi. They are stone-cutters and bricklayers, digging wells, blasting rocks, and breaking stones. Their houses are like those of cultivating Marathas. The men wear the loin cloth, waist cloth, and short tight trousers or *cholnas,* the jacket, and the Maratha turban; and the women dress in the ordinary Maratha robe and bodice and do not tuck the end of the robe back between the feet. They eat fish and flesh and drink liquor. They are hard working, orderly, and hospitable but fond of drink. They have caste councils, do not send their boys to school, and are a steady people earning enough to maintain themselves ".—*Gazetteer of the Bombay Presidency,* Vol. XX, pp. 91-92. *Lugada* means a robber or plunderer. *Beldar Lugare* therefore stands for a plunderer of the Beldar caste.

Bildar—The same as Beldar, but when used in relation to the army the word means a digger or pioneer. See *Hobson Jobson*, p. 94, Irvine, *The Army of the Indian Moghuls*, pp. 173-174.

Bhaldar—A mace-bearer. " An attendant on great men who waits with a wand in his hand,—an usher ".—Molesworth, *A Dictionary Marathi and English*, p. 611.

Bunga—The baggage of an army. See p. 149, also Molesworth, *A Dictionary Marathi and English*, p. 572.

Cafilla—" Arabic *Kafila*; a body or convoy of travellers. Also used for a sea convoy ".—*Hobson Jobson*, p. 142. Dalgado, *Glossario duso-Asiatico*, Vol. I, pp. 169-170.

Cartaz—A permit or passport.

Charrua—A ship of burden, a merchant ship, a store ship.

Chitnis—(From *Chithi*, letter, and *navishtan*, to write). A correspondence clerk or secretary.

Cozzy—Arabic *Kadi*, a judge.

Daftardar—" An ancient public officer. His duty was to collect and frame in order the accounts of the waste-book as prepared by the Fadnis, and to transmit monthly abstract accounts to the Huzur ".—Molesworth, *A Dictionary Marathi and English*, p. 402.

Dakshini—A southerner, a man hailing from the Deccan.

Darakhdar—" A holder of a hereditary public office especially Diwan, Mazumdar, Fadnis, Sabnis, Karkhannis, Chitnis, Jamdar and Potnis ".—Sen, *Administrative System of the Marathas* ", p. 665.

Desy—More correctly Desai. " An hereditary Officer, the head of a Pergunnah. He is the same as the Deshmukh ". Molesworth, *A Dictionary Marathi and English*, p. 426. " In W. and S. India a native official in charge of a district, often held hereditarily, a petty chief ".—*Hobson Jobson*, p. 306.

Dhal—Shield. A shield was made of either steel or hide. Brahmans often used a shield made of forty or fifty folds of silk.—Irvine, *The Army of the Indian Moghuls*, pp. 77-88; Egerton of Tatton, *Indian and Oriental Armour*, pp. 111-118, 134, 139.

Duan—More correctly, Diwan or Dewan. " A prime minister ".—Molesworth, *A Dictionary Marathi and English* p. 413. " The head financial minister, whether of the state or a province . . . . . charged, in the latter, with the collection of the revenue, the remittance of it to the imperial treasury, and invested with extensive judicial powers in all civil and financial causes ".—Wilson quoted in *Hobson Jobson*, p. 309.

Durbar—More correctly, Darbar. A court or levee.

Fadnis—" A public officer,—the keeper of the registers, etc. By him were issued all grants, commissions, and orders; and to him were rendered all accounts from the other departments".—Molesworth, *A Dictionary Marathi and English*, pp. 547.

Farman—A royal mandate, grant or patent.

Faujdari—The Faujdar was a military governor of a small district Faujdari was an *abwab* or abwabs exacted by the Faujdar.

Gariwan—A carter.

Ghat—A mountain pass, a landing place.

Golandaz—(From *gola*, a ball, and *andakhtan*, to throw) a gunner.

Gumashta—An agent or factor.

Hon—A gold coin, from Canarese *honnu*, gold. Wilson quoted in *Hobson Jobson*, p. 425. The value of this coin varied at different places and different times. From a manuscript in the Bodleian Library (Rawlinson Manuscript 841, fol. 1) it appears that the weight of a Kaveripak pagoda (or hon) was 2 dw. 5 gr. 8m. ½ atts and its value in Madras currency (in 1679-80) was 18 fanams 1 cash. "Accounts at Madras down to 1818 were kept in *pagodas*, *fanams* and *Kas*; and 8 *Kas* = 1 fanam, 42 fanams = 1 pagoda. In the year named the rupee was made the standard coin. The pagoda was then reckoned as equivalent to 3½ rupees".—*Hobson Jobson*, p. 653.

Houdah—A seat carried by an elephant.

Howda—See Houdah.

Inam—" Arabic. *in'am*, 'a gift' (from a superior), 'a favour' but specially in India a gift of rent free land; also land so held".—*Hobson Jobson*, p. 433.

Jahgir—(from *Jah*, a place, and *giriftan*, to take). "An assignment of the land revenue of a certain number of villages or of a sub-division".—Irvine. *The Army of the Indian Moghuls*, p. 14.

Jamadar—A petty officer.

Jamdar—Treasurer.

Jari Patka—" The Banner, 'Zari-patta' which was always carried before Ragobah, was small and swallow-tailed of crimson and gold tissue with gold fringes and tassels".—Egerton of Tatton, *Indian and Oriental Armour*, p. 114.

Jasud—A scout.

Jejala—(*Jajail* or *Gingall*). " A wall-piece or swivel gun".—Irvine, *The Army of the Indian Moghuls*, pp. 109—111. " They use large heavy wall pieces called gingalls, which send a ball of two or more ounces to a very considerable distance".—Fitzclarence, *Journal of a Route across India*, p. 246.

Jinsa—The grand park of artillery. See p. 149.—Irvine interprets *Jinsi* as " the artillery attached to the emperor's person".—*The Army of the Indian Moghuls*, pp. 133.

Karbhari—" A manager or Major domo". Molesworth.—*A Dictionary Marathi and English*, p. 159. " An agent, a manager ".—*Hobson Jobson*, p. 475.

Karkonnas—More correctly, Karkhana, a workshop, a manufactory. The word, when applied to a state department, means a royal establishment. See Sen, *Administrative System of the Marathas*, p. 668.

Kaul—A writing of assurance, agreement or engagements as granted by Government.

Kaveripak Hon—See *Hon*.

Khalasi—A seaman, a chainman, a tentpitcher, a gunner or artilleryman.

Khandi—A measure of weight, equivalent to twenty maunds.

Khasnis—A private scribe of a king or a grandee.

Khijmatgar—More correctly, *khidmatgar* (from Arabic *Khidmat*—service); A servant.

Kuran—Ground preserved for growing grass.

Laskar—An army or camp; also, a soldier or a gunner as well as a sailor.

Mahmudi—A silver coin current in Gujarat and the west coast of India. According to Herbert, a Mahmudi was worth eight pence in English money. Fryer says, " Mamodies are current only in Surat, and Parts adjacent; they are worth somewhat less than an English Shilling". Mahmudi chaparis carried a higher exchange value than Mahmudi chalanis. See Dalgado, *Glossario Luso-Asiatico*, Vol. II, pp. 18-19.

Mansab—" The word *Mansab* is literally the place where anything is put or erected; and then, as a secondary meaning the state or condition of holding a place, dignity or office ". Irvine, " *The Army of the Indian Moghuls*, p. 3.

Mukkadam—A village headman.

Mulukgiri—(From *mulk*, a country, and *giriftan*, to take). Foreign expedition; generally, a plundering raid.

Musnad—" The large cushion, etc., used by native Princes in India, in place of a throne ". *Hobson Jobson*, p. 600.

Nakhoda—(From Persian *ná-khude*, Lord of the boat). Skipper or captain of a ship.

Nalbandi—Literally the price of shoeing a horse. " A small advance of pay made to horse-soldiers on engaging them, or on dispatching them upon any service ". Molesworth. *A Dictionary Marathi and English* pp. 460.

Nishan—A letter written by an imperial prince.

Najeebs—(From Ar. *najib* 'noble'). " A kind of half-disciplined infantry soldiers under some of the native Government ".—*Hobson Jobson*, p. 631. Also see Irvine, *The Army of the Indian Moghuls*, pp. 164-165.

Ol—Hostage.

Pal—" A cloth or a large blanket, etc. stretched across a pole, forming a sort of tent with two sloping sides and two open ends ". Molesworth, *A Dictionary Marathi and English*, p. 512.

Parangue—(Probably derived from Tamil *padagu*). A small boat, used for transporting provision on the Malabar coast. See Dalgado, *Glossario Luso-Asiatico*, Vol. II, p. 169.

Parasnis—A Persian secretary.

Pataxo—" A pinnace. It is generally used for any tender that waits upon fleets and men of war ".—Lacerda, *A New Dictionary of the Portuguese and English Languages*, p. 681.

Peshkash—" Persian *Pesh-kash*. Wilson interprets this as literally 'first fruits'. It is used as an offering or tribute but with many specific and technical senses which will be found in Wilson, *e.g.*, a fine on appointment, renewal, or investiture; a quit-rent, a payment exacted on lands formerly rent-free, or in substitution for service no longer exacted; sometimes a present to a great man, or (loosely) for the ordinary Government demand on land ".—*Hobson Jobson*, p. 701.

Potdar—An officer whose duty was to assay all money paid into the treasury.

Pradhan—A minister.

Purvia—One belonging to the eastern provinces. The Marathas applied this term generally to recruits from Oudh.

Rahdari—Transit dues, originally meant for paying travelling guards. See Moreland, *From Akbar to Aurangzib*, p. 286.

Rojmura—Wages.

Ramoshi—" They claim descent from Ram, who they say created them when he pased through the Deccan to Ceylon. Their rites, ceremonies, and home speech seem to show a Telegu origin. They are divided into Chavans and Jadhavs. Like Kunbis they eat fish, fowls, and the flesh of goats and deer, and differ little from them in house, dress, or customs. They have a bad name for committing thefts burglaries and gang and highway robberies, and stealing cattle and crops. Their children are petty thieves and robbers. They act as village watchmen and in return for their services hold rent-free lands and receive grain allowances. Some are labourers and others husbandmen. Their favourite god is Khandoba, but they worship the usual Brahmanic gods and goddesses. Their priests are ordinary village Brahmans. They practise bigamy and have to pay for their wives. They bury their dead ".—" *Gazetteer of the Bombay Presidency*, Vol. XXIV, p. 107.

Saranjam—" Lands held in surinjam involve the condition of military service; the term is of Persian origin, meaning 'furniture,' 'apparatus'; implying that the lands are to defray the expense of equipment; in fact

Surinjam is synonymous with military Jagheer ".—Sykes, *Special Report on the Statistics of the Four Collectorates of Dukhan under the British Government*, p. 286.

Sartandel—An officer superior to Tandel.

Serang—" A native boatswain, or chief of a lascar crew; the skipper of a small native vessel ".—*Hobson Jobson*, p. 812.

Shikkdari—A shikkdar is a revenue collector of a small subdivision. Shikkadari is an *abwab* levied by a Shikkdar.

Shutarnal—" *Shutarnal, Zamburak, Shahin*. These words seem all three to refer to the same weapon, what we should call a swivel-gun or wall-piece. *Shutarnal* is literally ' camel-gun barrel ', and denotes the fact that they were sometimes carried on and fired from camels' backs. *Zamburak* is derived from *Zambur*, a bee or wasp, with a diminutive added, and thus means ' a little wasp ', probably in allusion to its sound when fired, or its power of stinging or wounding. *Shahin* literally ' falcon ', seems a later name for the same thing; a name which was brought into India by Nadir Shah ".—Irvine, *The Army of the Indian Moghuls*, pp. 135-136.

Tandel—" Malayal. *Tandal*. Telugu, *Tandelu*. The head or commander of a body of men; but in ordinary specific application a native petty officer of lascars, whether on board ship (boatswain) or in the ordinace department, and sometimes the head of a gang of labourers on public works ".—*Hobson Jobson*, p. 923.

Tindal—See *Tandel*.

Varat—Assignment either on a person or on a treasury.

Zamburak—See Shutarnal.

Ziyafat—Literally means an invitation or a dinner, hence an *abwab* levied to meet the expenses of a dinner; an entertainment or dinner tax.

INDEX

C.

T.

U.

V.

W.

X.

Y.

Printed by A. C. Biswas at the Modern Art Press, Calcutta and published by Girindranath Mitra, 4/4A, College Square, Calcutta.

ERRATA

Page	31	Line	33	*for*	as however	*read*	However as,
,,	38	,,	30	,,	*mul-kgiri*	,,	*mulukgiri*
,,	43	,,	6	,,	Hussain Ali	,,	Husain Ali
,,	47	Footnote Line 1.	30	,,	*Rellacao*		*Relacao*
,,	,,	Footnote Line 10.	30	,,	Marathas	,,	Maratha
,,	71	Line	9	,,	*mulukhgiri*	,,	*mulukgiri*
,,	76	Line	20	*put*	a comma after Carwar		
,,	76	,,	21	*for*	the Phonda	*read*	Phonda
,,	77	Footnote 7		,,	Scot	,,	Scott
,,	78	,,	14	,,	Muzaffarzung	,,	Muzaffar Jang
,,	81	,,	15	,,	the war	,,	war
,,	83	,,	15	,,	quite	,,	quit
,,	,,	,,	28	,,	bandooks	,,	banduks
,,	105	,,	14	,,	was	,,	were
,,	116	Footnote	22	,,	Livrts	,,	Livros
,,	137	Line	27	,,	embarrasments	,,	embarrassments
,,	147	,,	11	*after*	"led in person"	*add*	after consolidation of his authority in the Maratha Country.
,,	149	Line	2	*for*	wallow	read	swallow
,,	152	,,	11	,,	write Forbes	,,	writes Forbes
,,	159	Footnote	34	,,	Aitihasig	,,	Aitihasik
,,	166	Line	3	,,	set on	,,	set out on
,,	173	,,	29	,,	the	,,	he
,,	179	,,	1	,,	port	,,	harbour
,,	233	,,	1	,,	the Peshwa	.	the Peshwas
,,	247	,,	12	,,	was	,,	were
,,	251	Footnote	35	,,	Vol. II	,,	Vol. XI
,,	252	,,	37	,,	Vol. II	,,	Vol. XI.

This list should not be treated as either complete or exhaustive.

BY THE SAME AUTHOR

Published by the Calcutta University

1. ADMINISTRATIVE SYSTEM OF THE MARATHAS
(From original sources)

Demy 8vo., pp. 730, *Second Edition*, **Rs. 10.**

PROF. JULES BLOCH (*in the Journal Asiatique*) C'est un ouvrage solide et important, qui fait honneur à l'auteur et à l'école ou il se rattache.

MR. C. A. KINCAID—Should long remain the classic text on the subject.

2. SIVA CHHATRAPATI

Demy. 8vo., pp. 284, **Rs. 4-14.**

PROF. RAMSAY MUIR—Your work bears all the marks of exact and scientific scholarship and both you and the University of Calcutta have every reason to be proud of the admirable beginning thus made in the rendering of an essential service to historical scholarship.

THE INDIAN DAILY NEWS—It is a capital book for history students.

3. A PRELIMINARY REPORT ON THE HISTORICAL RECORDS AT GOA

Royal 8vo., pp. 88, **Rs. 1-12.**

PRINCIPAL H. G. RAWLINSON—It marks a real advance in our knowledge, and I hope it will lead other workers to take up the torch.

PROF. EDGAR PRESTAGE—It will be useful to all students of Indian history of the period with which it deals.

THE BOOK COMPANY LTD.,

4/4A, College Square, Calcutta.